WARTIME MISSION IN SPAIN

THE MACMILLAN COMPANY
NEW YORK · BOSTON · CHICAGO · DALLAS
ATLANTA · SAN FRANCISCO

MACMILLAN AND CO., Limited
LONDON · BOMBAY · CALCUTTA · MADRAS
MELBOURNE

THE MACMILLAN COMPANY
OF CANADA, Limited
TORONTO

WARTIME
MISSION IN SPAIN

1942–1945

BY

Carlton J. H. Hayes

Late American Ambassador to Spain

223792

THE MACMILLAN COMPANY · NEW YORK

1945

To

E. C. H., M. E. H., *and* C. J. J. H.

WHO SHARED AND
IMMEASURABLY AIDED
THE MISSION

PREFATORY NOTE

In the following pages I present a personal account of my diplomatic mission in Spain from May, 1942, to January, 1945. It deals only incidentally with Spain's internal affairs. Its central concern is with American policy toward Spain during those three wartime years, and with Spain's response.

The book is not "official," and has not been written as an apologia for an Ambassador or for the State Department or for Spain. It is, rather, an historian's candid and factual record of what he saw and knew at first hand. Now that the war is happily over, there would seem to be no reason, either military or diplomatic, why this record should not be disclosed. It should serve to dissipate some of the dense fog which propaganda and ignorance have cast over the relations of Spain with the two sets of belligerents and to let in some light on an important aspect of American foreign policy.

In writing the book, I have relied upon a detailed personal diary I kept during my three years in Spain, upon contemporaneous memoranda of conversations, upon personal correspondence with the President and others, and upon a trained historical memory. I have not utilized any documents of the State Department, except in so far as they have elsewhere been published, or as paraphrased extracts of them were incorporated in my personal diary. In the latter instances, I have indicated them usually by single quotation marks, in order to warn the reader that the quotations do not reproduce the exact form or wording of the originals.

Some of the statements in the book might have been more strongly buttressed, if I could have quoted from the archives of the State Department. The Department was naturally reluctant to afford me any special privileges or to appear to lend official countenance to what I might write. The alternative would have been for me to submit my manuscript to review and possible censorship by officials of the Department, and this I was unwilling to do, and have not done.

It is preferable that the account be entirely mine. I believe, how-ever, that if and when, at some future time, the official records are open to the public, they will but confirm, in all essential respects, the accuracy of the following narrative.

Let me add that with the State Department, as with the President, my relations, both personal and official, were always pleasant and agreeable. About two or three matters I thought the Department, or certain of its officials, made tactical errors, and I have frankly said so and explained what they were in the course of the story. But they were the exception, not the rule. On the whole, I have only respect and admiration for our Department of State and for our Foreign Service, and I esteem it an honor to have been, during trying times, a collaborator with them.

CARLTON J. H. HAYES

Jericho Farm
Afton, New York
September 15, 1945

Contents

WARTIME MISSION IN SPAIN

CHAPTER I

HOW I HAPPENED TO GO TO SPAIN

I

Since 1910 I had been a professor of modern European history in Columbia University. International law had been one of the subjects I had previously presented for the doctorate; and I continued to take a lively interest in international relations, especially after I, along with several million other Americans, was drawn, as active participant, into the First World War. That experience taught me the practical futility of isolationism for the United States.

I was henceforth a convinced and outspoken advocate of the League of Nations and of any agency or measure which might forward the cause of collective security and lessen the danger of another World War in which many more millions of Americans were sure to be involved. It seemed to me then, and it still does, that we who were decried in the partisan strife of 1920 as "idealists" and "dreamers" were far more realistic than those "realists" who wrecked the League of Nations and pursued narrowly nationalist ends.

Unfortunately for the present generation, there proved to be more "realists" in those days than "idealists." From the first advent of Fascism and Nazism in the 1920's and the first aggression of Japanese militarism in Manchuria in the early 1930's, it should have been obvious that a Second World War, of even greater dimensions than the First, was in the offing. Some of us recognized and warned of the peril. I did my little bit.[1]

The Second World War broke with Hitler's *Blitzkrieg* against

---

[1] See, for example, *Essays on Nationalism* (1926); *Historical Evolution of Modern Nationalism* (1931); *Patriotism, Nationalism, and the Brotherhood of Man* (1937); *The Novelty of Totalitarianism in the History of Western Civilization* (1939); *This Inevitable Conflict* (1941).

Poland in September, 1939. Followed in due course, less than two years later, the naval and air blitz at faraway Pearl Harbor; and in December, 1941, the United States found itself, to its surprise and consternation, at war with the embattled and hitherto victorious Axis Powers of Germany, Italy, and Japan.

II

On March 17, 1942, I received in my study at the University a letter, dated March 16 and marked "personal and confidential," from the Under Secretary of State, Mr. Sumner Welles, who was Acting Secretary during a temporary absence of Mr. Cordell Hull. It read: "The President has asked me to have an informal talk with you regarding a possibility which he is now considering. Unfortunately, at the present moment, it is impossible for me to leave Washington, and I wonder, therefore, if it would be convenient for you, within the next few days, to come down to Washington to have a brief talk with me regarding the matter. I shall be happy to arrange an appointment any day that proves convenient for you, and I shall appreciate it if you will be kind enough to telegraph me the day before you are planning to come so that a time can be set aside."

I naturally speculated on what the "possibility" might be which the President was considering, but with meager results. The more I thought about it, the more mystified I became. I knew Mr. Welles, and in 1936 I had received from him an invitation to be one of the American delegates to the Pan-American Conference in Buenos Aires, which I had then declined. Very recently, indeed just a few days before this latest letter from Mr. Welles, one of his associates, Mr. Charles A. Thomson, the Chief of the Division of Cultural Relations, had asked me to make a two to three months' visit to Brazil. Could the President be considering me for some special mission in South America? That was the nearest I could guess as to what was in store for me.

The letter from Mr. Welles came on a Tuesday. The next day was the only comparatively free day I had for a week. On Thursday

I was booked full with university lectures and seminars. On Saturday I was scheduled to give a lecture at Wheaton College in Massachusetts. Accordingly, I telephoned Mr. Welles that I would call on him the next day, Wednesday.

I went to Washington on Wednesday morning, March 18, expecting to return to New York the same night, and unhampered therefore by any luggage save a brief-case containing some student manuscript and a blue pencil. Mr. Welles received me most cordially, and opened discussion by remarking, and repeating with emphasis, that what President Roosevelt wanted me to do would entail heavy sacrifices on my part. Would I be willing in the grave crisis confronting our nation to make unusual sacrifices? I replied that I too recognized the extreme gravity of the current situation and that, of course, no American's personal interests should now stand in the way of his serving the Government in any position for which he might be fitted. Mr. Welles then got to the point. He said the President wanted to send me as his Ambassador to Spain. It would be a very difficult assignment, but extremely important and critical for our future military fortunes, and one which the President thought I, if anyone, could successfully discharge.

My first reaction was astonishment and something close to panic. Why should *I* be sent to Spain? True, I had read a good deal of Spanish history and had even written some; and I was a Catholic. But except for a glimpse from Gibraltar over the barbed-wire entanglements of "No-man's Land" while I was on a Mediterranean cruise in 1938, I had never seen Spain. All that came at the moment to my confused mind was, curiously enough, a recollection of a prank of my youth, when, in the midst of the Spanish-American War of 1898, a school-chum and I had secretly manufactured a big Spanish flag and run it up in the night on the village flagpole to the amazement next morning of the whole community. What this reveals, I must leave to the psychiatrists. Perhaps at an early age I already had a perverse liking for Spain and the Spanish people. Possibly it was a gesture in favor of an "underdog." More likely, it may only have been an exuberant show of youthful animal spirits.

When the first shock of Mr. Welles's proposal was over, and as discussion of it developed, I advanced against it several arguments which I regarded as convincing but which he more or less gently brushed aside. I pointed out that I was not a career man, that I had had no experience in the State Department, that I was not trained or used to being a diplomat. To which he rejoined, rather jauntily, that there was no mystery about being a diplomat, that I would be provided with competent foreign-service aides and could learn what was needful of State Department practice within a month, and that, anyway, the President wanted for the emergency in Spain not a routine man but a professor presumed to have imagination, initiative, and a broad knowledge of international affairs.

I said further that while I could read Spanish, I could not speak it, and it seemed highly desirable, if not absolutely requisite, that an Ambassador to Spain should be able to converse fluently with any and every Spaniard. Mr. Welles expressed regret that I did not speak Spanish but insisted that this was no insuperable obstacle to my going to Spain. It would be better, he said, to speak no Spanish than to speak it badly or haltingly, and I would find that many Spaniards spoke English or French. In any event, it was the rule that our Ambassadors and Ministers should make their official representations in English.

Likewise I explained that I was not wealthy and could not afford to maintain such an establishment as might be required to uphold the dignity and advance the prestige of the United States in Spain. Mr. Welles tried to be reassuring about finances. While the ambassadorial salary might hardly suffice to cover my official and family expenses, the exceptionally high cost of living in Spain could be reduced by importation of staple foodstuffs from America and Portugal, and I could count on additional "representation allowances" from the State Department. The President, he said, was anxious that financial obstacles should not stand in the way of a man's serving wherever he was most needed.

I expressed serious doubt as to whether the existing Spanish Government would be willing to receive me if I were willing to go. I reminded Mr. Welles that I had never been a partisan of

General Franco or the Falange. During the Spanish Civil War, while I had signed a protest of American co-religionists of mine against a published statement of other Americans which attacked the Spanish bishops and appeared to condone the killing of priests and nuns by Spanish "Loyalists," I had also protested in writing against the pro-Franco and pro-Nationalist campaigns which certain publications and individuals were then conducting in the United States.[1] I had never concealed my faith in democracy and individual liberty or my hostility to totalitarianism in any of its forms. In view of the record, I would be surprised if General Franco and his Foreign Minister should not regard me as *persona non grata*. And with a rebuff from Spain in prospect, would President Roosevelt wish to nominate me? After questioning me about certain details of the record, and remarking on the very small number of our fellow countrymen who had maintained a disinterested and judicious attitude toward the contending forces in the Spanish Civil War, Mr. Welles asked me to leave the question of my acceptability to the Spanish Government. He was sure the President would not hesitate to name me, and while the response from Spain might be slow, he thought it would be favorable. He relied on Spain's desire, as well as on our need, in the present juncture of affairs, to preserve friendly diplomatic relations between the two countries.

I had no illusions about the difficulties of the task which I was being asked to shoulder. I foresaw difficulties in Spain with a dictatorship which owed its existence in part to Axis military aid and which by common repute was unfriendly to the democracies and sympathetic with Hitler and Mussolini. I likewise foresaw difficulties at home, where the bulk of public opinion was still inflamed

[1] I had written on May 4, 1937, to the Editor of the *Commonweal*: "You advertise, in the issue of May 7th, a mass meeting to be held at Madison Square Garden on May 19th 'under the auspices of *The Commonweal* and The Calvert Associates.' I judge from the advertisement that the meeting will be wholly favorable to General Franco and his following and that it will engender more heat than light. I believe it will do grave harm.

"What immediately troubles me is your commitment of *The Commonweal* and The Calvert Associates to what I can only regard as an ill-considered and mistaken line of action. You have obviously not consulted either the Editorial Council of the former or the Board of Directors of the latter. In the circumstances, I must ask you to withdraw my name from both immediately."

over the Spanish Civil War and antagonistic to General Franco and his Falange, and where a considerable number of influential publicists would tend to regard any American Ambassador to Spain as a Fascist or at least as a collaborator with Fascism and hence to campaign against any line of action he might follow. And in view of the current military situation and of the patent advantage to the Axis of its early forceful occupation of the Iberian peninsula, the chances of any new American Ambassador's getting to Spain and being able to stay for any length of time seemed very slim indeed.

Mr. Welles had no illusions, either. He frankly admitted and even enlarged on the difficulties. But these, he said, were a challenge to the United States and to me personally. Wouldn't I accept the challenge? At any rate, President Roosevelt wanted to talk directly with me about it and requested that I come to his office the next morning.

When I left Mr. Welles's office I was pretty well convinced that I should not attempt the mission to Spain. Nevertheless, I could not decline to see the President. So, after telephoning to my wife and to the University that I would not be back in New York until Thursday evening, and after buying a toothbrush and a pair of pyjamas, I spent three hours riding about Washington in search of a vacant hotel-room. Washington was already a war-casualty, an over-occupied town. Finally, thanks to the intercession of an old friend, I was accommodated at the modest but comfortable Carroll Arms, between the Capitol and the railway station. Having no burden of luggage, I paid for my night's lodging in advance. I slept fitfully, alternating a wakeful array of reasons why I should remain at home with dreams of fantastic and forbidding castles in Spain.

On Thursday morning, March 19, 1942, I went to the White House offices and was promptly ushered into the President's beautiful oval room. He was sitting with his back to the large windows and in front of a small desk on which were toys and ship-models but no papers. He received me with his usual affability and charm. I had met him casually some years before, but my admiration for the man and for his achievements, both foreign and domestic, was based on general reading and observation rather than on any personal intimacy. Though I had voted for him in 1932 and 1936 and again in 1940, I had never taken an active part in politics, and my adherence to the Democratic Party had been more "independent" than "regular." At no time then or afterwards did he or any other official of our Government ask me about my "politics."

My conference with the President lasted an hour. I repeated, I thought with greater cogency, the arguments I had advanced with Mr. Welles, the day before, why I was not the man to go to Spain. The President said he had considered all those arguments and found them unconvincing. He recognized the difficulties—the very serious difficulties—but he was insisting that I could and should grapple with them and surmount them. I should know the great importance he attached to keeping Spain neutral and out of the war and in persuading it to resist to the utmost of its strength any attempt of the Axis to invade and occupy the peninsula. Quite possibly, despite our best endeavors, General Franco would join Hitler or at any rate offer only token resistance to the entrance of Nazi armies. In that event, the whole peninsula—Portugal as well as Spain—would be overrun; the Portuguese Government would probably seek refuge in the Azores; Gibraltar would be doomed, and with it any likelihood of early and successful Allied operations in the Mediterranean or North Africa. It was our urgent business to prevent or, failing that, to postpone as long as possible any such development. Time was of the essence, and we must gain time. He counted on me, he said.

I told the President that I appreciated the confidence he was reposing in me, but I doubted my ability to do what he wanted done. I would need a week to decide finally if I would go. The President said I might have a week in which to think about it, but "the question was not *if* but *when* I would go."

Before leaving Washington that day, I saw Mr. Welles again and told him I would make my decision of "yes" or "no" within the week. He asked me not to talk about the matter with anyone except members of my immediate family, and perhaps with the President of Columbia, Dr. Nicholas Murray Butler, in order to seek possible leave of absence from the university.

III

During the ensuing week, even while I was keeping my engagement at Wheaton College, I kept turning over in my mind the pros and cons of President Roosevelt's proposal. The cons were so self-evident. I had seen them clearly in my conversations with Mr. Welles and the President, and the more I reflected upon them the more unanswerable they appeared. How could I, a convinced democrat and life-long champion of individual liberty, have any success with a totalitarian government, and at the same time retain the confidence and needful support of those fellow Americans who believed and expected the worst of the existing Spanish regime?

Yet the President had put it up to me so strongly. He apparently had no misgivings, or, if he did, he masterfully concealed them. He was drafting me for a war job. How could I in conscience resist the draft, especially since I had publicly urged for two years past that this Second World War demanded American participation and the drafting of men and materials in the United States with consequent personal sacrifice on the part of all Americans, young and old.

It was conscience and a sense of duty, coupled with a sporting desire to meet a first-rate challenge, which finally decided me. After confidentially informing President Butler and receiving from him the requested leave of absence from Columbia, I notified Mr. Welles, and through him President Roosevelt, on March 25, 1942, that my decision was "yes." I would go to Spain. Two days later I left New York with my family to spend the Easter holidays at our upstate country home.

The State Department must have acted with extraordinary speed, and obtained quick favorable response from the Spanish Government. On the morning of Thursday, April 2, I read in the paper the news of the resignation of Mr. Alexander Weddell, our previous Ambassador to Spain. On the afternoon of Friday, April 3, which happened to be Good Friday, Dr. Edward Danforth, a local physician and friend, telephoned me he had just heard over the radio that the President had announced my nomination. That evening as my family and I gathered around our own radio at Jericho Farm in Afton, we heard the same news from the broadcast of Mr. Elmer Davis.

There followed a hectic day of packing at the farm, and on Easter Sunday, April 5, we motored back to New York. The ensuing month was a very busy one. I had to arrange for quitting my university work in mid-term. I had to make repeated trips to Washington for instruction and consultation. The house in New York had to be closed and preparations made for removal to Madrid. And hundreds of congratulatory letters and telegrams had to be acknowledged. It was nice to know that my wife and I had so many friends with such good wishes for us, but I could not help wondering, as I read their messages, whether they really understood what we were up against and whether they shouldn't have sent us condolences instead of congratulations.

The newspaper comment was almost universally favorable and commendatory of the President's choice. So far as I know, only one editorial expressed dissatisfaction, and that was in the weekly *Nation,* which could hardly be satisfied by any action of our Government affecting Spain short of a declaration of war. Illustrative of the general comment was the following editorial from the *New York Times* of April 4:

. The President has shown wisdom and tact in appointing Carlton J. Hayes to succeed Alexander W. Weddell as Ambassador to Madrid. From the American point of view Spain is a post of capital importance. Aside from our interest in keeping the westernmost peninsula of Europe out of the war on the Axis side, the cultural and traditional influence of Spain in South America makes its policy of vital concern to the United States. Through a difficult and dubious period we have managed to keep on good terms with the Spanish Government, and whether our diplomacy or Nazi arrogance deserves the chief credit, the fact is that the Franco Government is today farther from casting its lot with Berlin and Rome than at any time since the war began. Professor Hayes is admirably fitted to carry on the good work. As a distinguished historian he has the perspective to relate the present to the past in a country with deep roots in history. As an uncompromising enemy of the totalitarian system, he will be able to make the mind of democracy and of America felt on the wavering margins of an Axis-dominated continent. As a Catholic who has done yeoman's work to break down intolerance in the inter-faith committee of Protestants, Catholics and Jews, he will bring a special comprehension to the religious problems that are fundamental to the understanding not only of Spain but of all Latin America. For these reasons and many others the President has made an excellent appointment, and we wish Professor Hayes well in the delicate and difficult task he assumes in turning from the interpretation and teaching to the making of history.

There was a slight delay in securing the Senate's confirmation of the President's nomination, attributable to a trip of the chairman of the Committee on Foreign Affairs, Senator Connally, to his home in Texas. Eventually, however, the nomination was favorably reported out of Committee, and at the end of April it was confirmed by the Senate unanimously and without debate. On May 2, 1942, I took the oath of office and became Ambassador to Spain.

Meanwhile I had been busy within the State Department, familiarizing myself with its organization and procedure and with the voluminous telegrams and despatches of recent years relating to Spain. I profited greatly from frequent conferences with Mr. Sumner Welles, Mr. James Dunn, Mr. Ray Atherton, Mr. Herbert Feis, Mr. Charles Thomson, and particularly with Mr. W. Perry George, who was in immediate charge of the "Spanish desk" in the Department and who not only acted as my guide through the maze of papers and documents but also gave me, from his past personal experience in Spain, much "inside" information not obtainable from written documents. Fortunately, too, Mr. Cordell Hull returned from his vacation while I was then in Washington, and I had the opportunity and pleasure of consulting him at length and obtaining his wise counsel about my mission.

Outside the State Department, I made useful contacts in Washington with the Secretaries of Commerce, Agriculture, and the Treasury, with the Board of Economic Warfare, and with the Coordinator of Information, General William Donovan, who at that time headed the organization which was later split into the Office of Strategic Services and the Office of War Information. Likewise I conferred with the British Ambassador, Lord Halifax; with the

Portuguese Minister, Mr. Bianchi; with the Apostolic Delegate, Mgr. Cicognani, whose brother was Nuncio in Madrid; and with the Spanish Ambassador, Señor Cardenas.

With the President I had another conversation, in which he reiterated his anxiety lest Spain be drawn into the war to the very serious detriment of pending Allied plans. He did not specify these plans, but from what happened six months afterwards, I infer that he already had in mind an Allied landing in North Africa close to Spain. He asked me to call on Dr. Salazar on my way through Portugal and to impress upon him the high prospects of ultimate Allied victory. The President added that he would be willing to meet and talk with General Franco in the Canary Islands or elsewhere outside of Spain if a real crisis threatened, and that, at my discretion, I might communicate this suggestion to the Chief of the Spanish State. He was, he said, a strong believer in the advantages to be derived from personal contacts between chiefs of state. It was quite obvious to me that the President would go to unusual lengths to forestall Spain's cooperating with the Axis.

On the eve of my final departure from Washington, I was fortunate enough to be a fellow-guest with the visiting President of Ecuador at tea at the White House. President Roosevelt chatted gaily and instructively about a variety of subjects, including the economic progress of Latin America and his own early travels and observations in Spain. Mrs. Roosevelt presided simply and charmingly at the tea table.

IV

Arrangements were made, soon after the Senate's confirmation of my appointment, for my departure for Spain. At first there was some talk of sending the Hayes family by a Portuguese or Spanish boat, chiefly in order that we might take with us all our personal luggage and likewise those housekeeping articles, such as silver, linen, blankets, etc., which the Government did not furnish for the Embassy. There was, however, a widespread belief throughout the State Department, which I then shared, that the Germans

might invade Spain at any moment and that consequently my mission to that country would be brief and even might be over before
I got there. With this prudently in mind, I had obtained from
Columbia a leave of absence only for the summer and autumn of
1942. If we couldn't reach Spain, or if we should shortly have to
leave it in a hurry, the less luggage we carried with us the better.
Besides, as the President had said, "time was of the essence," and a
boat trip to Spain took much time.

Hence it was ultimately decided that we should go by Pan-
American clipper from New York to Lisbon, and thence by rail
or air to Madrid. We were allowed fifty-five pounds of luggage
per person. By the time all my ceremonial clothes were packed,
little space remained for anything else. As a result, the other members of the family, on our entry into Madrid, had but scant advantage, in the way of clothes, over the uprooted war refugees who
had entered before us.

We had been warned of the serious shortage of foodstuffs in
Spain and of conditions there bordering on famine and starvation.
So we placed a large order with an American wholesale grocery
firm for flour, sugar, cereals, oil, canned milk, butter, vegetables,
and other supplies to be shipped, together with our extra clothing,
a few house-furnishings, and our automobile, by Portuguese boat
from Philadelphia. On urgent recommendations from Washington
and from the Rockefeller Foundation in New York, we carried
with us an assortment of vitamin tablets (which we never used) and
a supply of vaccines against smallpox, typhoid fever, and typhus.
Despite remarkable subsequent improvement of living and sanitary
conditions in Spain, and despite repeated reporting of the facts
by the Embassy, none of the several hundred American officials
who landed in Madrid during the next three years failed to bring
a mental picture of "starving Spain" and a bottle of vitamin pills.
By now there must be a big surplus of vitamins in Spain.

In view of current opinion about Spain and its dangers, I was
a bit surprised by the number of persons who appealed to me to
help them get jobs in the Embassy at Madrid and to take them
over with me. Evidently Spain fascinated them, but I don't know

whether the fascination was associated with novel wartime perils in Spain or with those proverbial old castles in Spain. At any rate, I couldn't have taken the applicants if I had wished to do so.

My own family were to go with me: my wife; my son, Carroll, then sixteen years of age and a student in the Canterbury School in Connecticut; and my daughter, Mary Elizabeth, eighteen years of age and just completing her freshman year in Barnard College. In addition, I had decided to take with me a personal secretary, and for this post I had selected Michael George, a son of the Foreign Service Officer in charge of the Spanish desk in the State Department. Michael was a young man who had lived and worked in Spain, who spoke fluently both Spanish and French, and who at the moment was attending the Georgetown School of Foreign Service.

On the afternoon of Tuesday, May 12, 1942, we received instruction in New York to be ready to depart on the Clipper at four o'clock the next morning. We passed on the word to Michael at Washington, and he arrived late that night. There was, of course, no sleep for us. At the strange and almost ominous hour of four the five of us bade farewell to home and passed through the deserted streets and avenues of New York. It was seven o'clock when the clipper, with drawn curtains, actually took off with us from La Guardia Field.

We found the clipper flight pleasant and comfortable, though somewhat monotonous and more tiring than we at first realized. We stopped for three hours in the afternoon at Bermuda, where we were officially welcomed and shown about the harbor in a launch. The next morning we were having breakfast at Horta in the Azores, and late the same afternoon we arrived in Lisbon. Here we were met by the American Minister to Portugal, the Honorable Bert Fish, with members of his staff, and were driven to the Palace Hotel in Estoril, a delightful seaside suburb.

The next day, in company with Mr. Fish and his Counselor, Mr. Hugh Millard, I called on Dr. Salazar, the Portuguese prime minister and "dictator." He didn't look like a regular dictator. Rather, he appeared a modest, quiet, and highly intelligent gentleman and scholar. I knew that he had been literally dragged from a professorial chair of political economy in the venerable University of Coimbra a dozen years previously in order to straighten out Portugal's finances, and that his almost miraculous success in this respect had led to the thrusting upon him of other major functions, including those of Foreign Minister and constitution-maker. We conversed more as professors than as diplomats; and the first half hour of our conversation was devoted to professional "shop talk"— universities, books, science, Jacques Maritain's philosophy. He quizzed me about the position of the Catholic church in the United States, and I had the pleasure of informing him that its hundred-odd bishops and the mass of American Catholics, like the rest of the American people, were solidly behind our Government in the prosecution of the war and in the will to overcome the menace of a world dominated by pagan Nazism.

During the second half hour the conversation with Dr. Salazar veered to political and international affairs. He asked my opinion of the current status of war-preparedness in the United States and of when our full armed strength would be employed and how long the war would last. I stressed the fact, in reply, that we were ahead of schedule in our preparedness, that President Roosevelt's seemingly incredible forecasts were being really surpassed in the production of airplanes, tanks, ships, and munitions of all kinds, and in the training of millions of soldiers. I said I had no idea how long the war would last, but however short or long it proved to be, the United States, with *all* its might and resources, was in it to the finish and to *victory*. He expressed misgivings about what Russian and other Communists might do with a victory in which they shared, adding, however, that the long-range chances favored the English-speaking peoples.

But what, Dr. Salazar queried, would we do with the peace? Would the United States stay with it, as with the war, or would America relapse into isolation as in 1919 and again lose peace for the entire world? I said I was going to make bold and ask him a question. What kind of a peace did he want? He indicated it should embody guarantees of the independence of states, small as well as large, through a strong Association of Nations and one not dominated by only two Great Powers. The League of 1920 broke down, he remarked, primarily because it was but a "Franco-British syndicate." The United States *must* be in the new Association, along with the defeated countries, if the Association was not to suffer the same sorry fate as the League. He took some comfort, he admitted, from information that Wendell Willkie and other Republican leaders, as well as our Democratic President, were now anti-isolationist. He emphasized the need of more specific statements of our war aims and peace plans. They would be helpful and should be reassuring to lesser Powers like Portugal.

Dr. Salazar also emphasized the need of better relations between the United States and Spain, particularly in the economic domain. We should not merely buy from Spain what we wanted, but supply Spain with what she most required—oil and cereals and fertilizer. The Iberian peninsula was in many respects a unit, and what helped Spain would also help Portugal. Commercial ties could draw Spain as well as Portugal toward America.

While I was in Lisbon, I paid my respects to Admiral Leahy, our Ambassador to Vichy, who was awaiting ship for a sad return home. He was much broken by the recent death of his wife, but extremely interesting and illuminating on the French situation. He voiced the opinion that Vichy's collaboration with the Axis was not likely to extend to the French fleet, though it might affect certain French African bases.

Finding that rail service to Madrid was extremely slow and unsatisfactory, I booked passage for us on a plane of the Spanish "Iberia Company" for the next day, Saturday, May 16, 1942, which happened to be my sixtieth birthday. We left the airport at Lisbon at 9:30 that morning. In two hours and a half we would be due in Madrid.

V

Since that first conversation with Mr. Sumner Welles on March 18, and throughout the crowded intervening two months, certain convictions had gradually crystallized in my mind about policies and methods which I would try to follow in Spain if I ever got there. I fully recognized, of course, that our basic policy toward Spain was not, and should not be, determined by me. It could be determined, properly and with due reference to the exigencies of the war and the over-all world situation, only by the President, the Department of State, and the Joint Chiefs of Staff. In basic policy, therefore, I would simply obey orders. If it was decided in Washington to abandon Spain to the Axis or to make war on Spain, and I was accordingly ordered to break off relations with the Spanish Government and leave the country, I would promptly break and (if possible) leave.

It had been made abundantly clear to me, however, that the basic policy of the President and the Joint Chiefs of Staff, and consequently of the State Department, was to keep Spain out of the war, as a neutral barrier to further German advance in the Mediterranean and Africa, and not to break, but rather to maintain, friendly relations with its Government. On just how this was to be done, I had received no instructions. As Ambassador, I would have to devise and employ the tactics best calculated to implement the basic policy—the strategy—which my superiors determined. If these didn't like my tactics they could countermand them or recall me.

I would, then, do everything I could (1) to keep Spain from joining the Axis, (2) to encourage Spain to offer all possible resistance to any Axis invasion or threat of invasion, and (3) to obtain from Spain every possible facility for our economic and military warfare against the Axis, and in particular against Germany. The success of this program would depend, I recognized, on our ability not only to influence Spanish "public opinion" in our favor but also to obtain the cooperation of the existing Spanish Government. We might not like the dictatorship of General Franco. It certainly, from what I had read and heard about it, did not conform with American ideals. Yet it was the actual Government of Spain and the Government to which President Roosevelt had accredited me. It was this Government which would decide for Spain whether or not to join the Axis, whether or not to resist German invasion, whether or not to accord special facilities to us. I would have to deal with the Spanish Government which was, and not with what many of my countrymen back home hoped would be a different regime.

In tactics, therefore, I would proceed on the assumption that our enemy was not the Spanish Government but the Axis. I would wage war in Spain against the Axis, not against Spaniards. To this end, I would sedulously refrain from interfering, or giving the appearance of interfering, in the internal affairs of Spain. I would show no partiality for or against any domestic party or faction—Nationalist, Monarchist, Republican, Socialist, Communist. I would consign the Spanish Civil War to history and leave the future of Spain to Spaniards.

In this way only could I hope to get the cooperation we needed from the existing Spanish Government. While I most surely would not dissemble, with General Franco or Serrano Suñer or anyone else, my own loyalty to democracy and repugnance to Fascism and totalitarianism, I would assume that these isms were foreign products and that to no Spaniard were they really congenial. With officials of the Spanish Government, as with private citizens, I would seek to develop the most courteous and cordial personal relations. I would especially stress the historic and cultural ties between Spain and America, and the advantages to be derived by Spain and the Spanish people from close commercial relations with the English-speaking countries. In soliciting any sort of cooperation from the Spanish Government, I would always endeavor to present the matter as being in the interest of Spain quite as much as in that of the United States or the United Nations. I well knew that no Government will ever do anything which it does not regard at the moment as in its own interest.

For the execution of this strategy and these tactics I counted on the loyal and efficient support of the experienced foreign-service staff of our Embassy at Madrid and our consulates throughout Spain, and in this, as events proved, I was not to be disappointed. And I rightfully counted, too, on helpful collaboration of the

British and other Allied Missions in Spain, especially on those from Hispanic America.

Almost two years afterwards, my good friend Charles A. Beard wrote me: "I belong to the old school of dodos who do not regard an Ambassador of the United States as a filibuster with a roving commission to reform the country to which he is accredited and otherwise make as much trouble as he can. I labor under the impression that he is to work within the frame of his Government's policy toward the accomplishment of certain major ends. Naturally in so far as that policy is under fire at home, he is likely to come under fire, but in all such cases personal criticisms seem to me to arise from a misapprehension of the Ambassador's duties."

What Beard thus wrote on March 24, 1944, exactly expressed my abiding conviction about ambassadorial functions. And whatever may be current or future criticism of the policy of our Government and of myself toward Spain and its Government, that policy was no novelty. Long ago it had been clearly stated by James Monroe. In the same message containing the famous "Monroe Doctrine," which he sent to the Congress on December 2, 1823, President Monroe made these remarks: "The late events in Spain . . . show that Europe is still unsettled. . . . Our policy in regard to Europe, which was adopted at an early stage of the wars which have so long agitated that quarter of the globe, nevertheless remains the same, which is, not to interfere in the internal concerns of any of its powers; to consider the Government de facto as the legitimate Government for us; to cultivate friendly relations with it, and to preserve those relations by a frank, firm, and manly policy, meeting, in all instances, the just claims of every power; submitting to injuries from none."

That had been said in 1823, but it provided the text and indicated the methods for me, as I, with my family, took off from Lisbon on May 16, 1942, on the last leg of the journey to a mission of dubious and perhaps crucial nature in Spain.

The pilot of the Spanish plane which bore us was a big fellow who looked exactly like the ideal Aryan German of the Nazis. Presently, however, as we passed beyond the smiling Portuguese landscape, dotted with whitewashed cottages, and reached the grimmer Castilian countryside with its steep high hills and barren wastes and huddled towns, I learned from the pilot that he was a native of Andalucia, that he had never been in Germany, that he spoke English fluently, and that he was pro-Ally. He was, in fact, a fine and agreeable Spaniard. Perhaps, I thought to myself, this mission to Spain may yet succeed.

CHAPTER II

FIRST CONTACTS AND IMPRESSIONS

I

May 16, 1942, was an auspiciously sunshiny day at Madrid. The Spanish plane, after flying across the city, landed us at Barajas Field, a few miles to the east, exactly at noon. As we emerged, our ears ringing from the noise of motors and the drop of altitude, we were greeted by the Spanish captain of the airport and, beyond the barrier, by the full array of the staff of the American Embassy and a representative of the Spanish Foreign Office, Señor Maycas, with his wife, who gallantly presented Mrs. Hayes with a bouquet of red (!) roses.

Among the American staff, which I now met as a group for the first time, were officers and attachés without whose competent assistance and loyal cooperation my mission would have been foredoomed to failure. I was especially fortunate in having from the outset a Counselor, or first assistant, of the caliber and experience of Willard Beaulac. He was a native of Rhode Island, and a veteran of the First World War and since then of the Foreign Service. He had spent years at various consular and diplomatic posts in Spanish America and had come from Havana to Madrid in the spring of 1941, a year ahead of me. Recently, between Ambassador Weddell's departure and my arrival, he had been Chargé d'Affaires. He knew Spaniards and liked them. He spoke Spanish fluently. Subsequently he would become our Ambassador to Paraguay. Meanwhile his name will frequently appear in this narrative.

The name of Ralph Ackerman will similarly appear. He had been our Commercial Attaché in Spain continuously since our recognition of General Franco's regime in the spring of 1939, and before that he had had wide South American experience in both public and private commercial affairs. I don't think I ever knew a man who combined as perfectly as Ackerman an unfailing memory of detailed facts and figures with a grasp of the economic situation as a whole. In view of the fundamental relationship of our economic and commercial policy to our political and military ends in Spain, it was providential that Ackerman headed the vitally important economic section of the Madrid Embassy.

There were also, as First Secretaries of the Embassy, two recently arrived Foreign Service men of unusual ability: George Haering, a meticulous investigator and reporter, whom I later relied upon to take immediate charge of aviation matters and to exercise needful supervision over certain of our auxiliary services; and Julian Harrington, who was our liaison officer with the United States Commercial Company and with the British Embassy in economic affairs. Another First Secretary was Frances Willis, one of the few women in the American Foreign Service, an exceptionally well-educated, devoted, and delightful collaborator, who had been transferred to Spain from Belgium in July, 1940, when the Germans closed up our Embassy in Brussels, and who at Madrid was responsible for protocol and for much of our inner administration, our code room, pouch and courier service, official financial accounts, etc.

Then, too, there was an outstanding and very outgoing Second Secretary, Earl Crain, a younger man whom everybody called "Tom," who already had had two years' experience in Spain, and who during the past year had undertaken, against great odds but with intense energy and no little success, to build up a "press and propaganda" section within the Embassy. His Spanish was faultless, and Spaniards instinctively liked him. Still younger were two Third Secretaries, Findley Burns and Robert Brandin, graduates of Princeton and recently appointed, who were to prove highly useful in a variety of jobs. The Naval Attaché at the time was Commander Byron Anderson, a likable and capable "sea dog." The Military Attaché was Colonel Ralph Dusenbury, a solid and sober adviser on military affairs, ably assisted by his second in command, Colonel Dorsey Stephens. Besides, honorable mention should be made of Lieutenant Donald Johnson, the competent pilot of the small naval

plane which was attached to the Embassy and on which I was
destined to make many flights about the country.

Introductions to the Embassy Staff and to the official representative of the Spanish Government being concluded, we all proceeded
in a cavalcade of motor cars, with American flags flying, on the
half-hour drive to the Embassy. Mr. Beaulac and Señor Maycas rode
with me in the first car. The others, with what there was of the
Hayes luggage, followed.

The approach to Madrid from the Barajas airport is not attractive. It leads through a narrow road and a slum quarter, and then
past the big bull-ring. Between admiration for the Spanish chauf-
feur's dexterity in dodging children and donkeys and dejection at
seeing so many signs of poverty and malnutrition, I entered Madrid
with very mixed emotions.

The city itself has a dignity and spaciousness and an appearance
of well-being befitting the essentially artificial capital which it is.
Like our own Washington, Madrid is not an ancient city or one
which has concentrated and symbolizes all phases of national
activity. It was arbitrarily selected by Philip II as the seat of his
government because it happened to be close to Spain's geographical
center, and was thus raised from insignificance barely two hundred
years before our national capital was similarly founded. I noted on
the way to the Embassy that the Civil War had left few if any
outward signs of destruction in the eastern half of the city.

Shortly before one o'clock on that May sixteenth of 1942, our
little procession of motor cars reached the Embassy precincts. Front
gates were drawn aside by a porter in uniform resplendent with brass
buttons bearing the American coat-of-arms. We drove into the
courtyard and were welcomed at the front steps by another array,
this time of the Spanish household servants, most of whom had been
with the Embassy for many years. After thanking and bidding goodbyes to our various escorts, my family and Michael George and I
entered, explored, and took possession of the Embassy.

The building, we found, was an extensive three-story chateau,
designed by a French architect in a style reminiscent of Versailles
and built by the Duke of Montellano and his wife, a Mexican

heiress, early in the present century. It had been held on lease as the United States Embassy since the fall of the monarchy in 1931, and during the Civil War from 1936 to 1939 it had provided safe haven for hundreds of refugees and dozens of great works of art. Some damage had been done at that time. A bomb had wrecked apartments on the second floor which Ambassador Claude Bowers had used as his personal quarters, and one or two other bombs had buried themselves in the adjoining garden. Repairs had been made, however, early in the tenure of Ambassador Weddell, and by the time I reached Madrid the tale of the confused and exciting happenings in the Embassy during the three years' Civil War already partook of the nature of legend.

The Embassy premises occupied an entire city block, along the broad thoroughfare of the Castellana (officially the "Avenue of the Generalissimo," though nobody called it by this name), in the best residential district of Madrid and within easy walking-distance of most of the other Embassies and Legations. The garden which spread out from the terrace in back of the residence was the finest and most beautiful in all Madrid and as we walked about it we were charmed by the fountain at the far end, the long intervening lines of rose-bushes in full bloom, and in back of these the double rows of horse-chestnut trees, and still further back the scattered rhododendrons and pine trees.

Externally, the residence, despite obvious need of extensive minor repairs, appeared palatial. Inside, too, it seemed admirably adapted for well nigh regal entertainment, and the furnishings, which, under our lease, went with the house, included numerous French and Spanish antiques and a remarkable collection of magnificent paintings—eight Goyas, four Guardis, two Zuloagas, etc. However, as we gradually discovered, the residence was not actually as palatial or appropriate as it appeared. The first (or ground) story could be used only for receptions and entertainment, and while its plan was excellent for this purpose, with state dining room at one end, ball-room at the other, and smaller salons between, all opening on the beautiful terrace and garden, the furnishings made one feel that this was not at all an *American* Embassy and the

antique French chairs and settees were so dilapidated and rickety
as to imperil the life and limb of anyone who sat upon them. The
third story, which once upon a time had decently housed the
servants, was now a bedlam of congested, badly ventilated, and
poorly furnished offices for the Chancery, which could be reached
only by an antiquated little elevator that was more often out
of commission than in, or by kitchen back stairs. Indeed, so great
was the congestion in the Chancery that the offices of the Ambassador and his secretary had to be removed to the second floor. The
servants had already been consigned to dingy lodgings in the base-
ment, and all that remained as possible living and working quarters
for the Ambassador's family—to say nothing of possible guests—
was five bedrooms, a diminutive library, and a drafty hallway on the
second story. In the midst of an apparent palace, therefore, the
five of us settled ourselves into a six-room apartment without anything material to remind us of America and without much privacy.
We counted that day rare when some would-be visitor to the
Chancery did not lose his way and visit one of our bedrooms instead.

I couldn't help but contrast the American Embassy in Madrid
with the Spanish Embassy in Washington. The latter, while externally comporting with other buildings in its American environment, was so thoroughly Spanish inside, with Spanish furniture,
Spanish silver, Spanish decoration, even with a Spanish patio, as
to make any visitor feel that he was in Spain, in a typical and very
attractive Spain. And nearby but apart from the residence stood
a commodious and again typically Spanish chancery, both owned
by the Spanish Government and cared for principally by Spanish
servants. On the other hand, the United States, a far richer and
more powerful country, with finely indigenous achievements in the
art of cabinet-maker and silversmith, of which it might well be
proud, was content, in the cultural center of the Spanish-speaking
world, with a makeshift, rented Embassy whose interior appoint-
ments and furnishings and exclusively Spanish help could only
serve to confirm the impression of visitors that the United States
had no culture of its own and must depend upon fragments bor-
rowed from Continental Europe. An appropriate *American* Em-

bassy is needed in Madrid and I kept saying so to our State Department throughout my stay in Spain. Better and more enduring propaganda for us from satisfying that need, I am convinced, than from spending millions on high-pressure salesmanship of ephemeral propagandist news-sheets and pamphlets.

After inspecting and sizing-up the Embassy and having an impromptu luncheon of scrambled eggs, we took our first walk on Madrid streets and found our way to the nearest church—the homelike Franciscan Church of San Fermin de los Navarros—where we offered thanks for our safe trip and a prayer for the success of the mission. As we returned, I became acutely aware of omnipresent Germans. Just beyond the church was a big social club for them; across the street, the headquarters of their local Gestapo; in a side street, a large German school; and directly opposite our Embassy, a Nazi Kulturinstitut with swastikas rampant. I would shortly discover that Madrid was dotted with dozens of other "annexes" to the German Embassy and that where these were lacking one was likely to find an Italian Fascist "annex" or "school" or "institute."

II

At noon on Tuesday, May 19, 1942, in company with our Counselor, Mr. Beaulac, I visited the Foreign Office for the first time and made the customary courtesy call on the Foreign Minister, Señor Serrano Suñer. The Foreign Office is housed in the old Palace of Santa Cruz, in a crowded and busy section of the city. It is an unpretentious-looking but massively built structure which had originally served as a prison for offending aristocrats. As we entered it and went up to the reception room and the Minister's office on the second floor, I noticed, with mingled amusement and annoyance, a succession of youthful guards, all dressed in Falange uniforms and all holding guns in one hand and stretching out the other in fascist salute to me. I recalled that Serrano Suñer was not only Foreign Minister but head of the Falange. He welcomed me with affability and promised to make arrangements for my prompt presentation of credentials to the Caudillo. We chatted for half an hour and he then introduced me to his chief assistants in the Foreign Office. Two days later, on May 21, he returned the call at the Embassy, and we had another brief conversation.

According to established protocol, I was to present to General Franco, at some time designated by him, the "letter of recall" of my predecessor and the "letter of credence" for myself, and on that occasion I was to make a short speech, presenting the letters, and General Franco another short speech, presumably perfunctory, accepting them. My speech was to be submitted to the Foreign Office in advance of delivery.

I prepared the speech with much care and, after incorporating some suggestions of Mr. Beaulac, despatched it to the Foreign Office. When it came back, accompanied by the reply which General Franco proposed to make, I was astonished to discover that the attack on totalitarian economics which I had inserted in my speech not only was not objected to but was clearly acknowledged and endorsed in the Caudillo's speech. Could it be that we were to have here the first declared departure of Spain from Axis tutelage?

The date finally set for the presentation of my credentials was Tuesday, June 9, and it proved to be quite an affair. At ten o'clock in the morning our official staff, twelve strong, assembled with me at the Embassy in full dress. At half past ten a hundred Moorish Guards, in splendid native costume, arrived in the courtyard and street outside mounted on magnificent and richly caparisoned stallions with hooves painted gold or silver. They made a striking spectacle. At a quarter of eleven came the Spanish Chief of Protocol, Introducer of Ambassadors, Baron de las Torres, with five automobiles. In these, with prancing Moorish Guards on either side, we picturesquely paraded across the city to the stately and formerly royal palace in the far west end. Here, as we passed into the spacious courtyard, detachments of soldiers presented arms and a military band played "The Star-Spangled Banner" and the Spanish national anthem.

Entering the palace, we were ushered up the grand staircase, through various halls, and presently into the long throne-room. In front of the throne stood General Franco; at his right, the entire cabinet, and at his left, various dignitaries of state, church, and university. I faced the Generalissimo from the middle of the room, with my staff fanned out in a semicircle in back of me. I read my speech, in English of course, and handed him the letters. I said:

It is my great honor and privilege to place in Your Excellency's hands the letter by which the President of the United States of America accredits me near Your Excellency as his Ambassador Extraordinary and Plenipotentiary. I beg at the same time to present to Your Excellency the letter of recall of my distinguished predecessor, the Honorable Alexander W. Weddell, who by reason of serious illness has been compelled to retire from public service. I know that he has resigned his post as Ambassador to Spain with profound regret.

The President of the United States has especially charged me to assure Your Excellency of his great personal esteem and of his cordial good wishes for your personal welfare and for that of the Spanish people. It is his fervent desire that the ties of friendship between Spain and the United States be further strengthened in the interest not only of our two countries but of our common civilization.

I am by profession, Sir, an historian, and one sympathetically familiar with the long proud history of Spain. As such I am particularly mindful of the great cultural debt which my country, together with its sister nations of the New World, owes to Spain. It was Spain whose celebrated Admiral exactly four and a half centuries ago discovered our continents and opened them to Christian settlement and Christian civilization. It was Spain which, during ensuing generations, implanted far and wide throughout America certain basic institutions, a graciousness of living, and the sense of personal dignity which is Spain's illustrious heritage. It was Spain, too—we Americans shall always gratefully remember—which gave invaluable aid to the United States in establishing its freedom and independence as a nation.

It is gratifying to be able to remark that at the present time every college and university in the United States supports professorships and libraries of Spanish language and literature, while for a score of years Spanish has been taught in our secondary schools more widely than any other foreign language.

My country, Excellency, is an idealistic country. It cherishes intellectual and spiritual values. It is thoroughly conscious at the same time of the high esteem in which these values have been held by the Spanish people during a long and glorious history.

The United States seeks the friendship of all peoples. It is devoted to the thesis that the security and well-being of every country are directly dependent upon the security and well-being of all other countries. Respect for the sovereignty of other nations is, therefore, a basic tenet of our foreign policy. We do not try to impose our system of government on any other people. Equally, we are always quick to resist any attempt of another government to impose its system on us.

My country is devoted also to the principle that international trade should be freed to the greatest possible extent from the restrictions which have barred the nations of the world from free access to raw materials which should in justice be made available to all peoples on an equal basis. No country is self-sufficient or is capable of becoming self-sufficient without disastrously lowering the living standards of its people. Therefore, within the limitations naturally imposed by the troubled circumstances in which we all live today, my country is prepared to engage in honorable trade with all countries which are in a position to trade with us, exchanging those commodities which we are free to export for those products which friendly nations can send to us without depriving their own people.

In seeking sincerely and to the best of my ability to interpret to Your Excellency's Government the aims and ideals of my Government, and to communicate and interpret to my Government the ideals and aspirations of Your Excellency's Government, I venture to express the hope that I may receive the understanding assistance of Your Excellency and of those persons whom Your Excellency has chosen to collaborate with you in your high endeavor.

The speech with which General Franco replied in Spanish did not depart from the text I had previously seen. It was, in English translation, as follows:

I receive with deep satisfaction from Your Excellency's hands the credential letters in which His Excellency the President of the United States of America accredits you to me as his Ambassador Extraordinary and Plenipotentiary, and I very gratefully reply to the kind words by which Your Excellency conveys to me the greeting and personal esteem of the First Magistrate of the American people. To these I cordially respond, joining to his my reciprocal good wishes for him personally and for the nation over which he presides.

I am especially thankful to the President of the United States for the delicate attention he has showed in selecting such an illustrious person as Your Excellency to represent him in Spain. We well know, and I and my Government appreciate, the qualifications and work of Your Excellency as an historian and the friendly sympathy with which throughout your cultural and professional life you have known how to estimate and set forth the true significance of Spanish achievements in America across the centuries, and the high disinterestedness and noble zeal with which our predecessors carried the sign of the Cross and the light of civilization to backward peoples that through the kindly forethought of the Catholic Queen [Isabella] were incorporated into the modern world by means of the brave action and intelligent thinking of so many famous pioneers whom Spain devoted to the great work of transfusing our soul and our blood into the immense American world. I am convinced of the fine promise and happy augury which such an appointment as yours indicates, inasmuch as no one is in a better position to build up good relations and make the existing situation in the world less delicate than he who, through his mastery of our history and his spiritual attitude toward it, knows us and can appreciate at their due worth the basic qualities of our race.

This conviction and the reciprocal confidence which proceeds from it makes me regard the beginning of Your Excellency's mission in Spain, which I desire should be long and fruitful, with a fundamental optimism which permits me to hope that, subject to the mutual respect for our different regimes to which you so understandingly allude, the collaboration of Your Excellency with my Government will be advantageous for both sides and conducive to the highest interests of humanity.

I believe also in the good of the economic interchange to which Your Excellency refers in the words you have just spoken, thanks to which the friendly spiritual relationship will have the solid support of a correlation of interests between the two countries, based on the principle that no people on earth can live normally by its own economy and that all need one another for the attainment of human ends.

In giving, then, to Your Excellency the most hearty welcome, and in thanking you for your complimentary words of salutation, I take note of your offer to communicate our aspirations and points of view, and I assure you, with my personal assistance, the friendly and sincere cooperation of my Government in the common labor.

At the conclusion of these remarks, the Generalissimo stepped down and shook hands with me. I presented my staff to him in order, and he introduced me to each member of the cabinet. He then invited me, with Señor Serrano Suñer and the Baron de las Torres, to an adjoining room, where it was his custom to spend a few minutes in polite and theoretically "intimate" conversation with newly received ambassadors. This time, however, the "few minutes" lengthened into full fifty, with the result, as I afterwards learned from members of my staff, that the waiting assemblage in the throne-room evinced growing wonder and uneasiness and that bets were made by the Counselor with the Commercial Attaché whether I or the Caudillo was being done away with.

What really happened during those fifty minutes was a spirited conversation between General Franco and myself, with the Baron de las Torres interpreting and Sr. Serrano Suñer sitting mute. The General, I soon perceived, differed notably from the caricatures of him current in the "leftist" press of the United States. Physically he was not so short or so stout and he did not "strut." Mentally he impressed me as being not at all a stupid or "me too" sort of person, but distinctly alert and possessing a good deal of both determination and caution and a rather lively and spontaneous sense of humor. He laughed easily and naturally, which, I imagine, a Hitler couldn't do and a Mussolini wouldn't do except in private.

It was evident throughout the conversation that the Caudillo was, above everything else, a professional military man and that, like so many others of his calling and training elsewhere, he had a limited knowledge of the complexities and potentialities of the world outside his own country and a most respectful admiration —or fear—of a superior and most successful foreign military machine such as Germany's had proved itself to be. He seemed certain that Germany had already practically won the war. I did my best to enlighten him about our resources of men and material, about our firm and united will to win, about the scale and speed of our preparations to wage war in Europe as well as in the Far East. I fear he thought I was telling him fairy stories. He insisted upon the "impregnability" of the "fortress of Europe" which German arms had constructed and against which all efforts of the British and the Russians and "even of the French" had proved vain. France was utterly defeated. Russia was being conquered. The British Empire was spent. Even if we could now train and equip large armies we couldn't repeat our feat of 1917–1918 and get them across the Atlantic, by reason of the vastly increased effectiveness of German submarines, and in any event there would now be no such possible landing place for us as France had provided in the First World War. The moral was that we should concentrate our strength against Japan in the Pacific and come to terms with the Axis in Europe.

I asked the Caudillo if he could contemplate with equanimity for Spain the lasting preponderance, all over the Continent, of Nazi Germany with its fanatical racialism and anti-Christian paganism. He admitted that that was not a pleasant prospect for himself or for Spain, but he trusted it would not materialize. He believed that Germany would make concessions if we would, and thus a kind of "balance of power" could be reestablished in Europe. The danger for Europe, and for Spain, he insisted, was not so much in Nazi Germany as in Russian Communism. Spain did not wish an Axis victory but it most ardently wished the defeat of Russia. Spain's "non-belligerency," he was at some pains to explain, meant that while it was not neutral in the struggle against Communism, and specifically in the war between Germany and Russia, it took no part in the conflict between the Axis on the one hand and the Western Powers on the other. Spain, he said, had no hostility toward the United States.

I am sure I made perfectly clear to General Franco the impossibility of his expecting me to agree with his diagnosis of the troubles afflicting the world or with his proposed remedies. I reminded him of the tryranny and vaulting ambition of Nazi Germany and its steady succession of broken pledges and forceful aggressions. I pointed out that it was not Russia which had attacked Germany, but Germany which had attacked Russia, and I stressed the futility of attempting to compromise with Germany or to aid it against one victim of its aggression while professing sympathy for others. Perhaps all this had no effect, though the Caudillo gave every appearance of being intensely interested, and I imagined at the time that he was somewhat moved. He was certainly most courteous in attitude and speech. His silent Foreign Minister, however, appeared dubious, even cynical; I felt that at heart Serrano Suñer was distinctly pro-Axis.

At the conclusion of the conversation I rejoined my staff and left the palace. We were escorted, again by Moorish guards, back to the Embassy, where, still in bright sunshine and full dress, we refreshed ourselves by drinking a toast to the victory of the United Nations.

Two features of that day were especially noteworthy. One was the obviously friendly attitude of the crowds of people that lined the streets through which our procession passed to and from the palace. There was much hand-clapping, and not infrequently the V sign was made. The other was the favorable publicity which the Government must have authorized and directed. The Spanish press and radio, which hitherto had been stridently pro-Axis and had almost totally ignored Allied news, now blossomed forth with pictures and detailed accounts of the ceremony and with the speeches in full. The Caudillo's implied criticism of totalitarian economics was widely commented upon and commended.

III

During the ensuing summer of 1942, I saw little of the Foreign Minister. Serrano Suñer was not noted for long or sustained work at the Foreign Office. He was away a large part of the time, looking after his beloved Falange organization in the country or vacationing with his family. I did manage to have fairly lengthy discussions with him at the Foreign Office on Monday, July 6, and on Saturday, August 29, and a brief conversation with him at the Caudillo's garden party at La Granja on Saturday, July 18. And I sent him several communications.

He was always courteous to me, but his habit of slouching in his chair and letting his eyes roam about the ceiling was a bit disconcerting, as continued to be the Fascist-saluting Falange youths who lined the pathway to him. He gradually responded to my emphatic protests against the completely pro-Axis tone and tenor of the Spanish press and instructed the Falange censorship first to permit, and later to enforce, the publication of our official war communiqués. Incidentally, too, I arranged with him for the transmission of the manuscript of George Santayana's autobiography, *Persons and Places,* in the Spanish diplomatic pouch from

Rome to Madrid, and thence it went to Santayana's publishers in America. The only request which Serrano Suñer made of me was for the delivery of thirty-odd Packard cars, which had previously been ordered and paid for by the Spanish Government. He got the cars, and I was glad that that summer the Caudillo and his high officials were riding about in American, rather than German, automobiles. It was not a bad advertisement.

Meanwhile, at the Embassy we were centering our attention on three things: (1) economic warfare with the Axis; (2) increased press and propaganda effort; and (3) social activities, with a view to enlarging our contacts and influence. In addition, of course, we were intent upon finding out everything we could about the internal situation and the different shades of opinion in the country in order that we might better guess what Spaniards would do if and when the feared German invasion should occur.

Our social contacts were many sided. To begin with, there were numerous social, as well as business, contacts with the Allied and neutral diplomats in Madrid. Soon after my arrival and before the presentation of my credentials, dinners were given for us by the British and Portuguese Ambassadors and the Turkish Minister; and after the presentation of credentials, formal visits were exchanged, and a round of luncheons and teas and dinners commenced, with official representatives of other countries: Switzerland, Egypt, Ireland, Sweden, the Latin American Republics, and those then occupied by the Germans—Poland, Czechoslovakia, Yugoslavia, Greece, Norway, Holland and Belgium. The representatives of this last group had been deprived of official recognition by Serrano Suñer but they were allowed to remain at their posts in Spain and to communicate in code with their respective Governments. We took special pains to treat them as Allies and equals.

With the Danish and Finnish Ministers our relations, in existing circumstances, were polite but more distant. I presently learned that at least the former was decidedly anti-German, though naturally cautious and circumspect. With the Vichy Ambassador, François Piétri, formal calls were duly exchanged, and Madame Piétri, who had been educated in England and professed great affection for the United States, entertained my wife at luncheon, on one occasion, in the French Embassy. Piétri himself cut a sorry figure. A slight man, with a troubled look, he attended every public function in court uniform with much gold braid and a sword that dragged on the ground and would casually trip him up. His hobnobbings with the German and Italian Ambassadors and his apologetic attitude toward the British Ambassador and me were merely ridiculous. He was undoubtedly loyal to Marshal Pétain, and a tireless patron of concerts and participant in religious processions. But the Spaniards have a keen sense of humor, and they too laughed at Piétri. Sometimes I felt sorry for him.

Certain persons in the friendly diplomatic corps merit particular mention. The British Embassy, which in 1942 was considerably larger than ours, had several capable officers with whom we were in especially close contact: the Minister-Counselor, Arthur Yencken, an Australian, with a most gracious and hospitable wife; the Commercial Attaché, Ellis-Rees; the Press Attaché, Tom Burns, half-British and half-Chilean; the Military Attaché, Brigadier Windham Torr, a great admirer of America; the Cultural Relations Attaché, Dr. Walter Starkie, an Irishman who conducted a large and important "British Institute" in Madrid. The whole was headed by the Ambassador, Sir Samuel Hoare. Sir Samuel, everybody knows, was one of Britain's Tory "elder statesmen," who had been a member of the House of Commons for many years and had held numerous cabinet posts including that of Foreign Secretary in which he had won fame or its reverse by the ill-fated "Hoare-Laval Agreement." He had been sent to Spain in the dark days of 1940 when France was collapsing before the German onslaught and when the British, left alone, were making their agonizing withdrawal from Dunkirk and expecting to see Spain follow Italy into an overwhelming attack upon them. Sir Samuel has told me that when he reached Lisbon en route to Madrid his Government, despairing of any possible success for his mission, instructed him to return home but that he ignored the instructions and went on to Madrid.

Sir Samuel Hoare certainly performed signal service for his

country and for the cause of the United Nations in Spain during those difficult and trying months and years following the French débâcle, although from what I later learned, I came to doubt if there had ever been any real justification for supposing, on the part of the British Government or of Sir Samuel himself, that Spain would voluntarily join the Axis. Be that as it may, he assumed from the outset, and steadily maintained with both suppleness and dignity, that he was a most distinguished representative of a truly Great Power which eventually and inevitably must defeat the Axis. He affected unconcern when Falange youths demonstrated before his Embassy, shouting "We want Gibraltar" and occasionally breaking the windows. Through his deserved reputation as an expert swimmer, tennis-player, and huntsman, and through his well-known support of the monarchist cause in Spain, he made many contacts with upper-class Spaniards and appreciably enlarged the number of Anglophiles. He incessantly worried Serrano Suñer, as a cat worries a mouse.

I naturally saw a good deal of Sir Samuel during ensuing months in his office or mine or at social affairs, usually twice or thrice a week when we were both in Madrid. He was always interesting and ingratiating. About many matters I profited greatly from his counsel and heartily agreed with him. About others, however, as this story will subsequently indicate, I could not see eye-to-eye with him, which irritated him. I hope I do him no injustice in venturing the opinion that, though he frequently complimented me on America's part in the war as an ally of Great Britain, he really didn't like Americans or seriously try to understand them. I believe that he had never been in the United States and that, as a kind of unreconstructed Tory, he still regarded Americans as rebellious subjects of George III. Besides, he doubtless felt, correctly enough, that he had borne the heat and burden of the "Peninsular Campaign" for a year and a half while the United States held aloof from the struggle and that the leadership he had then assumed and had since so ably exercised should be unquestioningly accepted and obeyed by a colleague from a country which had just begun to fight Germans. At any rate he seldom spoke of the "United Nations," but habitually of "Great Britain and its Allies." And he acted accordingly.

From the beginning of our association, Sir Samuel sought to persuade me that a restoration of the monarchy in Spain would be most helpful to the Allies during and after the war, and that I should join him in encouraging the Monarchists. I explained that I could not take sides in Spain's internal affairs. I was sure my Government would not intervene to effect a change in the existing regime but would recognize any, whether monarchist or republican, which the Spaniards themselves chose to substitute for the existing one and which could demonstrate its ability to maintain order at home and to fulfill its duties abroad. This principle I frequently reiterated and rigidly adhered to thoroughout my sojourn in Spain.

The Portuguese Ambassador, Dr. Theotonio Pereira, who, next to the Papal Nuncio, was dean of the diplomatic corps, proved to be a good friend and very helpful associate. Still youthful in years as well as in spirit, he, like the Portuguese prime minister, Dr. Salazar, had been drafted from a professorship (that of mathematics) at the University of Coimbra into his country's public life. After serving in cabinet posts at Lisbon, he had been accredited to General Franco early in the Spanish Civil War; and his protracted stay in Spain, together with his continuing personal intimacy with Dr. Salazar, enabled him to exert a significant influence in both countries. His strong patriotism was at all times evident as was also his loyalty to the historic Anglo-Portuguese alliance. He recognized, as fully as we did, the danger both to Portugal and to the Allied cause in any Axis intervention in Spain or in any unneutral collaboration of Spain with the Axis. Though he distrusted Serrano Suñer and heartily disliked the Falange, his long and close association with other influential advisers of General Franco and with large segments of the Spanish people stood us, as well as himself, in good stead. In his constant endeavor to draw Spain with Portugal into a really neutral Peninsular *bloc,* he contributed immeasurably, at a time when the British and ourselves had much less influence, toward counteracting the propaganda and pleas of our enemies.

As early as May 23, 1942—only a week after I first arrived in Madrid—the Portuguese Ambassador made me a lengthy call in the course of which he said Dr. Salazar wished him to supplement the conversation I had had with the Prime Minister on my way through Lisbon with some important statements of Portuguese fears and policy. First, they feared a grave threat of communism in the Peninsula in the event of a Russian victory and believed the best means of removing it would be a successful Anglo-American military offensive on the Continent, so that when Germany eventually collapsed the Anglo-Americans rather than the Russians would be the dominant force in central and western Europe. I said, in reply, that I appreciated the apprehension in both Spain and Portugal, but that, as I saw it, a Communist threat could hardly become acute except among peoples utterly exhausted and starving as the result of war and that during the critical period accompanying and immediately succeeding the cessation of hostilities a victorious America would be in vastly better condition than a victorious Germany to rescue western Europe from starvation and to reestablish popular morale.

Secondly, the Ambassador stated, rumors were widely prevalent in the Peninsula, presumably inspired by German propaganda, that the Allies planned an early offensive through Morocco as a diversion for the Russians and a means of appropriating French North Africa. Dr. Salazar earnestly hoped such rumors were without foundation, because an Allied invasion of Morocco, he greatly feared, would instantly result in German occupation of Spain and Portugal, and, surely, it was to our advantage to keep the Peninsula out of the war. I said that so far as I knew the rumors were baseless (which at the time was quite true), but that I could conceive of some counter-action by the Allies *if* the Vichy Government should allow the Axis to utilize the French fleet or any bases in French North Africa, and that I hoped the Peninsular Powers, in their own interests, would give salutary advice to Vichy and to Berlin.

Finally, the Ambassador wished it thoroughly understood that the "unpublished agreement" concluded between Portugal and Spain in February, 1942, had been directed toward the establishment of Peninsular solidarity on the basis of genuine non-belligerency. He thought that the Serrano Suñer of 1942 was less chauvinist and possessed a greater sense of responsibility than the Serrano of 1941. I thanked the Ambassador for the statements and communicated them to Washington.

In addition to the Portuguese and British Ambassadors, I saw, from the start, a good deal of the Nuncio, Mgr. Cicognani, a genial and kindly man who had been long in Spain. As official representative of the Vatican and a high dignitary of a supra-national church, he preserved an air of detachment from partisanship in the war and in domestic politics. Yet he left me in no doubt about his real and deep-seated aversion to Nazism and Fascism and the Spanish Falange. In subsequent negotiations with the Spanish Government about refugee problems and a number of other matters he was of incalculable assistance to us.

With the Latin-American diplomats in Madrid, our relations were markedly close and cordial. Ambassador Weddell had instituted, before I arrived, a series of informal Pan-American luncheons, held every two or three weeks and presided over, in turn, by the various chiefs of mission in the Spanish alphabetical order of the countries they represented. I found upon my arrival that it was next the turn of the United States' representative to be host, and this pleasant duty I performed, with the seasoned assistance of Messrs. Beaulac and Ackerman, at our Embassy on Wednesday, June 17, 1942. It was the first of a succession of these affairs in which I participated and took a great interest and which, from their very informality, were particularly delightful and, I think, mutually informing and advantageous.

By reason of Spain's special susceptibility to her daughter-nations in the New World we frequently relied upon our Latin American colleagues effectively to reënforce our own representations. The Brazilian Ambassador, though easy-going, was a shrewd and humorous critic of the Spanish scene and a reassuring optimist about Allied success. The Chilean Ambassador, on the other hand, was at first a pessimist, although he later plucked up courage and became an enthusiastic ally. The Argentine Ambassador when I arrived was Dr. Escobar, who, with no trace of humor, entertained the notion that Argentina, at the head of a confederation of neutrals, could step in between the warring Axis and Allies and bring peace to the world. Dr. Escobar was subsequently replaced at Madrid by Palacios Costa, who, throughout his stay, was a flaming champion of the Allied cause and a frankly indiscreet scoffer at the Falange. As he said, he was "a democrat in Argentina and a monarchist in Spain." Among other Latin-American diplomats, the collaboration of the Colombian and Salvadorean Ministers and the Cuban Chargé was notably constant and dependable.

Naturally I had no personal contacts with Axis diplomats in Spain. I first saw them at a state function in the old Senate Chamber on Friday, July 17, at which the Caudillo made an address and to which the entire diplomatic corps was invited. They sat in a ground-floor box, and the Allies in a box above, with the neutrals distributed between the two. I could easily look over the railing of my box and survey the enemy below. The German Ambassador, Von Stohrer, wrapped in a huge military cloak, was at least six feet seven inches tall; curiously enough, he had a reputation for timidity and was usually accompanied by six or eight strapping young men of the Gestapo almost as tall as himself. The Italian was a little sickly man, who shortly afterwards went home to die. The Japanese Minister, Suma, was the most disgusting and also the funniest of the lot. He was fat and oily, incessantly smiling and hissing, and his affectation of being a connoisseur of Spanish art immensely amused the Spaniards and enabled them to sell him at fantastic prices their worst pictures. There were also, in the Axis box, consumptive-looking "ministers" of the puppet governments which Japan had set up in Manchuria and at Nanking, a youthful Croatian Minister, and obviously uncomfortable Ministers of Rumania and Hungary. Piétri, with his gold braid and dragging sword, sat with the Axis.

There were certain state functions which all of us were expected to attend. On July 17-18, for example, the anniversary of the Nationalist uprising of 1936 was observed, on the first day by a Te Deum in the splendid state church of San Francisco el Grande, a session of the Falange Council in the Senate building (which I have just mentioned), and a reception at the royal palace of the

Oriente, and on the second day, by an evening banquet and garden-party amid the chilly ponds and fountains of Philip V's eighteenth-century country seat at La Granja, some thirty miles from Madrid. How pained on this occasion was Sir Samuel Hoare that General Franco should use the *royal* plate!

On October 1, another Te Deum and another reception in the royal palace; it was the anniversary of General Franco's designation by fellow generals as "Caudillo and Generalissimo." On January 6, the Feast of the Epiphany, a gala state dinner and concert at the palace for the cabinet and the entire diplomatic corps with their wives; this put such strain upon protocol in seating the guests so as to keep Allies and Axis apart that after two years it was discontinued. On April 1, a big military parade down the broad avenue of the Castellana, past reviewing stands for the Caudillo and all officialdom, including ourselves; it was the anniversary of the Nationalist "liberation" of Madrid in 1939.

Except on these formal and official occasions, I seldom saw General Franco. He lived in a relatively modest palace at El Pardo, which had been a shooting-lodge of the Kings, some fifteen miles northwest of Madrid, and he came into the city only for ceremonial appearances. He held his conferences and cabinet meetings and transacted state business at El Pardo. I heard of this or that Ambassador's occasionally playing golf or tennis out there or accompanying the Caudillo on a hunting excursion. I am not sure how true this was. I am sure, however, that throughout the three years of my stay in Spain my personal calls on him were limited to six at El Pardo, of which five had strictly to do with governmental business. Most of our negotiations, like those of other embassies and legations, were carried on with the Foreign Minister at the Foreign Office in Madrid.

IV

Social contacts of the Hayes family and the Embassy staff were by no means exclusively with diplomatic colleagues and ranking Spanish officials. Those were, indeed, necessary and frequently very useful. But from the start we recognized that we must foster the widest possible contacts with all sorts of Spaniards if we would make a truly *American* impression upon the country and successfully counteract pro-Axis propaganda and influence.

We did our best to make the American Embassy in Madrid a representative American home. Tea was served in American, rather than Spanish, fashion; and the Spanish chef was taught to prepare typically American dishes. We couldn't change the traditional Spanish hours without provoking riot and revolution, and we didn't try; we merely suffered, and at first almost died, from them. Luncheon was at two o'clock; tea at six; a cocktail hour at nine; dinner at nine-thirty or ten; theatre, cinema, and opera from eleven until two a.m.; flamenco parties until six a.m. However, all Madrid offices and shops were tightly shut from 1:30 to 4:30 every afternoon, when Spaniards followed lunch with a siesta. Gradually, in this respect, the American home in our Embassy yielded to environment and turned Spanish.

Our contacts were numerous and varied, depending upon the training, background, and connections of different members of the Hayes family, of the Embassy staff, and of the American "colony" in Madrid. For example, it soon became well known that Mrs. Hayes was at home several afternoons a week at six o'clock and delighted to welcome friends and acquaintances for a cup of tea at that time. These afternoon teas at the Embassy were always pleasant, usually interesting, and sometimes amusing and difficult. At first certain Spanish guests showed surprise and even resentment at the presence of other Spaniards of quite different political hue, but it was soon understood that everybody was welcome and no questions asked. Mr. Roosevelt's succinct advice, "If you want a friend, be one," was followed, and the tea hours from six to eight were devoted to learning to know Spaniards and enabling them to know Americans and American ways.

We never knowingly discriminated for or against any political group or tendency. We received monarchists, traditionalists, republicans, socialists, Falangistas. We listened to everybody. Our aim was not only to confirm the faith of those who already believed in the Allied cause but to make new converts to it. I think we made satisfactory progress.

Not all our Madrid contacts were centered in the Embassy. We stirred about a good deal throughout the city, visiting shops and bookstalls, the Prado and other art-museums, and many Spanish homes. We occasionally attended bull-fights. And wherever we went the bright-red Buick convertible roadster, which I had brought to Spain and which was the only car at our disposal until the Government a year later furnished a sedate official car, drew admiring crowds and proved a brilliant asset.

Desiring to learn first-hand all I could about Spain and to make personal contacts outside of Madrid, I early began a series of tours which eventually familiarized me with all parts of the country. Shortly after our arrival, I visited the Escorial, with its somber fortress-like memorial of Philip II, and Toledo, with its rich cathedral and ruined castle. In July, in company with my children and Michael George, I made an extensive trip through Old Castile, the Basque country, Navarra, Aragon, and Catalonia. We spent some time, and met a number of people, at Burgos, Santillana del Mar (whence we visited the famous prehistoric cave-paintings), Santander, Bilbao, Guernica, San Sebastian, Pamplona, Zaragosa, Lérida, Montserrat, and Barcelona. At Bilbao and Barcelona, resident American consuls tendered us receptions, and at the latter city, the commercial metropolis of Spain, I was guest of the vigorous American Chamber of Commerce at a large luncheon presided over by its acting president, Don Ramón Pañella, a remarkably eloquent and intensely pro-American gentleman. The principal provincial and municipal officials attended and spoke.

Two months after this tour through northern Spain, my wife and I made a similar tour south of Madrid across La Mancha, the windmill region immortalized by Don Quixote, and through the extensive agricultural province of Andalucia. We rambled about Granada and Córdoba; we visited Málaga and our consulate there; we spent several busy days in Sevilla and its environs as guests of Consul and Mrs. John Hamlin in their very attractive consular home. This is the one consulate in all Spain which is owned by the

United States Government and is really worthy of America. Mainly through the efforts of Congressman Sol Bloom, it had been built, in the California mission style, and provided with fine colonial furnishings, so that it could serve temporarily as our exhibit at the Sevilla World's Fair of 1929 and permanently as appropriate office and residence for our consul.

Later we made still another tour through eastern Spain, visiting our consulate in Valencia, stopping in the government *parador* (or inn) at Benicarló, and riding miles and miles through the groves of orange and almond trees with which the whole Mediterranean coast of the Levante abounds. I was impressed, as many previous travellers to Valencia had been, by seeing the peasants of the region still conducting their own court, independent of any state authority, to adjudicate the precious irrigation and water rights. This voluntarily cooperative and semi-communist institution goes back to early medieval days, perhaps to Roman or even Carthaginian times; it has survived monarchy, republic, and the Falange; it seems indestructible.

Needless to say, the impressions I gathered from all these journeyings and contacts were multitudinous. As this is not a travelbook, or a critique of Spanish life, but only an account of a diplomatic mission, I shall mention here only those impressions which are directly pertinent to the business in hand and which grew stronger in my mind the longer I remained and the more I observed in Spain.

I liked Spaniards. I always found them, regardless of class or calling, extraordinarily courteous and charming. They are a very approachable and frank people, with a high sense of individual dignity and worth. It was patent to me that by habit and temperament they were instinctively and stubbornly resistant to any such regimentation as obtained in Nazi Germany (or Communist Russia) or as at home the Falange minority sought to impose.

But just as an extreme individualism was a great virtue of the mass of Spaniards, so was it, especially in political matters, a vice. They simply couldn't or wouldn't think alike or act together. And every one was so sure he was right that he was apt to be intolerant of dissent or opposition. Compromise was alien and unpopular. You were either a "patriot" or a "red."

Yet there were almost as many hardy varieties within the categories of "patriot" and "red" as there were individual Spaniards. There were Falangistas, Traditionalists, Conservative Monarchists, Liberal Monarchists, Conservative Republicans, Liberal Republicans, Radical Republicans, Socialists, Syndicalists, Anarchists, Communists, Basque Nationalists, Catalan Nationalists. Even these subdivisions, with the possible exception of the Falangistas at one extreme and the Communists at the other, represented only general colorings which comprised innumerable shades and tints.

The mass of Spaniards were, first and foremost, Spanish in that they preferred their own country to any other, resented foreign dictation or patronizing, and distrusted any alien who assumed superior airs. After being Spanish first, they might have secondary predilections for this or that foreign country.

The large majority, I soon discovered, were more partial to the United States and Great Britain than to the Axis. This was the case not only with the "reds"—the "Loyalists" of Civil War days— but also with many supporters of General Franco, notably among Monarchists and Conservative Republicans. Among the Rightists, there was, of course, a sentimental regard, in greater or lesser degree, for the military aid they had received in the Civil War from Germany and Italy, and among the army officers a vast respect for Germany as a great military power. I gathered, nevertheless, that relatively few Spaniards really liked Germans and that almost none had anything but contempt for Italians and repugnance to Japanese. The Falangistas, it is true, usually professed preference for the Axis and cooperated in Axis propaganda, and they were influential in Government circles both nationally and locally. But numerically they were a small minority of the Spanish people. The aristocracy and business men, no less than the mass of peasants and artisans, were in general hostile to the Falange and inclined to oppose its policies. I got the impression that German and pro-German Falange propaganda had been too abundant, that it had overreached itself.

Pro-Allied sympathies varied a good deal in degree and in different parts of the country. Pro-American sentiment was especially marked in Barcelona and throughout Catalonia; pro-British, in Bilbao and the Basque country, and also in Andalucia. The upper classes, many of whom had lived in England and still employed English governesses in Spain, were apt to be decidedly Anglophile, while the middle and lower classes looked more to America. Persons of monarchist leanings were customarily pro-British; those of republican proclivities, pro-American. Altogether, despite official indications to the contrary and despite every resource and device of experienced Nazi propagandists, I reached the conclusion that at least eighty per cent of the Spanish people were sympathetic to Great Britain or the United States rather than to Germany.

Another kind of impression I got with great vividness. Wherever I went, whether in Madrid or in the provinces, everybody recalled the tragedy of the Spanish Civil War and recounted the holocaust of relatives and personal possessions. I don't believe there is a single Spaniard, no matter what his past or present political views, who didn't suffer in that terrible recent struggle the loss, by assassination or death in battle, or by exile or imprisonment, of some one near and dear to him. You couldn't so catastrophically sacrifice a million lives out of a population of twenty-six millions without profoundly affecting the survivors and leaving them not only with grief but with the bitterest hatreds. In Spanish minds, the Civil War remained. "Leftists" hated "Rightists"; "Rightists" feared and denounced "Leftists."

I don't propose to engage now, any more than I did then, in discussion of the rights and wrongs of the Spanish Civil War or of what led up to it. I must remark, however, on the basis of careful and, I believe, objective investigation and study in Spain for a fairly long time, that it was not as simple as many foreign publicists and commentators have represented it to be. It was not a clear-cut struggle between democracy and fascism, or merely a first round in the Second World War. It was certainly not a conflict between "pure black" and "pure white"; there were admixtures of grey in each. Neither side was at all homogeneous, and shocking atrocities were committed on both sides.

Moreover, from what I know of Spanish history and temperament and of the actual course of events in the country between 1931 and 1939, I am convinced that whichever side had been victorious in the Civil War it would have speedily passed under the domination of its most extreme elements and inflicted on the vanquished the same kind of proscription and punishment. Actually, the "Nationalist" coalition won, and its extremist Falange wing promptly proceeded to exert an influence far beyond its numerical strength, with the result that in 1942, three years after the Civil War, hundreds of thousands of "Loyalists" were still in jail or exile, and scores were still being executed. No one can be absolutely sure what would have happened if the "Loyalist" coalition had won, for that involves an *if*, but I strongly suspect that, in such an event, other groups of extremists, Communist and Anarchist, would have come out on top and displayed no less intolerance and vindictiveness.

The Civil War involved heavy loss of life for all classes and kinds of Spaniards. It also cost Spain vast material destruction, the repair of which was rendered exceptionally difficult if not impossible by the World War which immediately followed the Civil War and effectually deprived Spain of requisite materials from abroad. Wherever the fighting in Spain had been severe and protracted, sorry ruins and debris and makeshift shelters and pill-boxes or utter barrenness still bore mute but eloquent witness. One saw the worst and most complete havoc in "University City" and the northwestern and southern suburbs of Madrid, in the Alcázar at Toledo, and all along the roads from Madrid to the Escorial, from Madrid to Valencia, from Valencia to Barcelona, and around Guernica and Irun in the Basque provinces. And through central and eastern Spain were hundreds of wrecked churches and private houses which had been stripped and looted and not infrequently reduced to rubble. The southern and western parts of Spain, where Nationalist forces effected early occupation and consequently where there was little fighting, fared better. In such cities as Sevilla, Granada,

Córdoba, Bádajoz, etc., one would scarcely guess from external appearances that a civil war had occurred.

V

President Roosevelt interested himself in the fate of the great Spanish art treasures. Amidst all his manifold cares and responsibilities at home and afield, he took time on July 9, 1942, to send me a special inquiry:

. . . Just for my personal interest, will you be good enough to get someone to give me a very brief résumé—one or two pages—as to what has happened to all of the art, paintings, etc., which were damaged or removed to other places during the Revolution? In other words, I have at the back of my head that some day Spain can become again a great mecca for tourists. In fact, it should be made infinitely more attractive for tourists than it ever has been in the past. . . . I have always felt that the economic situation in Spain could be greatly helped by a Spanish catering to visiting firemen!

To this, I replied on August 3:

Your letter of July 9 was brought to me last week while I was journeying through the Basque and Catalan regions of Spain and inspecting our consulates at Bilbao and Barcelona. Your question about what has happened to the art treasures of Spain I asked myself shortly after my arrival, and I will give you, in answer, a résumé of my observations.

Surprisingly little happened. Both parties to the Civil War seemed to have shared the normal Spaniard's respect for art. Thus, the priceless paintings in the Prado—the Goyas, El Grecos, Velasquez's, Murillos, Brueghels, etc.—were packed up and stored away by the Loyalists at the beginning of the conflict, and at the close were all recovered and replaced by the Nationalists. Not a one was lost, though some are in need of repair and restoration.

A large number of churches were rifled or razed, especially in Madrid, Valencia, and Barcelona, but in the main they were parish or conventual churches of relatively minor artistic or historic importance. In Madrid, it is true, the Cathedral was demolished, although the sumptuous church of San Francisco el Grande is still intact. In Lérida, too, while the eighteenth-century baroque cathedral was gutted by fire, the far more interesting "old cathedral" of the twelfth century was only slightly damaged and is now repaired and in use.

I have recently visited the beautiful old monastery of Montserrat with its magnificent library, the vast pile of the Escorial with its big collections of paintings and manuscripts, and the charming cathedrals at Burgos, Pamplona, and Toledo, and can testify that all of them are quite unharmed. And from the Embassy Counselor I have similar testimony about the chief monuments in Granada, Córdoba, and Sevilla (including the rich Archives of the Indies).

Many private residences were destroyed; and despite much rebuilding during the past three years, some of the Madrid suburbs (including "University City") and a section in the middle of Barcelona, for example, are still ugly with debris. There probably was considerable loss of art objects in looted houses of noble families, although some such families had the foresight at the start of the Civil War to entrust their most valuable things to the safekeeping of some embassy or legation in Madrid. . . .

The other day the sixteen-year-old Duke of Veragua—who bears the name of Christopher Columbus and the title of "Admiral"— proudly exhibited to me at his home a whole set of original parchment charters issued to his ancestors by Ferdinand and Isabella, Philip I, and Charles V, which had been stored during the Civil War in a Madrid bank safe that the "Reds" neglected to blow up!

Altogether I am reassured that if Spain escapes from the present World War . . . she should be a most alluring mecca for future tourists. You may recall that back in the early 1920's Primo de Rivera made a serious effort to improve tourist facilities in Spain. Some of his disciples with whom I have talked hope after the war to renew and redouble his effort. Even now there are fairly clean and comfortable hotels in the larger cities, and several attractive "paradors"—government inns—at strategic half-way points.

The great drawbacks now, of course, are: (1) indescribably bad transportation; and (2) scarcity and extreme expensiveness of food. Railways are thoroughly dilapidated, and motor roads cry for resurfacing. Almost no private automobiles are to be seen, and the few buses and trucks and taxis chug along with contraptions known as "gasogenos." The lack of transportation facilities, combined with the lack for six years past of fertilizers, explains the dire shortage of foodstuffs. . . .

The President subsequently gave out at one of his press-conferences the gist of my report on the Spanish art-treasures. So far as

I know, it elicited no adverse comment. In Spain, Serrano Suñer and the pro-Axis press ignored it, although I have no doubt that many Spaniards, including officials, learned of it and were flattered that the President of the United States should be so interested in their culture. A humorous touch was added by several of our enterprising travel agencies and advertising firms which promptly solicited my advice and assistance in developing American tourist traffic to Spain. I politely intimated to them that they better wait until after the war.

As my letter to the President stated, I found the food situation pretty bad in 1942. For two months after my arrival, even at the American Embassy we could get almost no meat in Madrid and had to subsist on fish and eggs until we brought in supplies, in our own truck, from Portugal. On our travels through the country that year we never saw butter or real bread in a Spanish hotel or home, and the inevitable olive oil was invariably rancid. For Spanish workingmen and others less favored than we, there was rationing at fixed minimal prices for whatever essential foods were available. But there was real and distressing scarcity; and how the masses of Spanish townsfolk managed to live I have no idea. The peasants were relatively a bit better off; and for the upper classes there was an extremely expensive, but very flourishing, "black market," which was called, in Spanish slang, "estraperlo." "Estraperlistas" were the butt of much sarcastic joking; they figured in cartoons as the "fat boys."

Gradually, after 1942, economic and living conditions in Spain perceptibly improved. There was more and better food. There was also a truly remarkable and, in the face of existing handicaps, almost miraculous repair of roads, rehabilitation of railways, reconstruction of churches and villages and public buildings (including University City at Madrid), and new erection of apartment houses and "model tenements."

But even such later betterment did not compensate the mass of Spaniards for their great personal and material losses in the Civil War or appreciably dull their memories of the horror and havoc of those dreadful years from 1936 to 1939. It was quite evident to me in 1942, and equally so afterwards, that the most ardent desire of the Spanish people as a whole was to avoid becoming involved in another war, either domestic or foreign. They had had enough fighting and knew too well its attendant chaos and misery and destruction. They wanted no more. They were definitely pacifist.

A very important aspect of this state of mind, I found, was an almost universal fear of communism, a fear which amounted to an obsession. The number of outright Spanish Communists had never been large, but they were the one group in Spain, aside from the Falange, which had been efficiently organized and disciplined, which had known precisely what they wanted, and which had not hesitated to use any means to achieve it. Their fanaticism and organization still persisted, all the more suspect because it was now clandestine, and they were the one group, again aside from the Falange, which was not pacifist.

Communists were feared by well-to-do Spaniards because of Marxian economic doctrines and program, and by Catholic Spaniards because of Marxian hostility to religion, desecration of churches, and proscription of priests. But they were also, and widely, feared because they were reputed to desire and to be working for foreign and especially Russian intervention, which could only mean what Spaniards feared most, their entanglement in the international conflict and a renewal of the frightful Civil War.

The fear—or obsession—was common to most "Leftists" as well as to the "Rightists." I particularly recall, for example, a conversation I had with a most resolute "Leftist," who had been mayor of Toledo under the Republic, had fought on the Loyalist side in the Civil War, and, taken prisoner by the Nationalists, had since languished in a variety of jails. He had no love for his prison-keepers and none for General Franco's regime. The fact that this regime was in power, however, he attributed less to any superior military prowess or strategy of the Nationalists in the Civil War, or any aid they had received from Italy and Germany, than to divisions and quarrels among the Republicans which the Communists had aggravated and exploited for their own selfish ends and which thereby had brought dishonor and eventual disaster to the cause of democracy and republicanism in Spain. He was fearful lest the underground Communist minority was gathering strength and preparing for another bloody uprising in which, under the guise of championing a popular "democratic front," they would again betray democracy.

The ex-mayor of Toledo was but one of several typical "Leftists" who expressed, in slightly variant forms, the same fear. I heard it from a Liberal Republican in Burgos, from a Socialist in Bilbao, from a Syndicalist in Barcelona, from a number of Basques and Catalans who had battled in the Republican ranks. It didn't surprise me to learn two years later, when an attempt was made to recreate a federation of groups opposed to the existing regime, ranging from Moderate Republicans to Socialists and Syndicalists, that its various leaders unanimously resolved to eschew violence and rigidly to exclude the Communist group.

How to deal with all these prevalent popular desires and fears so as to ensure the widest possible sympathy and support for the United States and the cause of the United Nations was a difficult and delicate problem. On one hand, there were advantages to us in the latent preference of the large majority of Spaniards for the English-speaking nations over those of the Axis and also in the anxious desire of the still larger number to keep out of the war. On the other hand, we were confronted with certain disadvantages. The popular will-to-peace might encourage the Spanish Government to continue "appeasing" the currently stronger set of belligerents, which in 1942 was the Axis, and might enable the Germans to invade and occupy the Peninsula without encountering serious resistance. Moreover, the anti-Communist complex, which also was an anti-Russian complex, might offset the popular inclination toward Britain and the United States and swell the Spanish minority who regarded Germany as the bulwark against Russia and hence against Communism. This, of course, was grist to the German propaganda mill in Spain.

In seeking answers to the "Russian problem," we fully appreciated that we could not and should not give the slightest hint of encouragement to any effort or tendency to separate the United

Nations and to array the western democracies with Germany against Russia. That, obviously, would be playing the Axis game. At the same time, we perceived that any frontal attack by us on the intense anti-Communist feeling in Spain or any appearance of collaboration on our part with Spanish Communists could only alienate that majority of Spaniards whom we would need as friends and allies if German invasion of the Peninsula was to be resisted.

The tactic we therefore followed in good conscience, both in personal conversation and in our publicity, was to distinguish between Russia and Communism; to defend and praise the former, and to dissociate ourselves and the cause of the United Nations from the latter. Communism, we always explained, was a domestic concern of Russia, one of our Allies, which should not be interfered with from outside, as the Germans, to their grief, were trying to do; it was not popular or important in the United States or in the British Commonwealth, neither of which had the least intention of fostering it elsewhere; and the surest defense against it was not fighting Russia but bettering the economic lot of the masses at home. After all, I was not in Spain to combat either Communists or Spaniards. I was enlisted in the war against the Axis.

VI

By the middle of August, 1942, I had been in Spain three months and had gathered some very definite impressions about the general internal situation, about the various social and political groupings, and about the popular attitude toward the war and the several belligerents. About the Government's attitude, however, my impressions were still dubious and conflicting. The Falange, though comprising a small minority of the population, was militantly organized and deeply entrenched in the Government. It was the only legally recognized political party in the country, and in this respect as well as in appearance and form—its shirts, salutes, youth movement, etc.—it was obviously patterned after the Fascist Parties of Italy and Germany. The Civil Governor of every Spanish province was a member of the party and its local "leader." In the central administration, there was a special ministry of the party, with a large independent budget of its own, while other party-members headed the key ministries of education (including press-censorship and propaganda), the interior (including the police), and labor (including direction of the syndical trade-unions). The organization as a whole was notoriously pro-Axis, and its most conspicuous chieftain was Serrano Suñer, brother-in-law of General Franco and Minister of Foreign Affairs.

How much influence did Serrano Suñer and his Falange colleagues have with General Franco? And just how far could and would they go in translating their pro-Axis sentiments into action? These were vitally important questions, on whose answers depended the success or failure of my mission and the future course of the war.

Serrano Suñer, on the few occasions on which I saw him in the spring and summer of 1942, impressed me as having something inscrutable about him. He seemed mysterious and never frank. We knew of his intimate associations with the German Ambassador, von Stohrer; and we had plenty of evidence of his fostering of Falangist activities against the United States in Latin America. On the other hand, General Franco's slowness and extreme caution, popularly ascribed to his "Gallego" qualities, were proverbial throughout Spain and in diplomatic circles. He was reputed to exercise a restraining influence on his impetuous brother-in-law. And the Portuguese Ambassador, who knew both men very well, was insistent that the Serrano Suñer of 1942 was "less chauvinist" than the Serrano of 1941. Perhaps he did see things differently after the entrance of the United States into the war.

General Franco himself had made speeches in 1940 and 1941 which sounded quite promising to the Axis and alarming to the Allies. Especially in his speech before the Falange Council on July 17, 1941, he had denounced "out-worn democracy" and lauded the "new order" in Europe and had declared that if the Russian Communists should succeed in invading Germany a million Spanish soldiers would rush to the defense of Berlin. So obnoxious was this speech that Sir Samuel Hoare told me he thought that Ambassador Weddell, who with the other foreign diplomats attended the meeting, should have ostentatiously withdrawn, and that I should absent myself from the meeting on July 17, 1942, and thus avoid any similar embarrassment. I dissented from the British Ambassador's implied criticism of my predecessor and did not follow his recommendation as to my own conduct. Both Mr. Weddell and I had been accredited to General Franco, and if he chose to say things we didn't like at a ceremonial meeting to which the entire diplomatic corps had been summoned, a mere gesture of withdrawing or absenting oneself would have rejoiced our enemy, the Axis, and been for General Franco only the petty discharge of a pop-gun. If we were to take his speech seriously and show our displeasure at all adequately, we might much better fire a cannon and break diplomatic relations altogether. But the United States was hardly in a position in 1941, or in 1942, to fire cannon in Spain.

As a matter of fact, the speech which the Caudillo made on July 17, 1942, proved surprisingly mild. It announced that the form of government suitable to one country was not necessarily suitable to others, and that the million Spanish soldiers would make their stand against Communism not before Berlin but at the Pyrenees. Perhaps, after "appeasing" the Axis for two years, General Franco was starting to "appease" the United States and Great Britain. Perhaps his earlier pro-Axis words had saved him from more fateful pro-Axis deeds. I didn't know, but I began to suspect as much.

I did discover, rather early, and with certainty, that General Franco's regime was by no means a unit. It was actually and essentially a coalition government in which the Falange was only one, albeit a significant, element. Nominally, ever since the Caudillo had decreed in Civil War times a fusion of his military and monarchical supporters with the then budding Falange, all his officials, both central and local, were listed as Falangistas and expected to appear on state occasions as such. Nevertheless, the "fusion" was hardly skin-deep, and clearly visible beneath it were still the diverse and mutually jealous factions of Traditionalists,[1] Liberal Monarchists, and former Clerical Republican followers of Gil Robles, to say nothing of professional military men and "independents." All these

---

[1] Conservative Monarchists, known also as Carlists or Requetés.

factions disliked and at least in private criticized the Falange, its ideology and most of its policies. Yet all of them were represented in the Government and had more or less weight in the councils of General Franco.

The Caudillo, I soon learned, had no inconsiderable talents as a "politician." He was adept at balancing army against Falange, and manipulating the divergent elements in the "Nationalist" coalition. For a proper understanding of the situation, it should be borne in mind that General Franco, unlike Hitler or Mussolini (or Lenin), had always been a career military man, that when he revolted in 1936 against the Republican regime he was not the leader of any party or the spokesman for any particular ideology, and that the supreme power to which he eventually succeeded more closely resembled the older type of military dictatorship traditional with Spain and Latin America than the newer type exemplified in Italy or Germany (or Russia).

To be sure, after the Italian Fascists and German Nazis began intervening in the Spanish Civil War and giving military aid to the Nationalists, they "sold" their ideology and party organization and methods to a number of Spaniards, including Serrano Suñer,[2] who adopted and adapted the hitherto insignificant Falange, and then got General Franco to engraft it upon his military dictatorship. In other words, fascism in Spain was an added trimming of government; whereas in contemporary Italy and Germany government issued from fascism and was completely dominated by it.

The Spanish cabinet, for example, usually consisted of five Falangistas and six others: two Traditionalists, two Liberal Monarchists, and two "independents"; and this balance General Franco appeared desirous to preserve. Moreover, while each major city in the country had a "civil governor" who was invariably Falangista, it also had a "military governor" who was a professional army officer likely to be contemptuous of the Falange, and a "mayor" who was almost always a Monarchist. And though Falan-

[2] Serrano Suñer had previously been a follower and lieutenant of Gil Robles, the Moderate Republican leader, who, since the outbreak of the Civil War, has been an exile in Portugal.

gistas might be pushed into what were regarded as minor diplomatic posts, the Duke of Alba, president of the Grandees and leader of the Liberal Monarchists, was kept as Spanish Ambassador in London.

Nor was there political uniformity within the several ministries. If a Minister was Falangista, his under secretary was apt to be a Traditionalist or a Liberal Monarchist, and his staff a congeries of Spanish individualists. The Foreign Office, with which, among all the Ministries, I naturally had most to do, had the reputedly pro-Axis Serrano Suñer at its head, but its Under Secretary, Señor Pan de Soraluce, who did the principal part of the detailed work and exerted considerable influence, was no Falangista. He had already proved himself, and would unchangeably remain, a staunch and very helpful friend of the Western democracies. His sympathy with the Allies, as against the Axis, was open and notorious. And under him, the staff of the Foreign Office, though cautious and reserved, were notably lacking in enthusiasm for the Falange or for the Axis.

Within such a coalition Government as General Franco's, partisan differences and conflicts were always latent. Outside the Government they were evinced, particularly by university youth, in spasmodic fisticuffs between the Falange and the Traditionalists. In the spring and summer of 1942 there was a veritable epidemic of student riots, brawls, and street fighting, so that Spanish jails began to bulge not alone with "reds" but with quarrelsome "patriots." I fear I took the matter too seriously at the time and drew premature conclusions, for in a letter to the President on June 30 I wrote: "No longer is it a prime question whether Spain will intervene in the war or give active aid to the Axis. The prime question is what will happen *inside Spain* within the next months or years." I went on to hazard "four conceivable answers," among which I rather starred a possible "restoration of the monarchy, either (a) through a military coup, or (b) under the patronage of Franco . . . The restored Monarchy would almost certainly be more liberal and more friendly to our cause. The British Ambassador is actively encouraging the Monarchists."

It then seemed to most of us in Madrid that a crisis was rapidly developing for the Falange and that the Traditionalists, with army support, would compel a monarchical restoration. The Minister of the Army was General Varela, a devoted Traditionalist.

The crisis culminated in August and September, 1942. In August General Varela went to Bilbao to attend a solemn requiem mass for the Traditionalists who had died during the Civil War. As he emerged from the church, a bomb was thrown from the street, killing or wounding several persons near him and narrowly missing him. Police investigations disclosed that the perpetrators of the outrage were Falangist youths, one or two of whom had been closely associated with Serrano Suñer. Although a rigid censorship was promptly imposed and no reference to the outrage was made by Spanish press or radio, exaggerated reports of it spread like wildfire all over Spain. Great was the excitement and many the recriminations. What would General Franco do? Dismiss Serrano Suñer and dissolve the Falange, as Traditionalists demanded? Or dismiss Varela and repress the Traditionalists, as Falangists demanded?

General Franco gave his answer—an unexpected but characteristically Franco answer—early in September, 1942. It took the form of a brief announcement in the official bulletin, repeated verbatim and without comment in the press, that both Serrano Suñer and General Varela were being replaced in the Ministries of Foreign Affairs and the Army, respectively, by Count Jordana and General Asensio, and that General Franco himself was taking over Serrano Suñer's leadership of the Falange. General Asensio was a soldier, inclined toward the Falange and the Axis. Count Jordana was also a General, but a Traditionalist sympathetic with Great Britain and the United States. There was thus a change of ministers without changing the balance in the coalition cabinet. A Falangista was succeeding a Traditionalist at the head of the army; a Traditionalist was succeeding a Falangista at the head of foreign affairs. Popular excitement at once died down, and regret that General Varela was out of office was lost in rejoicing that Serrano Suñer was out.

Probably the retirement of Serrano Suñer was not intended by the Caudillo to lead to any shift in Spanish foreign policy. He doubtless regarded it primarily as a needful manoeuvre in domestic politics. We now know, however, that, whatever may have been its purpose, the replacement of Serrano Suñer by Count Jordana, almost precisely two months before the Allied landing in North Africa, proved an epochal event of prime importance to us and likewise to Spain.

I saw Serrano Suñer casually several times after his departure from the Foreign Office, and many stories and rumors reached me concerning him. He returned to his private law practice and ceased to take any active part in public affairs, even in the Falange. For a long time he seldom or never visited his brother-in-law. For a while it was rumored that he was trying to ingratiate himself with the Monarchists, and in January, 1944, he volunteered to a friend of ours some reminiscences about Spanish-German relations in 1940-1941 to which I shall later refer. Otherwise, after September, 1942, Serrano Suñer was merely a memory and a bit of a myth.

VII

At noon on Tuesday, September 8, 1942, I went to the Foreign Office to meet Count Jordana for the first time. On entering the building, I was pleasantly surprised to find that I no longer had to face a gantlet of Falange youths. These were gone completely and for good. A single liveried porter politely showed me up the elevator, and above I was greeted cordially by an aide in military, not Falangist, uniform, and promptly ushered into the Minister's office.

The first glimpse of the new Minister disclosed a man about sixty-five years of age and very short of stature—even shorter than the late Newton Baker. He was obviously a gentleman, with engaging manners and a fine sense of humor. He also gave the impression of being frank and sincere. He was dressed then, and usually afterwards, in ordinary civilian clothes; and when on a few ceremonial occasions he wore a uniform, it was that of a general in the army.

Count Jordana was not of the "old aristocracy." He belonged

to a professional military family and the title of "count" had first been conferred on his father, also a general. He had spent most of his life in the army. As a lad, he had fought in Cuba in 1895. In 1898 he had graduated from the Spanish Military Academy, and, after rising through the various officer grades he had served in the 1920's as High Commissioner of Spanish Morocco. Though a Traditionalist Monarchist, he supported the Republic in its early days, but in 1936, like practically all the Traditionalists, he cast his lot with the Nationalists and Franco. To the Caudillo he was thoroughly loyal.

He was not new to the Foreign Office. He had been Foreign Minister under the Monarchy for a brief term in the 1920's. He had again been Foreign Minister under Franco in 1938-1939; and we were reliably, reassuringly informed that his retirement from the post in 1939 resulted from his disapproval of the fawning attitude of some of his cabinet colleagues, notably Serrano Suñer, then Minister of the Interior, toward Italy and particularly toward Ciano (whom Jordana specially disliked and distrusted). Now, after an interregnum of three years while Colonel Beigbeder and Serrano Suñer in turn occupied the Foreign Office, Count Jordana was back for the third time. Unlike his immediate predecessor, he was experienced, responsible, hard-working, and "simpatico" to the Under-Secretary and career staff of the Foreign Office.

In our first conversation, Count Jordana made clear his anxiety to have better relations with the United States. He took special pride, he said, in having helped to arrange, when he was Foreign Minister previously, for the reception of the first American Ambassador accredited to General Franco. He stated that he had then been, and still was, a sincere admirer of the United States, and that his greatest wish was to do everything in his power to keep Spain out of the war and to improve Spanish-American relations. He remarked how grateful he was, and how grateful Spaniards as a whole should be, that the United States had observed strict neutrality during the Spanish Civil War; and how just it was, therefore, that Spain should observe real neutrality in the current international conflict. This was indeed quite a different refrain from what Serrano Suñer had ever been chanting about America's supporting the "Reds" and thus obliging Spain to support the Axis.

Some other little straws indicated that in September, 1942, the wind was beginning to blow in Spain from a different direction. The Countess Jordana, rather ostentatiously and contrary to protocol, received my wife ahead of the German Ambassadress. The first official appearance of the new Foreign Minister outside his office was at a state dinner at the American Embassy on September 29 in honor of Mr. Myron Taylor, who was stopping with us on his way home from the Vatican.

Optimism was starting to suffuse the pessimism which had hung over the Embassy. Perhaps my stay in Spain would be longer than I or the Department of State had originally imagined. In September I wrote to Dr. Butler requesting that my leave of absence from Columbia be extended to June 30, 1943.

CHAPTER III

COPING WITH SPANISH NON-BELLIGERENCY

I

When I arrived in Spain, and for over a year afterwards, the official attitude of the Spanish Government toward the War continued to be defined as "non-belligerency." What did this mean? General Franco, in my first conversation with him on June 9, 1942, had offered an explanation,[1] but it left us in considerable doubt. How could Spain favor Germany against Russia and be at least semi-belligerent against the latter, and at the same time not help Germany against Russia's allies—the United States and Great Britain?

International law and usage had long provided for "belligerency" and for "neutrality," and had endowed each status with certain rights and duties. Customarily, on the outbreak of a war, every nation chose and publicly stated whether it was *in* the war, that is "belligerent," or *out* of it, that is, "neutral"; and it was presumed to act and to be treated accordingly. But "non-belligerency" was something new, with no established rules of behavior. The outstanding example of it was Italy's declared position at the beginning of the Second World War in September, 1939.

Mussolini had then refrained from proclaiming either war or neutrality. He merely announced that Italy was "non-belligerent." This seemed to imply that, while Italy would not be neutral in the conflict, it would not at once engage in fighting. Actually, Italy's "non-belligerency" proved but a prelude to full-fledged belligerency. It was only a nine-month gestation. For, as everybody knows, Mussolini in June, 1940, put his country squarely alongside his Axis partner, Germany, in the war against the Allies. The Italian precedent hardly reassured us concerning Spain's "non-belligerency." Indeed, it had been generally expected, back in 1940, that

[1] See above, p. 31.

Spain, under General Franco, would speedily join the Axis and follow Italy into the war. The temptation to do so must have been very great. During the Spanish Civil War, General Franco's Nationalist forces had received military assistance from Italy and Germany, and in many respects his ensuing regime resembled theirs. Spain was already associated with them in the "anti-Comintern pact" against Russian Communism. By sharing in the spectacular triumph of Axis arms in the spring of 1940, Spain might seize a unique opportunity to recover long-lost Gibraltar and to gratify expansionist appetite in North Africa.

The military situation in July, 1940, was inviting. France had just collapsed. Victorious German armies stood poised at the Pyrenean frontier between France and Spain. Resistance to the Germans was everywhere broken or non-existent. Practically all central and western Europe was "occupied territory": Czechoslovakia, Poland, Norway, Denmark, Holland, Belgium. Russia, still appeasing and collaborating with Germany, was busy at the moment with a campaign against Finland. Italy had just joined Germany. The United States was far away, unprepared and notoriously reluctant to go to war. Great Britain was isolated and apparently at the mercy of German aircraft, submarines, and landing barges. Its only remaining foothold on the Continent of Europe was Gibraltar. And against Spanish attack, aided by the overwhelming superiority in bombers and tanks which Germany possessed, Gibraltar was no longer tenable. Spanish artillery was in place and pointed at Gibraltar; and to take advantage of obvious British weakness in order to recover it was urged upon General Franco within Spain, particularly by the Falange and the university youth.

Why, then, did not General Franco follow the example of Mussolini and utilize the golden opportunity to attack the isolated and hard-pressed British at Gibraltar and the vanquished and dispirited French in North Africa? No conclusive answer is possible until all pertinent evidence, including the diplomatic, can be examined and sifted. Meanwhile, some light may be thrown on the problem by what the Italian Ambassador Paulucci told me toward the end of 1943.

Paulucci was a distinguished career diplomat, with a half-English wife. He had served his country before, as well as after, the advent of Mussolini. When Italy entered the war in June, 1940, he was in a key position in the Foreign Office at Rome to know a vast deal about Axis negotiations, including those with Spain. According to Paulucci, Franco was extremely reluctant to follow Italy into the war—for two principal reasons. First, he was anxious that Spain should recover from the devastating effects of its own Civil War before embarking on any foreign war. Second, he feared lest if Spain entered the war in its weakened condition, it would be subjected to occupation and control by Germany and Italy and hence lose its national independence and perhaps more of its patrimony. He had already resisted, very stubbornly, Italy's request for a base in the Balearic Islands as compensation for Italian help to him in the Civil War. He had almost a psychosis about similar requests being made in the future.

According to Paulucci, the attitude of General Franco was reflected and fully shared by his first two Foreign Ministers—Count Jordana and Colonel Beigbeder—who were strongly opposed to any entangling alliance with the Axis or to Spanish participation in the war on any terms. Both of these men had resisted the blandishments and entreaties of Count Ciano, the Italian Foreign Minister and ill-fated son-in-law of Mussolini. On Ciano's state visit to Spain, he had derived some comfort, however, from Franco's brother-in-law, Serrano Suñer, who then was Minister of the Interior (Gobernación) but who shortly afterwards succeeded Beigbeder as Spanish Foreign Minister, and who gave him to understand that General Franco could be persuaded actively to support the Axis if Mussolini and Hitler would take him into full partnership and offer him extraordinary guarantees and such liberal territorial inducements as Gibraltar, all of Morocco, and the Oran district of Algeria.

This may be the basis for the statements in Ciano's posthumously published *Diary* to the effect that General Franco sought, for a price, to engage in the war. There is no other evidence, so far as I know.

Ciano was overly optimistic, according to Paulucci, about the chances of General Franco's cooperation, and he urged Ribbentrop and Hitler to offer what he deemed the requisite inducements. In this he failed. For, following the military collapse of France in the spring of 1940, Hitler and Ribbentrop had the idea that Vichy would collaborate with them and that consequently the French colonial empire should not be dismembered but held intact as a useful ward of Germany. Ciano's program, on the other hand, was predicated on the assumption that France would not collaborate and that at best its North African dependencies should be divided between Italy and Spain.

Paulucci's account is confirmed and supplemented by a report I received in 1944 of certain confidential disclosures of Serrano Suñer concerning the famous meeting of General Franco with Hitler at Hendaye, on the Spanish-French border, in September, 1940. According to this report, the Führer was kept waiting and otherwise treated with scant courtesy by the Caudillo. In the course of the conversation, Hitler reminded Franco of the close sympathy between their two regimes and of Spain's debt to Germany and Italy, and asked him if he did not wish to enter into a political alliance with the Axis. Hitler did not, in so many words, ask Franco to enter the war, but Franco interpreted this as his meaning, and, after pointing out the weak and delicate situation in which Spain found itself so soon after the Civil War, said that Spain could not possibly justify its entering the war unless some substantial territorial gain would result. Hitler asked Franco what he deemed a substantial territorial gain, and Franco replied that it might be French Morocco and went into considerable detail about Spain's historical claims to it. Hitler's response was that, although he had defeated France and held it at his mercy, he was convinced that the New Europe could not exist without the willing cooperation of France. He declared that even in defeat France was still a great nation, alike from cultural, economic, and political points of view, and that he wished French collaboration and alliance. He was not prepared to discuss any question of French territory until he had seen Marshal Pétain, and had fully explored the situation with him.

Franco, according to the report, appeared to be "greatly relieved" at having his overture rejected, and assured Hitler that Pétain was a good friend of Spain's and that he, Franco, would certainly do nothing to injure or embarrass him just as he was taking over the government of France and its colonial empire. Franco, in Serrano Suñer's reported words, "said he had mentioned the Moroccan matter merely to illustrate the difficulties in Spain's position; he took this weak stand because he did not wish to risk war." Also, according to Serrano, Hitler told his staff before leaving Hendaye in September, 1940, that "Spain could not be expected to offer military help in the war."

There are conflicting accounts of the subsequent trip of Serrano Suñer to Berlin in December, 1940. The one current in Madrid in 1944, and attested by Paulucci, was that the Spanish Foreign Minister wanted to make some deal with the Germans for Spain's entrance into the war, but that Franco sent along with him another Minister to check him and prevent him from making any such deal. Another account, recently provided by the German General Jodl, is that Serrano Suñer, in agreement with Franco, was adamant against pressure of Ribbentrop and Hitler for Spain's participation in the war.

From all accounts available to me, and from conversations I had with Count Jordana and with the Caudillo himself, I feel reasonably certain that General Franco, unlike Mussolini, was determined in 1940 not to enter the war. Temperamentally he was a very cautious man, a typical "Gallego," or, as we in the United States would express it, a "man from Missouri." He was, too, a very practical "realist," in that he had no illusions about the weakness and exhaustion which the preceding three years of horrible civil war had brought to Spain. Nor had he any illusions about the continuing deep-seated divisions among Spaniards and the danger to his recently established and still insecure regime in its taking thoroughly unpopular action. He knew that the vast majority of the Spanish people wanted peace, not war, whether civil or foreign.

It is likely, furthermore, that Franco had some real chivalrous feeling for France, especially for Marshal Pétain. The only country outside Spain which he knew first-hand was France, where he had received part of his military training and attended lectures in the War College by both Marshal Foch and Marshal Pétain. He undoubtedly liked France and immensely admired its military traditions, and the accrediting of Marshal Pétain as first French Ambassador to him in 1939 enabled him to renew and strengthen a personal friendship of which he was obviously proud. When the French army went down in dire defeat in June, 1940, and Pétain left Madrid to take charge of a sorely humiliated France, it would have been most unnatural for Franco to follow the example of Mussolini and give France (and Pétain) a "stab in the back." "No Spanish hidalgo would have done that," the Caudillo once said to me.

Doubtless Franco felt a need in 1940 of humoring the Germans, who were at the Spanish frontier in full force and flushed with victory. He therefore may well have conveyed an impression of willingness to consider territorial offers at French expense as a price for Spain's entry into the war and may actually have broached the matter to Hitler in September, 1940, although even Serrano Suñer, who has reported this, admits, very significantly, the "relief" Franco showed when nothing came of it.

If Hitler had been more urgent in September, 1940, and had offered Franco everything which Ciano thought should have been offered, Franco would undoubtedly have been placed in a difficult position. Just how he would have acted in the circumstances, no one can be sure. My own guess is that he would have delayed and drawn out the negotiations to interminable length. He was chary of more war; and, let me emphasize, he was very cautious.

II

But the supposition is academic. Hitler made no offers to Franco at their memorable meeting, and appeared curiously unconcerned about Spain. In this, he was much less wise and less farsighted than Ciano—or perhaps Serrano Suñer. By neglecting to extend Germany's military sway from France over the Iberian Peninsula in 1940 when he could easily have done so, with or without Spanish cooperation, he committed the first of a series of fateful strategic blunders.

The root of Hitler's miscalculation lay in an overestimating of France and an underestimating of Great Britain—and Russia. Apparently he had imagined that France was the one country whose armies would put up a really serious and sustained resistance to Germany. Then when these same French armies showed their utter inability to withstand his *Blitzkrieg* by collapsing and capitulating within a month, he must have concluded that everything else would be easy for him. The British had depended upon the French; without the French they would be powerless. The Russians had their hands full at the moment with the little Finnish nation; how quickly the big all-powerful German nation could dispose of them!

It is perfectly obvious, after the event, that what Hitler should have done in 1940, immediately after conquering France, was to concentrate all German forces and resources against Great Britain. With its air superiority and submarine strength, Germany should have been able in the summer and autumn of 1940 and the winter of 1941 to prepare and launch large-scale amphibious operations from the Channel ports against England itself. Simultaneously, Germany, with its surplus of mechanized arms, could readily have overrun the Iberian peninsula, regardless of Franco's wishes. Almost certainly Gibraltar would have been quickly appropriated; and, through timely and effective German aid to the Italians, the Suez Canal also. Thereby the British "life-line" through the Mediterannean would have been cut at both ends, and no "soft under-belly" of Europe would have been left exposed to a possible "come-back" of Britain or any other enemy of Hitler's. From what we know of the relative ease with which at a later date the Allies made successful landings in Europe, there is good reason to believe that the Germans could have invaded England in the spring of 1941 with at least equal ease and success. British armor in those days was neither heavy nor plentiful, and the United States was still on a peace basis and enforcing the rule of "cash and carry" for any material aid to Britain.

But instead of polishing off England in the spring of 1941,

Hitler attacked Russia! This proved, of course, his ultimate and most colossal blunder. It was probably because he was already planning this blunder that he committed the blunders in 1940 of not concentrating against Great Britain and of not occupying Spain and taking Gibraltar.

Undoubtedly the trouble which Soviet Russia had had in subjugating Finland, in contrast with the facility with which Nazi Germany had conquered France, misled Hitler into thinking that the German military machine could make short work of the sprawling Soviet Union. Easily and quickly, he imagined, he could remove all possibility of Russia's playing him false and upsetting his "New Order," and as easily and quickly he would realize his lifelong ambition of securing for the *Herrenvolk* the rich grain of the Ukraine and oil of the Caucasus. So he suddenly dropped the mask of collaboration with Stalin and dashed gaily into war with Russia. I have been told by Ambassador Paulucci that Hitler didn't even bother to inform his Italian ally beforehand.

The Führer could not have overlooked the necessity of coping, sooner or later, with Great Britain. He may have thought that the air blitz which he kept up against England in 1940–1941 would suffice to convince the British of the helplessness of their isolated position and bring them to terms. In any event he must have reasoned that, once his incursion into Russia was rewarded with the speedy success and big prizes which he anticipated, there would still be plenty of time to attend to the Mediterranean and to England. As for Spain, holding one of the two master keys to the Mediterranean, he was sure he had it in his pocket. Franco was already under military and financial obligations to the Axis and he should welcome the vanquishing of Russia and the final uprooting of Communism. He shouldn't require additional bribes. It didn't matter whether he recognized his obligations and immediately allied himself with the Axis. Germany held trump cards it could use against him any time it wished: Panzer divisions at his land frontier; submarines around his coastal waters; bombers over his towns. He could not be so foolish or stubborn as to resist Germany when the time came for the Axis to take over the Iberian Peninsula and close the western end of the Mediterranean. Yes, Franco had better be cautious and watch his step.

I have no doubt that Franco was glad to have Germany attack Russia in June, 1941. It promised a decisive blow at Communism, and it postponed decisive events in Spain. Yet Franco and his Government, no less than the Spanish people, were quite aware that grave danger remained of Spain's eventually becoming an "occupied country" and perhaps a major battle-ground.

The danger remained serious and acute through 1942, my first year in Spain. True, America had just been brought into the war and into close alliance with Great Britain. True, too, Russia was displaying unexpected strength and pluck and was keeping the principal German forces heavily engaged far from Spanish soil. Nevertheless, the general military situation during the spring and summer of 1942 was distinctly favorable to the Axis and unfavorable to the Allies. There was not a single Allied victory to relieve the gloom or to reassure our Spanish friends.

On the other hand, the Japanese, with lightning rapidity and seemingly at will, were extending their conquests to the Philippines, the Dutch East Indies, Siam, and Burma; they were isolating Chungking and menacing India and Australia. The Germans were deep into Russia, already in complete possession of the great granary of the Ukraine and now threatening not only Moscow and Leningrad but also Stalingrad and the all-important oil fields of the Caucasus. The Italians were occupying Greece and obviously preparing, with German assistance, for a final effort to dislodge the British from Egypt and the eastern Mediterranean.

To Spain and to the mass of Spaniards, the Axis was all-encompassing and apparently all-powerful. To the north of them, strong German divisions stood guard in France and at the Pyrenees. To the south, supposedly collaborationist Frenchmen, dependent upon Vichy, held Morocco and Algeria. The only Allied troops anywhere near Spain were the little British garrison at Gibraltar and the desert fighters of General Montgomery beleaguered at Tobruk or falling back from Tripoli into Egypt toward the Suez Canal.

For Spain, at that time, to have avowed any partiality for the

Allies would have been as suicidal as for Turkey or Sweden or Switzerland. The lot of the few European neutrals was not a happy one. Instinctively fearful of what Germany might do to them, they all pursued a policy of "appeasing" the Axis. Spain's "appeasement" took the nominal form of "non-belligerency," connoting that it was not neutral and might eventually imitate Italy and join Germany. Actually the "appeasement" involved giving the Axis many words and a few deeds. In public speeches, General Franco lauded German exploits and the "New Order" in Europe. In the Spanish press and over the Spanish radio and through the Spanish postal system, favoritism was shown to Axis, as against Allied, news and propaganda. Falangist youths were permitted to demonstrate against the "despoilers" of Gibraltar and Cuba—the British and the Americans. A thinly veiled "volunteer" division of Spanish troops—the so-called "Blue Division"—was sent, together with a token squadron of Spanish airmen, to join Germany's "anti-Communist front" against Russia, while the bulk of the Spanish armed forces were concentrated, not along the Pyrenees where they might disturb the Germans, but in Spanish Morocco where they did disturb the Allies. German propagandists, whose number in Spain was legion, were constantly spreading stories about Spaniards' having nothing to fear from the virtuous Axis but very much to fear from the wicked and imperialistic Allies.

III

In early September, 1942, the dismissal of Serrano Suñer from the Foreign Office lifted our hopes, although in existing circumstances we could hardly expect his successor, Count Jordana, to effect any sudden shift in foreign policy. Spanish "non-belligerency" continued.

A visit we received toward the end of the same month from Mr. Myron Taylor, President Roosevelt's personal representative at the Vatican, served to accentuate the doubts we had about the attitude and possible future action of the Spanish Government. In accordance with instructions from the President, and with exceptional arrangements for "safe conduct" between the Vatican and

the Italian Government, Mr. Taylor passed through Madrid in an
Italian commercial plane en route to Rome for important and
urgent conferences with the Pope. I saw him briefly at the Madrid
airport and arranged for him to stop over with us at the Embassy
on his return. This occurred on Monday, September 28th; and the
next day I accompanied him on calls on the Nuncio and the Foreign Minister, and in the evening the Foreign Minister attended a
dinner I gave at the Embassy in Mr. Taylor's honor. Count Jordana
obviously liked him personally and was greatly impressed by him,
but, aside from expatiating on the menace of Communism, he was
quite noncommittal about Spain's attitude and policy.

Mr. Taylor had planned to leave Madrid for Lisbon, by Spanish
plane, on Wednesday, September 30. But when we reached the airport we were informed that some "high official" had cancelled the
flight for that day, and on returning to the Embassy we found a
message from the Caudillo saying he wanted to talk with Mr. Taylor
at the Pardo.

Consequently out to the Pardo Mr. Taylor and I went; and with
General Franco, Count Jordana, and an interpreter we were closeted
for an hour and a half. It was not altogether a comforting session.
We were seated in the Caudillo's spacious and beautifully tapestried
study so that we faced the windows and between them three conspicuous autographed photographs—the Pope's in the middle, and
(amazing company for him) Hitler's on the right and Mussolini's
on the left.

The conversation was almost exclusively between General
Franco and Mr. Taylor. The General began by delivering a lengthy
speech, which he had doubtless prepared in advance. The main
points in it were that the war of the United States with Japan was
separate and distinct from the war in Europe, which was a struggle
against Communism and in which we should not mix; that Hitler
was an honorable gentleman who had no quarrel with Great Britain
and no thought of impairing its independence; and that the great
enemy of Britain and the United States, as well as of Germany and
Italy and all Christendom, was "barbarous and oriental, commu-
nistic Russia."

Mr. Taylor's rebuttal was masterful. Gradually, by a series of questions, he drew admissions from the Caudillo that the United States had to fight a war which the entire Axis, and not merely Japan, had precipitated; that Hitler had not respected the independence of nations and did not intend to respect the integrity of the British Empire; and that it was Nazi Germany rather than Communist Russia which had gone on the war-path. Furthermore, the Caudillo paid close and respectful attention to Mr. Taylor's extended defense of Russia and frank discussion of the "bogey" of communism, and to his emphatic account of America's power and determination to win the war.

On our way back to the Embassy, Mr. Taylor confessed to a feeling of grave apprehension about General Franco's apparent sympathy with Fascism and swallowing of Nazi propaganda. Needless to say, I too was apprehensive. Yet, as I was later to discover, the bark of the Caudillo was worse than his bite, and the bark on that occasion was his worst. That it afterwards softened is attributable in no small degree, I believe, to the opportunity the Caudillo seized, on September 30, of meeting and hearing Myron Taylor. The next day the Spanish plane for Lisbon took off from Madrid as usual, and on it Mr. Taylor departed.

In a letter to President Roosevelt on September 30 I reported

the immense current interest in the trip of Myron Taylor to the Vatican, widely advertised and commented upon in the Spanish press. German-owned and Falangist papers interpret it as a peace-overture of the United Nations. More moderate papers perceive in it an effort of the United States to detach Italy from the Axis and make a separate peace with her. Gossip—which in Spain is more informative than the controlled press—has it that the trip is "sensational" and "bodes no good to Germany." I have been deluged by Spanish requests to meet "the great Myrón Taylór," and my dinner last night, originally planned for eighteen guests, turned out to be for thirty—including Jordana with his chef de cabinet and military aide, the Under Secretary Pan de Soraluce, the Papal Nuncio, the Chilean Ambassador, the British and Irish Ministers—strange bed-fellows, but all anxious to be in bed with Taylor and to catch what he might say in his sleep. The Taylor visit, aside from being a great personal boon to me, has come at the right psychological moment for the American cause in Spain. We need here an occasional visit of just this sort.

In the same letter I mentioned to the President another matter which at that critical time proved as beneficial to us as it was damaging to Germany.

Aside from Mr. Taylor's visit, the subject most discussed (in conversation, *not* in the press) is the sinking of the Spanish ship *Monte Gorbea* off Martinique. Everybody assumes that the sinking was done by a German submarine, and many express the belief that it was in the nature of a warning to Spain not to flirt with America or otherwise to alter the pro-Axis policy of Serrano Suñer. The feeling is very bitter, and I wouldn't be surprised if the sinking, with its relatively heavy loss of life, reacts sharply against the Germans. Jordana told me last Thursday that he was going to get to the bottom of the matter and find out, if humanly possible, how and why the sinking occurred. He said he had already consulted the German Ambassador, who, on behalf of his Government, had categorically denied that any German submarine was responsible. Jordana implied that he did not believe that the disaster could have been caused by any American mine or submarine, and said he hoped I would supply him as soon as possible with an official categorical denial and that my Government would cooperate promptly in repatriating the survivors to Spain.

I may add that we did furnish Jordana with a prompt denial and did cooperate in getting the survivors home, and that Germany, after considerable wrangling, finally admitted responsibility for the sinking and paid Spain an indemnity.

The very fact, however, that the Spanish press never so much as hinted that the Germans had destroyed the *Monte Gorbea,* with the majority of its Spanish passengers and with all its precious cargo of wheat from Argentina, indicated only too clearly how fearful the Spanish Government was of Germany and how anxious not to arouse public opinion against it. We had to recognize that until the Allies should win some decisive military successes we would be seriously disadvantaged in coping with Spanish non-belligerency.

IV

Nevertheless, we did cope with it during the dark days of 1942. In the absence of military weapons, we used others. One was what

Sir Samuel Hoare had employed with consummate art during the even darker days (for him and for England) of 1940 and 1941. It was *poise*, the assumption of an air at once of impenetrability and of assurance. I and my family and the entire staff of the American Embassy simply took it for granted that the United Nations could and inevitably must win the war, and by our every word and deed we sedulously sought to communicate that conviction to Spaniards whether in or out of the Government. We merely dismissed, with a laugh or a shrug, any expression of doubt or any report of Axis gains in Russia or in Egypt or in Burma. We were impenetrable about unfortunate details and perfectly assured about the general outcome. Our poise was sustained with no little conscious effort and nervous strain, but I am sure it had an important, if intangible, effect upon Spain.

Another weapon was a steadily intensifying and expanding barrage of propaganda. As early as June 1, 1942, I wrote to General William Donovan, who then headed the organization from which the Office of War Information was later formed:

Two weeks in Madrid have convinced me that the present opportunity is golden for greatly enlarged and more effective propaganda in Spain. The British have a large organization which is doing splendid work, but its director, Mr. T. F. Burns, frankly admits that Spaniards will pay more attention to Americans than to Britishers and that the British work does not touch certain basic matters which American propaganda can and should deal with, such as American war preparedness and production, American scientific developments, American films, attitude of American Catholic prelates and intellectuals toward Nazism, the relations of the United States to Latin America (and vice versa), and the grim determination of America to win the war and to help impose a just peace. . . . The [Spanish] Government, as it is at present, is still outwardly pro-Axis in word, but the Spanish masses are *Spanish* and more anti-German than anti-American. And with impending Allied offensives on the European Continent, the need for adequate American propaganda here would appear imperative.

The only American propaganda now being carried on here is that directed by Mr. Crain, a Second Secretary of the Embassy. He is a hard worker and is doing everything he can do with the aid of a few clerks and messengers whom he impresses into running a mimeograph and occasionally displaying some films at the Embassy. Yet, despite dearth of means and facilities, he does manage to get out a valuable weekly bulletin in English and Spanish, which is mailed to a large select list, and to distribute some American magazines and illustrations, and to conduct a large correspondence. Nevertheless this is but a beginning—useful chiefly in making contacts, obtaining experience, and discovering what can and what cannot be done. It should lead at once into something more intensive and extensive.

I have sent you, through the State Department, a telegram outlining the program which I should like to have inaugurated as soon as possible. It starts with the renting of a house (the Byne house) four short blocks from the Embassy. Mr. Byne was an American architect long resident in Madrid and his wife was a collector and seller of Spanish antiques. Both are now dead, and the house with its beautiful furnishings is part of an estate administered . . . in New York. . . . I don't know what the rental would be, but I imagine that the total annual expenditure for it should not exceed $12,000, and might be considerably less, especially if the rental were paid in dollars in America rather than in pesetas in Spain. . . .

Three persons should constitute the main staff. The Director or Chief should be a judicious, experienced journalist. . . . There should be a First Assistant, . . . and for this post I have suggested Emmet Hughes, who is now with the research department of your office. . . . There should also be an attaché . . . to specialize on cinema and films. . . . Aiding the Chief and his Assistant and the Attaché will have to be a number of stenographers, clerks, and handy men—just how many only experience can show. Most of these, of Spanish nationality, can be procured in Madrid at relatively small expense. Perhaps two or three would have to be imported from America.

Any such establishment would have to function, of course, in harmony with the Embassy here, and I would expect to designate Mr. Crain as the liaison officer between myself and the Embassy on the one hand, and the establishment and its chief on the other. . . . It will also of course be necessary for collaboration between the Department [of State] and your office in inaugurating the program as well as in carrying it into effect. . . .

Almost simultaneously with the despatch of this letter to General Donovan, I wrote to Mr. Charles A. Thomson of the Division of Cultural Relations of the State Department, requesting the appointment of a qualified Cultural Relations Attaché to Madrid, and also to Dr. Nicholas Murray Butler, soliciting from the Carnegie Endowment the gift of some books for a contemplated library and reading room. Likewise I discussed with Mrs. Charles Foltz, the wife of our A P correspondent in Madrid and herself a delightful person and trained librarian, the possibility of her taking charge of the library and social activities of any "Casa Americana" which we might be able to open as an Embassy annex.

It took time to bring these projects to fruition. Dr. Butler, not being hampered by governmental red tape, was the first to respond, and he responded handsomely by providing us with standard works in American history, economics, and political science as the nucleus for what became, in a relatively short while, a flourishing and much frequented American library in Madrid. From General Donovan and later from his successor in the Office of War Information, Mr. Elmer Davis, came expressions of lively interest and promises of assistance. Gradually, the promises were fulfilled.

In the summer of 1942 Mr. Emmet Hughes arrived, at first as assistant to Mr. Crain, and then, after the latter unfortunately fell ill from overwork and had to return to America, as acting chief of the Press Section. Early in September I was enabled to sign a lease for the Byne House, and in it was duly installed our Press and Propaganda Section (or "OWI Madrid Outpost"). Before long, this was a humming and attractive hive of activities. On the third floor were, in addition to offices, the library and reading room in charge of Mrs. Foltz. On the first floor and in the adjacent garage building were the mimeographing, photographic, and printing machinery and the distributing rooms whence emanated daily bulletins in English, semi-weekly bulletins in Spanish, a weekly "Carta de America," thousands of copies of monthlies in Spanish—En Guardia and Reader's Digest—and large numbers of pictures and feature articles for Spanish newspapers and for "Efe," the Spanish news agency. On the second floor were social rooms, where American news-reels and feature films were exhibited nightly to many different invited groups and where in the afternoons conferences and tea parties were held, including Mrs. Hayes's weekly "knitting circle" of Spanish and Latin-American ladies, and another weekly "party" for Spanish young people. All the ladies of the Embassy cooperated in making the Casa Americana the great success it undoubtedly was. The regular staff of the Casa steadily augmented until it comprised, besides Mr. Hughes and Mrs. Foltz, six Americans in charge respectively of films, bulletins, photography, feature articles, distribution, and finance; three American clerks; and some sixty Spanish employees.

There was greater delay in the State Department's obtaining a Cultural Relations Attaché for us. Finally, in 1943, Professor John Van Horne of the University of Illinois, a specialist in Spanish language and literature, arrived. By making special contacts with Spanish scholars, he nicely supplemented the work of the Press Section.

Meanwhile, the Embassy Chancery had been expanding and distributing its activities among a variety of "sections" (political, economic, press, petroleum, refugee, cultural relations, etc.) and affiliated offices (Military and Naval Attachés, Office of War Information, Office of Strategic Services, United States Commercial Company, Board of Economic Warfare, etc.). To hold all these sections and offices together and to relate each of them to our central objective of drawing Spain away from the Axis and toward the Allies, we early instituted weekly conferences of the senior chancery officers, the attachés, and the chief representatives of affiliated organizations. In view of the difficulty and delicacy of our mission in Spain, my Counselor and I were insistent (I believe, most properly) that all should proceed as a unit, subject, in policy and tactics, to central direction and control.

There was no trouble about this with the trained foreign-service officers or with experienced attachés who understood local conditions. But it was sometimes difficult and time-consuming to make new and untrained arrivals from OWI and OSS, and some of their officials back home, understand that we were in Spain not to fight Spaniards or overturn their government but to help win the war against the Axis and to enlist all possible support for this purpose from both the Spanish people and the Spanish Government. Over and over again I told members of the staff whose missionary zeal outstripped their judgment that they might entertain any ideas they wished about the existing Spanish regime, but they must preserve, in word and act, a strict neutrality. After all, it was the regime with which we had to deal, the regime which ultimately determined Spain's fateful policy toward us and the war. I knew that the Spanish "Leftists" were sympathetic with us anyway. They didn't have to be converted, and for us to have encouraged them to revolt would have been suicidal for us and flatly contrary to instructions from President Roosevelt and to the clearly and repeatedly expressed wishes of our Joint and Combined General Staffs. No forceful overturn of the existing Spanish regime was likely or even possible, and the only result of our advocating it would have been our expulsion from the country and the surrender of strategic Spain to Germany.

It was peculiarly important that our press and propaganda work in Spain should serve Allied war-ends and not, through ignorance or misplaced enthusiasm, give aid or comfort to the Axis; and I am confident it did serve our war-ends and serve them intelligently and effectively. Of course it was not carried on exclusively by the OWI or at the Casa Americana in Madrid. All members of the Embassy staff, both men and women, and most of the American colony in Spain, especially our newspaper correspondents, were propagandists for us; and thanks to continuous and devoted assistance of all our consulates throughout Spain, the distribution of our propaganda and its resulting influence were nation-wide.

Please don't think that "propaganda," as here used, has any sinister meaning. We were not trying to "put over" on the Spaniards any falsehoods or deceptions. Rather we sought only to provide them with reliable factual information about why America was at war with the Axis, what it was doing to win the war, and how it was planning to cooperate with all nations of good will to establish after the war a just and durable peace.

Naturally the Nazis in Spain and the pro-Axis Falangistas did everything they could to impede and counteract our propaganda. They blocked, from time to time, its distribution through the post-office and frequently terrorized Spaniards who carried it. During

1942 they successfully prevented any exhibition or sale of it at Spanish newsstands or in other public places. Yet it did get about; and for its circulation we could always rely upon collaboration of the British and also of the Latin Americans.

V

I have now spoken of two weapons which, in the absence of Allied military victories, we employed in Spain in 1942 against the Axis. One was factual propaganda and the other was psychological poise. But there was a third, by far the most telling of all. It was economic. It had already been developed by the British two years before.

In 1940, when the German armies, after plunging through France, halted at the Pyrenees, and Spain, unlike Italy, refrained from entering the war on Germany's side, it had occurred to the British that there might be a chance, however slight, that Spain would be able to keep out of the war indefinitely, especially if its commercial ties with Britain were maintained and tightened.

Spain, the British knew, was dependent on overseas sources of supply for certain commodities, such as petroleum, rubber, wheat, etc., which it must obtain if it were even partially to restore its economy, still disrupted after three years of destructive civil war. Britain could supply some needed commodities and help to make others available from its Empire, allies, or friends. Spain, on its part, could repay Britain with iron ore, potash, citrus fruits, and other products which were greatly needed in the British Isles and which, because of the relatively short distance, could be brought from Spain much more advantageously than from across the Atlantic. So the British traded with Spain, and backed the United States, while we were still neutral, in doing likewise. In 1940–1941, two years before I went as Ambassador to Spain, the United States was supplying it with petroleum, trucks and tractors, and also with raw cotton, for the purchase of which we granted Spain a substantial credit. This credit Spain promptly repaid, and for the commodities it received from us it paid in its own products which found a ready market in America.

In July, 1941, however, as a result of serious friction between the Spanish Government and my predecessor, Ambassador Alexander Weddell,[1] and of mounting criticism within the United States of what was represented as an "appeasing" of the Franco regime, we stopped petroleum shipments to Spain [2] and imposed practically an embargo on other shipments. This did not please the British, and by the autumn of 1941 they convinced our State Department that a continuation of our embargo, particularly on petroleum, would play into the hands of the Axis. As Secretary Hull explained to the President: "The food situation is so bad in Spain, and so dependent on transportation within the country, that a curtailment of minimum gasoline requirements risks producing civil disorder which might conceivably result in presenting Germany with an excuse for 'restoring order.'" In November, 1941, therefore, our Government began negotiations with the Spanish Government for the lifting of the petroleum embargo; and early in 1942, not long after our entrance into the war, these negotiations culminated in an agreement.

What we were most anxious about was that none of the petroleum which reached Spain should be passed on to the Axis. Consequently we insisted upon two major precautions. One was restricting the amount of petroleum which we would make available to Spain to such a minimum as would barely suffice to meet most urgent Spanish needs and would thus leave no surplus for re-export to our enemies.[3] The other was ensuring that the shipment of

[1] Serrano Suñer, then Foreign Minister, was quite unpardonable in his attitude toward Mr. Weddell and for several months prevented him from seeing General Franco.

[2] Theoretically Spain, when cut off from petroleum in the United States, could still obtain it from Latin America. But our participation in the British navicert control and our ownership of Latin-American refineries actually operated to effect a total embargo, which we could maintain or lift at will.

[3] The maximal amount of all petroleum products which the Spaniards might import in a year was fixed at sixty per cent of the annual average for the five years from 1931 to 1936, despite the fact that Spanish needs were much greater after the Civil War than before. Moreover, this maximal allotment was quite theoretical. It was never officially communicated to the Spanish Govern-

petroleum to Spain and its distribution and use within the country should be controlled by American officials to the end that none of it might escape to German submarines or otherwise to our foes. This second precaution involved, of course, Spain's granting to us such extraordinary facilities for inspecting and supervising its domestic economy as could be interpreted as an impairment of its national sovereignty. Indeed, the British Ambassador at Madrid counseled against our insisting upon this. He feared it would antagonize, if not outrage, the Spaniards. Insist we did, nevertheless; and so desirous were the Spaniards of rebuilding their domestic economy and so essential was a supply of petroleum that they finally accepted all our conditions, and accepted them gracefully.

Our agreement further provided that the petroleum for Spain must come from surpluses in the Caribbean and be transported by Spanish tankers, inasmuch as we could divert none of our own oil or shipping from our war-effort. What Spain got, Spain would have to procure outside the United States and over and above all Allied requirements.

As for the American control commission, it was fortunate to have been headed from the outset by Mr. Walter Smith, a veteran technical oil-man, who spoke Spanish like a native, and who was at once forceful and resourceful, conscientious and intensely patriotic. He was already in Madrid as an attaché of our Embassy when I arrived in May, 1942, and before long his "petroleum section" comprised fourteen other attachés, all being experienced oil men, and all enjoying diplomatic privileges. These aides to Mr. Smith were stationed at strategic points throughout metropolitan Spain and in the Canary Islands and Spanish Morocco. Their business was to unseal and recheck arriving Spanish tankers, which had previously been checked and sealed by our people in the Caribbean, to follow the distribution of the petroleum from the port of entry through the various installations to the ultimate Spanish consumers,

---

ment; and by reason of the slowness and limited capacity of the Spanish tankers in which petroleum supplies had to be brought from America, the actual amount reaching Spain during the next three years fell considerably short of the sixty per cent.

and to investigate and report any evidence or rumor of infractions of our oil agreement with Spain.

Many rumors reached us, especially from opponents of the existing Spanish Government, that Spain was supplying petroleum to German submarines and to the Germans in France. Such rumors were always investigated but were invariably found to be baseless. The only case we ever succeeded in proving against Spaniards had to do with a black-market sale of a small quantity of gasoline to German consular officials at Tangier. The persons implicated were promptly punished by the Spanish Government. I must say that in carrying out the petroleum program with Spain, we had the constant and effective cooperation not only of Mr. Walter Smith but also of the Spanish Petroleum Commissioner, General Roldán.

The Spanish Government of General Franco thoroughly appreciated the country's cardinal need for petroleum and its dependence upon the United States for making a supply of that commodity available to Spain. It likewise appreciated what would happen to the supply if it allowed our enemies to get any bit of it. Spanish self-interest was our best guarantee in the matter of petroleum; and petroleum was our ace among the economic cards we held and played in Spain.

There were other economic controls which the United States, in conjunction with Great Britain, exercised in Spain. One was the system of navicerts which was administered by the British but on the content of which our counsel was sought and usually followed. It was a control of Spanish shipping—crews, passengers, cargo. It enabled the Allies not only to prevent the Spanish merchant marine from being used for Axis purposes but also to ensure its utilization for transportation of persons and commodities favorable to the Allies as well as to Spain.

Another was the "blacklisting," either public or confidential, of Spanish individuals and firms that "traded with the enemy." This was a joint Anglo-American undertaking in the field of "economic warfare." Both the American and British Embassies had "blacklisting" sections, which made the investigations and recommendations on which was based, for Spain, the final action by a committee in London. Against persons on the "blacklist" we applied whatever economic sanctions we could. We would not buy anything from them, and eventually we denied petroleum supplies to them. As time went on, more and more Spaniards sought to escape or be removed from the "blacklist," and the number of those trading with the Axis correspondingly declined.

Still another, and peculiarly significant, phase of our economic warfare in Spain was "preemptive buying." This meant trying to buy up those strategic materials which the Axis, and especially the Germans, most wanted for their war effort, such as wolfram, mercury, fluorspar, sheepskins, woolen textiles, fleece-lined gloves, etc. A few of these articles, but only a few, we wanted for ourselves. The main object was to keep them from the enemy.

Spain presented a favorable field for preemptive buying. Unlike Portugal and most other neutrals, it preserved an "open market," allowing anyone, whether of the Allies or of the Axis, to purchase whatever he wanted and could pay for, instead of allocating quotas to various belligerents. Proverbially unbusiness-like, Spain, at least in this respect, had an excellent eye for business. It perceived economic advantages to itself in selling competitively to both sides and thereby accumulating larger foreign credits for goods it required from both sides.

On the Allied side, Great Britain inaugurated preemptive buying in Spain through a Madrid branch of the United Kingdom Commercial Corporation. Then, shortly after our entry into the war and about the time of my arrival at Madrid, our Government, through the United States Commercial Company, a subsidiary of the Reconstruction Finance Corporation,[1] embarked on a joint program with the British. The UKCC and USCC had offices together, pooled their information, shared in negotiations with the Spaniards, and divided costs evenly. Both had competent and experienced staffs, who set a high standard for loyal and effective Anglo-American cooperation. From June, 1942, the director of the USCC for the whole Iberian peninsula was Mr. Walton Butterworth, a career

[1] Later, of the Board of Economic Warfare, and later still of the Foreign Economic Administration.

Foreign Service officer who simultaneously ranked as a First Secretary of the Madrid Embassy; his first assistant for Spain was another Embassy First Secretary, Mr. Julian Harrington; and the executive head of the Madrid office was a remarkably able and astute business-man of Swiss origin, Mr. Paul Walser.

There has been a good deal of misunderstanding about Spain's continuing to trade with Germany. In some quarters it has been assumed and stated that Spain sent vast amounts of produce to Germany in order to help the Axis wage war against us. The fact is that what produce actually went from Spain to Germany in 1942 and 1943 (the quantity and variety have been grossly exaggerated) was always exported for financial considerations and in payment for imports which Spain vitally needed for its domestic economy and which the Allies, for war reasons, were unable or unwilling to furnish —heavy machinery, precision tools, buses and streetcars, chemicals and drugs, seed-potatoes. Spain did *not* export wheat to Germany; as late as January, 1944, Germany exported 20,000 tons of wheat to Spain.

Our objective in preemptive buying was not to reduce Spanish imports from Germany, but rather to reduce the volume of materials which Spain must furnish to Germany in payment. The device principally resorted to was to raise prices of Spanish products which the Germans wished to acquire. Thus, if Germany was purchasing a strategic ore at, say, $20 a ton, the Allies offered $60 a ton. As a result, Spanish producers of the ore began either to sell it to the Allies or to charge the Germans the same high price the Allies were offering. Consequently the Germans, with only a limited amount of pesetas available from their exports to Spain with which to purchase the ore, could buy only a third of the quantity they otherwise could have bought. If they wished to overcome this handicap, they must increase their exports to Spain and thus further burden their own economy to the advantage of the Allies.

The economic competition thus initiated by the Allies operated, of course, as a potent stimulus to the production of certain materials, most notably wolfram, so that the Allies had to purchase steadily increasing amounts at the high prices they themselves fixed. Presently the Spanish Government helped further to raise the price of wolfram by levying a tax of a hundred pesetas a kilo on its production. This added still more to Germany's payment problem.

I think I never heard of wolfram before I went to Spain. I soon learned, however. In fact, all of us at the Embassy in Madrid had perforce to make it a topic of daily conversation and some of us dreamed about it at night. It is the ore from which tungsten is derived, and tungsten is a strategic material of the highest order. It is used to harden steel and is an essential element in the manufacture of machine tools, armor plate, armor-piercing projectiles, etc. For it, Germany was almost entirely dependent upon Spain and Portugal.

By the end of 1942 the USCC and UKCC had jointly purchased in Spain 350,000 kilos of wolfram. Besides, by the same date, we had jointly purchased one and a half million kilos of sheepskins; 20,000 flasks of mercury; 28,000 pairs of fleece-lined gloves; 15,000 tons of fluorspar; 1,300 tons of strontium; and large quantities of woolen cloth, blankets, and sweaters. We had kept all these strategic materials from the Axis. It was economic warfare in action.[1]

Of course, the British and ourselves, no less than the Germans, had to sell things to Spain in order to pay for what was purchased in Spain. Had we withheld petroleum, and quotas of rubber, cotton, fertilizers, wheat, and other products which Spain sought from sources under Allied control, we could not have waged in the Iberian peninsula that economic struggle with Germany which was so advantageous to our over-all war effort. In fact, by withholding them and thereby reducing Spain to utter economic chaos, we would, in all probability, have forced General Franco and his Government into the arms of Germany, with disastrous effects, by the end of 1942, on our military projects in North Africa.

As it was, our buying from, and selling to, Spain, and our active and increasingly successful commercial competition with the Germans throughout the Peninsula, forged links between Spain and the Allies and demonstrated to the former the large measure of its dependence upon the latter for its own economic recovery and

[1] Cf. the important article by David Gordon, "How We Blockaded Germany," Harper's Magazine, December, 1944, pp. 14-22.

material well-being. Higher prices for Spanish products, and increased production stimulated by the higher prices, created a mild boom in the country, particularly in wolfram-producing areas. This, with accompanying increase of helpful imports from the Allies as well as from the Germans, immeasurably strengthened Spanish economy. Gradually, foodstuffs and textiles became less scarce. Rationing was reduced. Transportation was improved. Simultaneously the Spanish army was enlarged, properly uniformed, and better equipped. Altogether, Spain was undergoing rehabilitation and becoming a nation whose power must be recognized. The Government's policy of staying out of the war, at a time when entry would have meant entry on the side of the Axis, was beginning to pay dividends. It received nearly universal support from the Spanish people, and fortified Spain's desire to continue trading with us and remaining out of the war.

For the practical operation of our manifold economic program in Spain, major credit is due our Commercial Attaché, Mr. Ralph Ackerman. He was chiefly responsible for supervising, checking, and coordinating the whole purchase-supply program, the detailed work of the petroleum, "blacklisting," and economic sections of the American Embassy, and the pertinent liaison with the British. Moreover, he was the immediate negotiator with the Spanish Minister of Industry and Commerce, Señor Carceller, a shrewd and competent business-man; and the fact that the two maintained cordial personal relations and respected each other certainly contributed to the success of the negotiations and of the economic warfare we waged against the Axis.

VI

The crucial—and dramatic—test of Spain's "non-belligerency" was the Allied landing in French North Africa on November 8, 1942. At my first meeting with General Franco early the preceding June he had expressed the greatest skepticism about our ability to get troops across the Atlantic. Apparently he then had no idea that we could land in North Africa. Nevertheless, it was rumored that we contemplated such an undertaking, and, as I have already indicated,[1] the Portuguese Ambassador had conveyed to me, at the beginning of June, his Government's hope that the rumors were not true and were only German propaganda. Eventually the Spanish Government must have given credence to them and also to German-inspired stories about a forthcoming attack by us on Spain itself. During October the Foreign Minister, Count Jordana, repeatedly expostulated, at considerable length and with unusual asperity, about the current agitation in certain American newspapers for a rupture of diplomatic relations with Spain and about the grave menace to Spain in any attempt by us to wage war at its doors, which could only invite disaster for ourselves. I could merely reply, at the moment, that I was sure we would respect Spanish territory (unless Spain aided the Axis) and that I would inform my Government of his views.

I had already been confidentially informed, at the end of September, that President Roosevelt and Prime Minister Churchill, with their Combined Chiefs of Staff, definitely planned an early invasion and occupation of French North Africa as a preliminary to putting Italy out of the war, and that the Allied plan might involve, as a precautionary measure, our seizure of the Canary Islands. Against this last possibility, I protested, as energetically as I knew how, directly to the President and the Secretary of State, warning them that any attack on the Canaries would be sure to embroil us with Spain and wipe out any chance we might have of keeping a buffer between the Germans in France and an expeditionary force of ours in North Africa. The danger was readily perceived; and our military authorities, if they ever really projected an attack on the Canaries, abandoned it. Eventually I received official word which enabled me, on November 2, to give these written assurances to Count Jordana:

Excellency:
Confirming and developing the statement I made to Your Excellency informally and verbally on October 30, I have the honor, on behalf of my Government, to transmit for Your Excellency's infor-

[1] See above, p. 37.

mation and for that of His Excellency the Chief of State and Generalissimo of the Armies the following declaration:

"Such articles and resolutions of organizations as have recently
appeared in the American press advocating the rupture of diplomatic
relations with Spain in no way represent the policy of the Government of the United States of America.

"It is the purpose of the Government of the United States of
America to do everything possible to prevent Spain from being
brought into the war, and Spain's desire to remain out of the war is
fully recognized by the United States. The Government of the United
States has no intention of infringing upon the sovereignty of Spain
or of any Spanish colonial possessions or islands or protectorates. The
United States will take no action of any sort which would in any way
violate Spanish territory.

"Moreover, the Government of the United States of America,
perceiving with much gratification the improvement of relations between the two countries which has been taking place in recent months,
strongly deprecates any activities by purely private organizations or
individuals within the United States which would seem intended to
prejudice the growth of good feeling between the Spanish people and
the people of the United States."

The foregoing declaration has been personally authorized by the
President of the United States and Commander-in-Chief of the
American Army and Navy.

I avail myself, etc.

Two days before the actual landing in North Africa, secret and
detailed instructions were sent me through a British code which was
deemed safer than any of ours and which was known in Madrid
only to Sir Samuel Hoare and to his Counselor, Mr. Arthur
Yencken. The instructions contained the text of a communication
from President Roosevelt for me to present in person to General
Franco and of another from Mr. Churchill for the British Ambassador to deliver to Count Jordana, and concluded (in rough para-
phrase) as follows: 'On receipt, by either of the Ambassadors, of
the word "Thunderbird" in cypher, followed by a time, they are
to concert together immediately and arrange to make their respective communications at, or as soon as possible after, the time given,
which will be the time of the start of the landing in North Africa.
The British Ambassador will report the delivery of his message to

Count Jordana by a code word *en clair* to London, repeating it to Gibraltar, Tangier, and Lisbon; his telegram to be "most immediate." The American Ambassador similarly is to report "most immediate" the delivery of his message to General Franco, using the code word "Jelly" *en clair* and repeating the telegram to Gibraltar, Tangier, and Lisbon, also *en clair*.'

On the afternoon of Saturday, November 7, both Sir Samuel and I received the mystic warning telegram "Thunderbird," followed by "Sunday, November 8, two a.m. Spanish time." We thus learned when the fateful landing would begin and knew that in the following night-hours there would be high business for us and for Spain. We consulted together and agreed that I should wait upon Count Jordana shortly before two a.m. and seek through him an immediate audience with General Franco, and that, following the presentation of the President's communication to the Caudillo, the British Ambassador should then present Mr. Churchill's to the Foreign Minister.

Meanwhile we had to recognize the possibility that General Franco and his Government might react violently against the *démarche* we were about to make and might utilize the big garrison in Spanish Morocco—150,000 strong—to reënforce French resistance. Personally, I discounted this possibility. But there remained, with no discounting by any of us in Madrid, the very great possibility that the Germans might make a dash in force over the Pyrenees and down across Spain onto our flank. Some precautions must be taken. I let into the secret two members of the Embassy: Mr. Beaulac, the Counselor; and Mr. Outerbridge Horsey, a Third Secretary. The latter was charged with perfecting arrangements, if need arose, for quick evacuation of the Embassy, and departure of its staff by automobiles toward Lisbon or Gibraltar. He was also charged with the stealthy burning of confidential documents; and for forty-eight hours prior to the decisive night, wisps of smoke rose intermittently from the chimneys of furnaces and fire-places in the Embassy. If things went wrong, my last task in Madrid would be, according to instructions, to call on the Swiss Minister and entrust to him the protection of American interests.

Both Beaulac and Horsey stayed up with me throughout the night of November 7–8, as did also my wife; and from time to time Mr. Yencken came and went with messages between us and the British Ambassador. So as not to inform or alarm the servants, we left them in their beds and did our conferring in a small sitting room with heavily curtained windows. Shortly after one o'clock in the morning we telephoned to the Foreign Office for Count Jordana. He was at home, they said. We telephoned to his house. He was in bed. I said I must see him at once. His consent sounded sleepily surprised.

In twenty minutes, in company with Beaulac, I arrived at Count Jordana's. He greeted us in pyjamas and bathrobe and with obvious anxiety. This was not lessened when I requested him to make an immediate appointment for me with General Franco so that I might present to the Caudillo, without delay, an urgent communication from President Roosevelt. The Foreign Minister tried to elicit from me the contents or at least the subject of the communication. I regretted, I said, that I could not divulge it except to the Caudillo. Count Jordana then tried calling the Palace of the Pardo from his telephone in the adjoining hallway. After half an hour, punctuated by his pacing the floor in and out of our room in ever deepening anxiety, he finally aroused the Pardo, only to learn that the Caudillo was out on a hunting party and wouldn't be back until early morning, at which time he would set an hour for receiving me.

It was then a little after two, and I knew our landing in North Africa was already under way. Count Jordana looked so inexpressibly distressed that I decided to take him into our confidence forthwith. So, "as a trusted friend," I then and there let him see the President's letter, and Beaulac interpreted it for him in Spanish. I have never seen a man's face change expression so quickly and so completely as Jordana's. From one of intense anxiety, it was now one of intense relief. "Ah!," he said, "so Spain is not involved."

Beaulac and I also felt relief, and with rising optimism we returned to the Embassy. Here the vigil continued. Finally, as dawn began to tinge the east, word came from the Pardo that General Franco would receive me at nine o'clock. I toop a nap, and at sharp nine o'clock on Sunday morning, November 8, 1942, I was in the Caudillo's study, facing him and Count Jordana and the official interpreter (Baron de las Torres), and again, above them on the wall, the photographs of Hitler and Mussolini. After expressing gratitude for his receiving me on such short notice and at such an unseemly hour, I handed General Franco the communication from President Roosevelt, which the interpreter rendered in Spanish. Its original was as follows:

Dear General Franco:

It is because your nation and mine are friends in the best sense of the word and because you and I are sincerely desirous of the continuation of that friendship for our mutual good that I want very simply to tell you of the compelling reasons that have forced me to send a powerful American military force to the assistance of the French possessions in North Africa.

We have accurate information to the effect that Germany and Italy intend at an early date to occupy with military force French North Africa.

With your wide military experience you will understand clearly that in the interests of the defense of both North America and South America it is essential that action be taken to prevent an Axis occupation of French Africa without delay.

To provide for America's defense I am sending a powerful army to French possessions and protectorates in North Africa with the sole purpose of preventing occupation by Germany and Italy and with the hope that these areas will not be devastated by the horror of war.

I hope you will accept my full assurance that these moves are in no shape, manner or form directed against the Government or people of Spain or Spanish Morocco or Spanish territories—metropolitan or overseas. I believe the Spanish Government and the Spanish people wish to maintain neutrality and to remain outside the war. Spain has nothing to fear from the United Nations.

I am, my dear General, your sincere friend

FRANKLIN D. ROOSEVELT.

General Franco was evidently prepared for the President's message and seemingly pleased with it. I subsequently heard that Count Jordana, following my talk with him at two o'clock that morning, had conferred with the Ministers of Army, Marine, and Air and got them to join him in advising the Caudillo. Be that as it may, General Franco, when I saw him, was very calm and cordial. He showed considerable interest, as a military man, in the landings, and did not conceal his admiration of the strategy involved. He expressed appreciation of the Allied guarantees and said that he accepted them. This he later confirmed in a personal letter to President Roosevelt which I duly transmitted.

Returning to the Embassy that Sunday morning, I telegraphed with satisfaction the little word "Jelly" to Washington, Gibraltar, Lisbon, and Tangier. The next morning all the newspapers throughout Spain published in bold type on their front pages President Roosevelt's letter embodying Allied guarantees to Spain and General Franco's reply accepting those guarantees. The Spanish people were thus told, in effect, that Spain had nothing to fear from the Allies. They were not told that Spain had nothing to fear from the Axis.

The Spanish Government of course tried to obtain guarantees from the Germans. The latter replied that guarantees were not needed among friends. The Spanish Government insisted that they were. Finally, after much procrastination and evasion, the German Government is said to have given oral guarantees similar to the written guarantees of the Allies. If this is true, the Spanish Government apparently did not think highly enough of the German guarantees to publish them.

There is no doubt that, despite their previous spreading of rumors about an Allied invasion of French Africa and even an attack on Spain, the Germans were taken unawares and were quite astounded by our actual landings. For several days the German Embassy in Madrid and its auxiliary propaganda machine were mute and obviously perplexed, which profited both us and the Spaniards. Eventually the Germans resumed their swagger, and our Embassy was informed that, after our landings and while our military position in French Morocco and Algeria was still insecure, they twice requested free passage of German troops through Spain and that Spain twice refused.

On December 7, just a month after our landings, Count Jordana gave me special assurances, which, with other significant developments, I reported to the President as follows:

The most important news from Spain, in my opinion, is the emphatic assurance given me last Monday afternoon by the Foreign Minister, Count Jordana—which I promptly telegraphed to the Department—that General Franco and his whole Government are determined to pursue a policy of "impartiality" toward the two sets of belligerents, to maintain the partly mobilized Spanish army strictly on the defensive within present Spanish frontiers, and to resist *forcefully* any attempt by *any* foreign Power to invade Spanish territory. This is a long stride for the Government here to take, and one which couldn't or wouldn't have been taken had it not been for the sensational military developments in North Africa and your own previous assurances to Spain.

Incidentally, Count Jordana suggested to me the propriety and advantage of our North African Commander's calling on General Orgaz, the High Commissioner of Spanish Morocco. Such a call, he said, would advance our cause with the general Spanish public and would also serve to obviate difficulties which might arise between the two zones in Morocco. Apparently Nogues [the French High Commissioner] and Orgaz get along very well with each other, and Jordana wants a similar personal relationship established between Orgaz and the American commander in French Morocco.

We must not expect any broadcast of Spain's shifting policy in the near future. . . .

Count Jordana tells me that, with General Franco's concurrence, he has instructed Spanish diplomatic missions in the American Republics not to tolerate any Falange activities. This probably marks the beginning of the end of "Falange Exterior," that brain-child of Serrano Suñer which did its bit to make trouble for us in Latin America. I have seen certain instructions issued to Spain's new special envoy to Cuba, . . . and they are quite explicit against his having anything to do with Falangist or other anti-American agents or intrigues.

Thanksgiving Day was observed by the American colony in Madrid with special fervor this year. We had so much in recent developments to be thankful for. At both the Mass in the Catholic Church and the service in St. George's Protestant Church, your proclamation was read and "America" and "The Star-Spangled Banner" were sung. In the afternoon, in the Embassy Annex (Casa Americana), we had a showing of the film "Abe Lincoln in Illinois." And in the evening, at the Embassy, there was dinner for everybody, with turkey—Spanish turkey (which is excellent).

At the present moment I am devoting my chief efforts to seeking satisfactory solutions of at least some of the complex refugee and internee problems here. I want to obtain release of the nearly 200 American internees—mainly aviators and paratroops—now in Spain and Spanish Morocco. I want to get Polish, Czech, and other war-prisoners out of Miranda and to encourage reform, if not abolition, of Miranda and similar prison-camps. I want to help with the Jewish refugees here, . . . and I am reliably informed that since November 8, some twelve thousand Frenchmen have entered Spain, hoping to pass on to the fighting in North Africa—which creates a major problem for Spain as well as for us. Count Jordana appears sympathetic, but negotiations are as yet only in an initial stage.

CHAPTER IV

OBTAINING FACILITIES IN SPAIN

I

The President wrote me on November 25, 1942 : "I am very satisfied with Spanish reactions to date, and with the capable way in which you have kept us informed and have handled your mission in general." But as I wrote Mr. Myron Taylor at about the same time : "For weeks and months ahead the situation here is bound to be tense, with Allied forces to the south and Axis forces to the north, and with aerial and submarine warfare very close to, if not actually within, the peninsula's area. The American Embassy at Madrid will have to be all eyes and ears—and, on occasion, many tongued."

The situation did remain tense throughout the winter of 1942–1943. Our successful landings in French North Africa had been accomplished by relatively small forces, and several months elapsed before supplies and communications and reinforcements were sufficiently available for the Allies to undertake a serious offensive against the Axis in Tunisia. Our military difficulties and exposed position during those months were well known to the Germans and could only increase their temptation to force their way across Spain and cut us off. Doubtless they would have yielded to the temptation if they could have counted on Spain's acquiescence. But Spain, through Count Jordana—and probably through General Franco himself—made clear to them that if they moved in, it would enter the war on the Allied side. Germany feared to run the risk.

The Spain which showed readiness to resist German aggression at the end of 1942 was a more powerful Spain than Hitler would have had to deal with in the spring of 1940. Spanish strength had been built up in the meantime with German as well as Allied help, but, when the test came, that strength was used to deter Germany. Spain's "non-belligerency" was becoming less ambiguous.

Further clarification of Spain's position was afforded by the state visit which Count Jordana made in December, 1942, to Dr. Salazar of Portugal, and the resulting formation of the so-called "Iberian bloc." Spain was now ostentatiously collaborating with Portugal, and Portugal, though neutral, was an old ally of Great Britain.

Yet the Germans, after their initial consternation over our entrance into North Africa, redoubled their efforts to halt and reverse the newer Spanish trend. They replaced their Ambassador at Madrid, von Stohrer, whom they deemed too "soft," with von Moltke, who, as last Nazi Ambassador to Poland, had a reputation for stiffness, for banging desks of Foreign Ministers, and for hastening the doom of a country which displeased the Führer. Simultaneously they flooded Spain with their propaganda, accusing us of being Communists, belittling our war effort, and stridently proclaiming their own invincibility. In this they possessed willing allies, or dupes, in the Spanish Falange, especially in the "Vice Secretariat of Popular Education," which had a stranglehold on the Spanish press and radio. Despite friendly assurances of Count Jordana and General Franco himself, the bulk of publicity in Spain was markedly hostile to the Allies throughout the winter of 1942; and the Caudillo's devotion to the Falange was frequently reiterated. In January, 1943, General Franco sent a most cordially worded message to Hitler, wishing him success against Communism; and in the same month Señor Arrese, secretary of the Falange and member of the Caudillo's cabinet, made a much-publicized visit to Berlin.

While I had reason to believe that the Caudillo and his Government were seeking to "appease" Germany with words rather than deeds, I feared the effect of the words upon large and influential segments of the Spanish people. Consequently we undertook a special counter-offensive against the German and Falangist propaganda. On December 7 I addressed a strongly-worded personal letter of protest to Count Jordana, and followed it up with verbal representations to him almost every week during the next three months.

On January 15, I made a speech at the Casa Americana in Madrid, before an invited audience of Allied and Latin American diplomats and of Spanish officials, on "American War Aims." On February 26, I made another speech at Barcelona, at the 25th anniversary celebration of the American Chamber of Commerce in Spain, on "Reciprocal Trade and Spain's Developing Economy." Thousands of copies of both speeches were circulated, in Spanish versions, all over the country; and I flatter myself that they did a vast deal of good at an extremely critical time.

Of course, as I expected, certain journalists and radio commentators in the United States, particularly those who had long been more concerned with waging civil war in Spain (from a safe distance) than with fighting Germany, tore phrases loose from their context and deduced from them that I and the State Department were engaged in most nefarious "appeasement" and that the United States should instantly break off all relations with the Spanish Government—and, by implication, leave the country to the Axis. This barrage back home struck me as both humorous and pitiful, although it undoubtedly gave aid and comfort to our German enemies in Spain.

Meanwhile, on February 12, we sponsored a gala and full-length showing of the American film, "Gone with the Wind," at one of the principal theaters in Madrid. The Germans warned against the film's "immorality" and employed young Falangist hoodlums to strew carpet-tacks in the path of the motor cars of such evil folks as might attend. But no less a personage than the Bishop of Madrid, a close friend of Franco's, dramatically belied the German charge by coming and occupying a front seat and remaining the full four hours; while a strong cordon of Spanish police kept to a minimum any trouble the paid hoodlums made. The family of the Foreign Minister attended, and so did a thousand other Spaniards. It proved, indeed, to be a gala affair, and one of our best bits of propaganda.[1]

At about the same time, Archbishop Francis J. Spellman of

[1] The film was also shown at the Pardo at Franco's personal request, and subsequently, under the auspices of our various consuls, in the chief cities throughout Spain.

New York arrived in Madrid, and his visit, most pleasant in itself, also provided us with excellent indirect propaganda. He was on an extended tour of inspection of Catholic chaplains with our armed forces, and stopped several days in Spain, while en route from Lisbon to North Africa, in order that arrangements might be completed for a side trip by him to the Vatican by the same Italian plane which Mr. Myron Taylor had previously used. He stood on no ceremony, and talked freely with many Spanish Catholics about the Church in America and its determined opposition to Nazism and support of our war effort. He was received, with special cordiality, by the Foreign Minister and by prominent ecclesiastics, including the Nuncio, the Spanish Primate (Archbishop of Toledo), the Bishops of Madrid and Barcelona, and Cardinal Segura of Sevilla, all of whom were naturally critical of Nazi doctrines and favorably disposed toward us. Finally, General Franco himself sent for Archbishop Spellman, and their conversation at the Pardo lasted two hours.[1]

According to the report I had of this conversation, the Caudillo dwelt on much the same topics with the Archbishop in February, 1943, as he had with Mr. Myron Taylor in September, 1942: the menace of Communism, the necessity of suppressing it by force, the regrettable conflict between civilized Britain and Germany when they should be united against barbarous Russia, the theory of the two wars (the one in Europe and the other in the Pacific), the destructiveness of aerial warfare, the disastrous effects of a long war, the desirability of a negotiated peace. The Archbishop apparently argued the points, and drew from the Caudillo an admission that Germany couldn't possibly win the war, though he suspected no one would really win it except Russia.

In April, 1943, two quite different events occurred which were of notable propagandist value to us in Spain. One was the publication by General Franco of a volume of his "memorable addresses," including the speech he made when I presented my credentials in June, 1942, but rigidly excluding his welcome to the German Am-

[1] Archbishop Spellman's own account of his sojourn in Spain is contained in his interesting *Action this Day* (New York, Scribners, 1943), pp. 10–28, 39–42.

bassador and all other indications of past alignment or sympathy
with the Axis. The other event was the sensational trip of President
Roosevelt to Casablanca and his conferences there with Mr. Churchill and General De Gaulle. The Germans, in this case, were unable
to prevent the Spanish press from displaying the news with big
headlines and evident satisfaction.

As I wrote to the President on May 3: "I am tempted to send
you a whole sheaf of comments which we have gathered on the
reaction of Spaniards to your North African visit, but I think it
can all be summed up in their favorite expression, 'Estupendo!'
These people admire, above everything, personal courage and they
are now convinced that we cannot lose while under your leadership.
No propaganda campaign would have won us the respect and admiration which your trip did.

"There is a slow but steady improvement in official relations.
My Barcelona speech, which was printed and widely distributed
here, has been influential, I am sure, in gaining friends for the reciprocal trade policy and for the principles of the Atlantic Charter.
I regret more than I can say that its incidental reference to petroleum supplies from America caused such a furor back home. I can
only plead that if the journalistic critics of our Spanish policy knew
the real facts about the situation here and were as intent upon winning the present war against the Axis as they are upon continuing
the seven-year-old Spanish civil war, they would be more charitable
and less voluble."

II

Although, during the spring of 1943, we obtained no marked
general improvement in the tone of the Spanish press or lessening
of German and pro-Axis Falangist influence on it, we did obtain
from the Spanish Government in that critical period a number of
facilities and favors highly helpful to our war effort. In all this, our
chief friend and collaborator was the Foreign Minister, Count Jordana. Unlike Serrano Suñer, he was in his office every day, working
hard from early to late, and there I could and did have easy access

to him at any time. I conferred at length with him on an average of once a week. Of course, the German Ambassador saw him frequently also, and I knew that every request I made was energetically and vehemently opposed, usually with at least implied threats, by that Ambassador. Jordana was a little man physically, but he possessed a moral strength and a pluck and a courage which stood him in good stead in dealing with any blustering German. He occasionally felt obliged, in the face of too ominous threats from the Axis or of difficulties with some of his Falangist colleagues, to retreat, but his retreats were temporary and he was sure to face about again. In emergencies, I found, he almost always had the Caudillo's backing.

Before describing the facilities and favors we obtained that spring, I must emphasize that they were obtained at the very time when Germany still had large and powerful forces at the Pyrenees and when numerous Americans as well as Spaniards feared and even expected that they were preparing to dash into the Peninsula and take possession of it. Throughout the month of March, for example, I received a series of urgent telegrams from Washington requesting instant information about such alarmist reports reaching our military authorities as that the German Foreign Minister was at San Sebastian, delivering an ultimatum to Jordana, and that 500 trains transporting German troops and equipment were moving to the Spanish Basque frontier from northern France through the Bayonne-Hendaye zone, while trucks and tanks were proceeding in the same direction by road.

Of course all such allegations were promptly investigated, and in establishing their truth or falsity we were immeasurably assisted by dependable "inside" contacts which our competent Military Attaché and our resourceful Counselor had within the Spanish Ministries of Army and Foreign Affairs respectively. Thus, I was enabled to wire to Washington and repeat to Algiers a report of this tenor: 'Alleged presence of Ribbentrop in San Sebastian is unknown to Foreign Office. It likewise disclaims knowledge of any 500 German troop trains enroute to Spanish border. It points out that, being in daily communication with Hendaye and Vichy, and in frequent communication with Spanish consulates throughout France, it would know of any significant movement which might occur. Spanish consular reports revealed some time ago important German troop concentrations along the railway connecting the Mediterranean with the Atlantic and passing through Port Vendres, Perpignan, Toulouse, Pau, etc., but there have been no recent shifts or additions of significance. The Spanish Ambassador in Berlin has telegraphed to the Foreign Office that he is unable to procure German laborers to move the chancery to its new building and that ten or twelve Spanish workmen should be sent to do the job and must bring their food and materials. This is considered by the Foreign Office as clear evidence of Germany's shortage in manpower and materials. Again this morning I have been assured that there is not the slightest doubt of Spain's resisting a German invasion and that it has so been reiterated several times to the German Ambassador by General Franco. I said I assumed from the foregoing that there had been German demands on Spain. The reply was that while there had probably been "insinuations," downright "demands" had been forestalled by General Franco's making it clear that he would grant no military facilities and would resist any aggression.'

I was under no illusions about the Germans, and I don't believe the Foreign Minister was, either. If they deemed it practical and advantageous to invade Spain, invade it they would, regardless of what Jordana or Franco or any other Spaniard might think or do. Fortunately for us, their Russian campaign was consuming too much of their time and effort and too many of their reserves. Their armies in France remained strong enough to worry and menace Spain and ourselves, but not strong enough, apparently, to risk giving full effect to the menace and bringing the whole Peninsula into war against them.

Besides the threat of armed invasion across the Pyrenees, the Germans held over Spain the threat of employing their submarines to sink Spanish merchantmen on the high seas. On occasion, in order to show their displeasure and give special warning, they actually attacked and sank a Spanish ship, as, for example, the *Monte Gorbea* just after Serrano Suñer was dismissed. Spain, being dependent on its own relatively small merchant marine for transportation of all the goods it so vitally needed from America, could ill afford the loss of any of its ships. It was naturally cautious about possible sacrifice of any.

Yet despite threats and pressure from our enemies upon a Government which was presumed to be sympathetic with them, that same Government gave them mainly flattering words while to our representations it accorded deeds of signal importance. First of all, in the matter of our airmen, the Spanish Air Ministry, under General Vigón, cooperated from the outset with the Foreign Minister and with ourselves. In November, 1942, at the time of our landings in North Africa, the pilots of three of our large army transport planes (Douglas C 3's), enroute from England with paratroopers, and not too well posted about Moroccan geography, landed their craft in the Spanish zone instead of the French. The Spaniards proceeded, in accordance with international law, to intern the planes and to bring them with their crews to the airport at Madrid for safekeeping. The crews, however, were not interned, as was the habitual practice then and afterwards in such neutral countries as Switzerland and Sweden, but were parolled in the immediate care of our Military Attaché and comfortably lodged in Madrid hotels. Mrs. Hayes and I had the pleasure of entertaining some twenty of these paratroopers at a Sunday luncheon at the Embassy in early January. "The toughest babies in the American army," their young Captain had warned us. They probably were, but they were also extraordinarily fine fellows.

I at once began a campaign to obtain permission from the Spanish Government for their release and departure. Here I encountered more difficulty with my British colleague than with the Spaniards. At an earlier time when the fortunes of war had been most favorable to the Axis, there were many more Axis than Allied crews liable to internment in Spain, as a result of more frequent forced landings of German and Italian bombers on their way to or from attacks on Gibraltar, and of submarines, putting in to Spanish ports to escape pursuit or to repair damages. At that time Sir Samuel Hoare had worked out an informal agreement with the

Spaniards whereby, for each member of a crew of an Axis plane or submarine whom they might release, they would release a member of a British crew. To this "one-for-one" arrangement, Sir Samuel continued to cling, when, as it seemed to me, the fortunes of war were radically changing and there was every prospect that in the very near future American internees in Spain (to say nothing of British and French) would greatly outnumber those of the Axis. We would then be seriously disadvantaged by the "one-for-one" procedure.

Despite the reluctance of my British colleague to go along with us and his prophecy that we would get nowhere with the Spaniards, Mr. Beaulac and I took the stand with the Foreign Office, and our Military Attaché with the Air Ministry, that forced-landed aviators were analogous to shipwrecked mariners rather than to fighting submarine crews and that therefore the former should be assisted to leave while the latter should be interned. The Spaniards, with slight delay, agreed with our interpretation, and early in February, 1943, the whole complement of our paratroopers were evacuated through Gibraltar to rejoin their command in French North Africa.

This established the precedent for Spanish treatment of increasing numbers of highly trained Allied aviators during 1943. Some made forced landings in Spain itself or were rescued by fishermen from its territorial waters. But, as time went on, the large majority consisted of those who, after being brought down in German-occupied France, Belgium, or Holland, were assisted by the French "underground" to elude the Germans and clandestinely to traverse France and the Pyrenees into Spain. Between our landings in North Africa in November, 1942, and our landings in Normandy in June, 1944, as many as eleven hundred trained American airmen found refuge in Spain, besides a sizable number of British airmen. Not a single one of these was refused admission to Spain, and not a single one was interned in Spain. All, on declaring their American nationality, were turned over to our consuls, and by these to our Military Attaché, who arranged for their care and transportation to Gibraltar. Some arrived in Spain suffering from wounds or malnutrition or from badly frozen feet acquired in wintry crossing of the

Pyrenees. Several of these were brought to us, with fine courtesy
and thoughtfulness, in official cars of the Spanish air ministry; and
Spanish hospitals as well as the small British-American Hospital in
Madrid took excellent care of all who needed medical or surgical
attention. As the system was perfected, it required, on the average,
only two weeks to get an ablebodied aviator of ours in from the
Pyrenees, through Spain, and out to Gibraltar and reunion with
our armed forces.

Of course, the Germans protested and fumed. All the satisfaction they got was the release of a mere handful of their own aviators.
They didn't even get the release of the crews of their two or three
submarines which put into Spanish waters during 1943.

Our military planes were provided with certain secret equipment which the War Department was anxious should not fall into
enemy hands. Though our airmen were under strict orders to destroy it in event of forced landings in enemy or neutral countries,
there were several instances in Spain of this not being done through
either inability or inadvertence of the commander. In the first instance of this kind (I think it was in March, 1943), the minute that
the plane commander reported to us his failure to remove the secret
equipment, Mr. Beaulac rushed over to the Foreign Office and
successfully solicited the intervention of the Under Secretary, Señor
Pan de Soraluce, with the Air Minister to obtain its return to us.
Almost immediately the Air Ministry informed our Naval Attaché
that the latter could take the equipment from the interned plane.
He did so, and found it still sealed and intact and obviously uncompromised. Here, again, a favorable precedent was established, and
it was invariably adhered to in later instances.

III

We likewise obtained in the spring of 1943 extremely helpful
cooperation of the Spanish Government in dealing with inter-related
and very important French problems which our landings in French
North Africa had created. One was the problem of receiving, caring
for, and evacuating thousands of French veterans and would-be

soldiers, who stole past German guards at the Pyrenees and sought to cross Spain in order to join French fighting forces in North Africa. This flood began in November, 1942, and within three months thereafter there were at least 10,000 "fighting Frenchmen" in Spain. And more were coming all the time. What to do with them? The Germans pressed the Spanish Government to turn them back into France, or, failing that, to intern them. To us, of course, it was imperative to do everything we could to ensure that they would not be turned back or interned, but rather that they be decently treated as refugees and permitted to pass on to North Africa as our allies.

Another problem was the relationship between Spain and the French regime which was being set up at Algiers with the support of the Allies and in intimate association with them. The Germans and the Vichy Ambassador at Madrid (M. Piétri) urged the Spanish Government to treat only with Vichy about all French affairs, and to regard the regime at Algiers as purely insurrectionary and temporary, and consequently to have no dealings whatsoever with it. We, on the other hand, were convinced that some amicable *modus vivendi* between Madrid and Algiers was essential for solving the problem of the thousands of French refugees in Spain and also for undermining Vichy influence and minimizing friction between the Spanish and French zones in Morocco.

These two problems were clearly inter-related, and negotiations looking to their solution proceeded simultaneously. For the sake of clarity, however, let me indicate first what happened in Spain concerning the North African regime, and afterwards what happened to the refugees.

On January 14, 1943, I talked at length with Foreign Minister Jordana about Spanish-French relations and left with him an elaborate written memorandum. The gist of what I presented on that occasion was as follows: There was urgent need for a *modus operandi* between Spain and French Africa, and my Government was greatly interested in forwarding it. There was need of, and mutual advantage in, resuming commercial relations: for Spain, so as to obtain from North Africa exportable surpluses of phosphate, barley, etc., and for North Africa, so as to get certain manufactured goods from Spain. Likewise there was need of safeguarding Spanish interests and consular representatives in French North Africa and therefore of Spain's affording reciprocal rights and opportunities to the Algiers regime. It was patent that the Vichy Government and its Embassy in Madrid wouldn't and couldn't meet these needs. They could be met only by agents of the Algiers regime. Three such were now in Spain. They had formerly been attached to the Vichy Embassy in Madrid, with diplomatic status, but immediately following Vichy's break with the United States in November they quit M. Piétri and his Embassy. One, Colonel Malaise, was chief and now serving as an informal attaché of the American Embassy and liaison officer between us and Algiers. The second, M. Pettit, a specialist in commercial matters, was already discussing them, on behalf of Algiers, with our Commercial Attaché and with the Economic Director of the Foreign Office, Señor Taberna. The third, Monsignor Boyer-Mas, as representative of the French Red Cross in Spain, was collaborating with us and with the Spanish Red Cross in caring for French refugees.

I said, further, that I knew the French Ambassador in Madrid, M. Piétri, was objecting to these men and asking the Spanish Government to expel them and any other Algiers representatives.[1] But the Vichy regime and its embassy in Madrid had no claim in international law to continued recognition by the Spanish or any other Government. All metropolitan France was now under German occupation and control, and Vichy could no longer claim to be anything but a puppet of Hitler's. My Government, aware of the delicacy of Spanish relations with the Axis, was not suggesting that Spain immediately withdraw recognition from Vichy and M. Piétri, although it did not believe that Spain should thereby be deterred from having at least informal relations with the French regime at Algiers. Specifically, we wished assurances that the three representatives I had named would not be disturbed in the work they were doing, and that duly authorized agents of the French African regime, such as Col. Malaise and his assistants, should be enabled

---

[1] We were kept fully informed of what M. Piétri did, by a pro-Allied member of his Embassy who, with our knowledge, stuck with it for this very purpose.

(a) to issue passports and visas, (b) to circulate freely like any diplomats, and (c) to represent and assist persons of French nationality professing loyalty to Algiers. I also entered a protest against M. Piétri's effort to establish a new Vichy consulate at Ceuta in Spanish Morocco.[1]

Count Jordana at once assured me that Spain recognized the need of a *modus vivendi* with the regime at Algiers and would not disturb Col. Malaise, M. Pettit, or Mgr. Boyer-Mas. He said, however, that he would have to give further study to the nature and extent of the privileges to be extended to them. Four days later— on January 18—I returned to the charge and left with the Foreign Minister another written memorandum, stressing the point that the empowering of an agent of a *de facto* Government to issue passports and visas, or other travel documents, did not imply, in international law, *de jure* recognition of the regime be represented. As yet, neither the United States nor Great Britain had so recognized the regime at Algiers, and we didn't ask Spain to do what we had not done. Nevertheless we dealt *de facto* with it, and we deemed it in Spanish interest, as well as in our own, for Spain to do the same. Count Jordana then made it perfectly patent to me that Spain would go along with us in this very important matter.

Consequently, the representatives in Spain of the French committee at Algiers—Col. Malaise, M. Pettit, and Mgr. Boyer-Mas— constituted themselves a "French Mission," in opposition to the Vichy French Embassy of M. Piétri, and opened negotiations for renting office quarters in Madrid.[2] We, of course, treated them as friends and allies, and sought their advice on all pending questions between us and the Spaniards which affected French North Africa. The "Mission" grew rapidly in size and prestige. In the latter part of March, I could report that only three officers remained with Piétri, and these included a press attaché subsidized by the Germans

---

[1] We had just established a consulate of our own there. Piétri's request to do likewise was denied by Jordana.

[2] They eventually succeeded in leasing the palace of the Duchess of Lecera in the east end of Madrid, and here the "French Mission" functioned until its removal to the regular French Embassy in the autumn of 1944, following the complete collapse of Vichy and the retirement of M. Piétri.

and an officer in our employ. Among the latest group to leave him and join Malaise were the Counselor, the Military Attaché, and a First Secretary.

Already on March 10, Count Jordana communicated to me the decision of the Spanish Government to accord the following facilities to the "French Mission." It might open offices and operate freely. Although its members would not have full diplomatic status, they would be treated in a representative capacity by Spanish authorities. While the Spanish Government was not yet prepared to agree to the mission's issuance of North African passports, it would respect visas and travel documents which the mission might grant to Frenchmen and to other persons. Colonel Malaise might bring two additional assistants from Algiers, and the Spanish Foreign Office hoped at an early date to agree to the French Mission's use of its own diplomatic code and couriers.

So we encountered no real difficulties with the Spaniards about the "French Mission." We did encounter them, however, with the British and with some of the officials at Algiers. The latter, irritated by past Spanish behavior and claims in Tangier and by delay in getting French refugees out of Spain, proposed to apply "sanctions" against Spain, including closure of Spanish schools and institutes in Oran and French Morocco and an embargo on exports to Spain. I heard about this on March 19 and at once telegraphed to Washington, repeating to London and Algiers, that in view of the progress we were making with the problems of refugees and Spanish-French relations I could think of nothing more ill-advised. Mr. Murphy, our diplomatic representative at Algiers, seconded me, and the State Department presently instructed him to inform the French High Command that such a grave retaliatory step against Spain as an embargo on exports from North Africa would be considered to be most inopportune and undesirable.

This question of retaliatory measures by Algiers against Spain was speedily and satisfactorily settled. Mr. Murphy informed the Department and myself on April 6 that, in view of the improved situation, no measures, even of a limited nature, were contemplated by the French High Command against Spain. I had just received from our Chargé at Tangier, Mr. Rives Childs, an account of the courtesy call of the American General Clark on the High Commissioner of Spanish Morocco, General Orgaz, on April 2. 'At eleven o'clock, Clark and his party were met at the frontier between Melilla and Oujda by Orgaz, a group of other high Spanish officers, and myself, and escorted to Tauima, where an impressive review of troops was held and luncheon served in the barracks. After lunch, the visitors were re-conducted to the frontier. General Orgaz outdid himself in an effort to show his friendly disposition. It could not, in my opinion, have been more gracious. A fine impression, too, was made by General Clark and his officers. If an appropriate occasion presents itself to the Ambassador in Madrid, it is suggested that it would be helpful to all concerned to have him express our Government's gratification with the very hospitable reception accorded to General Clark by General Orgaz.' I acted upon the suggestion gladly and at once.

The difficulty with the British about Spanish-French relations was not so easily overcome. While Sir Samuel Hoare was kept informed by me of the steps the American Embassy was taking from early January onwards to establish a mission of the North African French in Madrid, to obtain informal Spanish acceptance of it, and to admit it to a share in pertinent commercial negotiations, we could not help but notice that the British Embassy was extremely cold to the French Mission. Neither Sir Samuel nor any of his subordinates would even receive its members, let alone admit them, as we did, to any joint discussion as allies. In March the Spanish Foreign Minister expressed surprise that the British Ambassador seemed so much more indifferent than I about relations between Spain and the French at Algiers. I reported all this to the State Department, which, toward the end of March, instructed Ambassador Winant to make representations about the matter in London, urging British support of the French mission in Madrid and collaboration with it in dealing with such problems as trade and refugees, without awaiting the conclusion of a basic agreement at Algiers between De Gaulle and Giraud.

As a result of these representations at London and of disclosures by the British Foreign Office, we learned that Sir Samuel Hoare had been hostile to the French Mission from the beginning and that as late as April 3 he was describing it to his Government as a "bureau," which in all probability would not be accepted by the Spanish Government, and which, if perchance it were accepted, should not engage in economic negotiations. Two days later, as a kind of postscript, he was reporting to London a discussion with me in which I was alleged to have admitted that neither Colonel Malaise nor M. Pettit was capable of directing the "bureau."

There followed more telegrams within the triangle of Madrid, London, and Washington. On April 19 I discussed anew and at length with Sir Samuel Hoare the matter of French representation in Spain. I said I gathered from recent telegrams that there was some misunderstanding between us and I was anxious to clear it up. It was my understanding that our two Governments agreed that the French should be treated as allies, that there should be (as actually there had been for some time) informal French representation in Spain, that negotiations on trade with French North Africa should be participated in by the French, and that Vichy influence in Spanish territory should be combated. The strengthening of representation of the French North African regime would be the surest way of accomplishing all these things. The British Ambassador said that this was true and that he agreed in principle, but he must raise the question of personnel. I then told him what I knew of Malaise, Pettit, and Boyer-Mas, no part of which was unfavorable. He astonished me by stating that the British Embassy had never had any word from Algiers or London about these men, or anyone else, acting in a representative capacity for French North Africa and that he thought their organization was "something to help out in refugee matters." I reminded him of the detailed accounts which, during preceding months, I had given him of the Mission and of my conversations with Count Jordana about its functions. Sir Samuel finally observed that he didn't see how the British could go ahead until London and Algiers advised him as to just what the French representation was. I left with him a written statement of our views.

London, doubtless prodded anew by Washington, must finally have instructed the British Embassy in Madrid to go along with us and the French. For towards the end of May, at long last, I could inform Washington that, under instructions from Algiers, Malaise had called on Taberna, the Economic Director of the Foreign Office, and notified him that Algiers, in agreement with both Americans and British, was ready to resume commercial interchange with Spain. Pettit had been called to Algiers, and Drouin, his successor, was due to arrive in Madrid on the 26th. Meanwhile, by common agreement of Americans, French, and British, 10,000 tons of phosphates were being made available to the Spanish. Great appreciation was expressed by Taberna, who, incidentally, knew Drouin well. After the call on Taberna, Boyer-Mas in company with Malaise saw the Spanish Under Secretary (Pan de Soraluce) and left with him a letter from Giraud to Franco and another from Saint Hardouin to Jordana. The Under Secretary told them the French Mission might issue passports, use its own codes, and send and receive diplomatic pouches. Malaise stated that Algiers would be glad to receive a Spanish representative of higher rank than that of Consul, and the Under Secretary replied that such a proposal was already before General Franco and would be discussed at the next meeting of the Council of Ministers.

Shortly afterwards, Señor Sangroniz, a career officer in the Spanish Foreign Service and formerly Minister to Venezuela, was sent as Spanish representative, with the rank of Minister, to Algiers. He and the French got along very well together, and by this time the British as well as ourselves and the Spaniards were in amicable and mutually helpful relationship with the Algiers French Mission at Madrid. Piétri, the Vichy Ambassador, continued his protests, but in vain.

IV

Meanwhile, we had been grappling with a difficult and complex refugee problem in Spain. This had become acute with the exodus of thousands of would-be fighting men from France following our

landings in North Africa in November, 1942. But there had been
something of a problem before that.

It should be borne in mind that thousands of men, women, and
children, fleeing before the Nazi conquerors as these swept over the
Low Countries and France, had managed to escape in the spring
of 1940 through Hendaye or over the Pyrenees into Spain, and
during the next two or three years a continuing trickle of such
refugees, with the aid of paid French guides, got past German
frontier guards and into the Peninsula. Probably a majority of these
refugees were "stateless," that is, persons (chiefly Jewish) whose
original German, Polish, Hungarian, or other citizenship had been
annulled by the Nazis and who therefore were without regular passports. In addition, however, there were groups of Dutch, Belgians,
and Czechs, a few Britishers and Americans, and a sizable remnant
of the Polish Legion which had fought in France to the bitter end.
The majority of those who had arrived in the spring of 1940 did
not remain in Spain, but merely crossed the country to Lisbon,
whence in time they departed for America or Britain.

Nevertheless, a considerable minority tarried in Spain, either
because (in a few cases) they found means of livelihood there and
preferred to be nearer their native countries, or because they lacked
visas or means for going elsewhere. The number of these miscellaneous refugees remaining in Spain in 1942 comprised between
1,500 and 2,000 "stateless" persons (almost wholly Jewish, except
for a group of Catholic Austrians), and approximately 800 Poles,
500 Dutch, 300 Belgians, and smaller contingents of other nationalities. The British Embassy at Madrid had long had a special and
highly competent "relief section," which, in conjunction with the
diplomatic representatives and Red Cross agents of Poland, Holland, Belgium, etc., cared for British and Allied refugees. The care
of the "stateless" refugees had been left to a variety of American
humanitarian organizations, including the Jewish Joint Distribution
Committee, the Quakers, and a special committee of Mrs. Weddell's. These organizations had done a splendid work, but there
was duplication and overlapping of effort among them and a lack
of needed contact with the Spanish Government and the several
diplomatic missions in Madrid.

The Spanish Government had not closed its frontiers to refugees but had allowed them to enter and cross the country with considerable freedom. Their "travel documents" were not too meticulously inspected. Yet, in view of the very bad economic and food conditions in Spain in 1940–1941, the Government was reluctant to play permanent host to any large number of alien refugees. It wanted them to move on, and if they didn't or couldn't, it put them in camps, such as the one at Miranda de Ebro, where they could be kept together and more economically provided for. Miranda, in itself, was not a bad concentration camp, as such things go. It had pretty decent accommodations for, say, from 1,000 to 1,500 persons, and could be (and was) regularly visited by the agents of the relief organizations concerned. The serious trouble came at Miranda and other Spanish camps with the sudden influx of a prodigious number of new refugees in the winter of 1942–1943, and resultant overcrowding.

Most of the new refugees were Frenchmen desirous of reaching North Africa and engaging in the fight there with the Germans and Italians. Some, on getting over the Pyrenees, frankly confessed their nationality; and, inasmuch as the Vichy Embassy in Madrid would naturally do nothing to assist them, they became unwelcome and embarrassing guests of Spain. A surprising number of others, being more prudent and farsighted, pretended they were French Canadians and thus thrust themselves on British bounty. Practically none of the thousands of these Frenchmen who began pouring into Spain in November and December, 1942, had any money or warm clothing, and many were half-starved. And, of course, the Germans promptly sought to alarm the Spanish Government about the danger of so many "wild" Frenchmen being in Spain and to persuade it to "treat them rough" and send them home.

In December Sir Samuel Hoare, in great distress, appealed to me for American assistance in meeting the rapidly mounting needs of refugee relief. I immediately set up a special "refugee and relief section" of our own under the direction of Mr. Niles Bond, a particularly fine and able Third Secretary who had recently been added to the staff of our Embassy and who was to prove, during the next two years, an extraordinarily sane and efficient manager of a most important business. Then, as a result of a joint emergency conference of the British Ambassador and myself with our respective Counselors and chiefs of refugee sections, arrangements were made for both cooperation and division of labor between the two Embassies. The British would continue to care for "declared" British and Canadian refugees, and the Americans, as soon as we could get the necessary funds and supplies, which we pledged to get by February 1, would assume responsibility for the French refugees as well as for our men. Meanwhile, we would turn over our largest truck to the British and give them all other possible assistance, and both Sir Samuel and I would press the Spanish Foreign Office to ensure proper reception and handling of refugees in Spain and their eventual evacuation to North Africa.

In undertaking responsibility for the care of French as well as American refugees, I and my associates in the American Embassy were prompted by more than purely humanitarian motives. We felt strongly that, at a time when the United States was committed to the struggle to free French North Africa from Axis military control and at a time when we were seeking the cooperation of the French people in the hope of laying in North Africa the basis for a free and democratic France, the abandonment by the American Government of thousands of French refugees who had fled from France into Spain in the expectation of our help might have a lastingly injurious effect upon their faith in us and consequently upon our efforts in North Africa and our future relations with France.

There was, too, the more immediate consideration that among these refugees were some of France's finest military leadership and thousands of her best fighting men, who could provide us with invaluable first-hand information about enemy movements and dispositions within France and who, if and when evacuated to North Africa, would be very useful in reconstituting French military strength and thus reënforcing our own. Besides, we hoped that in due course the diplomatic representation of the French North African régime, for whose establishment and strengthening we were simultaneously working, would be able to take over from us the care of the French refugees and thus to fortify in Spain its own position and that of the France it represented.

The State Department promptly approved our reasoning and recommendations, and in the emergency turned to the American Red Cross for immediate concrete aid. This was forthcoming in the best Red Cross tradition. At least two financial allotments of $25,000. were placed at our disposal, and as these were speedily exhausted, the President himself made available another $50,000.[1] Moreover, the Red Cross despatched large shipments of foodstuffs and medicines on Spanish boats from America and sent over one of its own experienced agents (Mr. Charles McDonald) to take immediate charge under the general direction of Mr. Bond and the Embassy. Besides, it made heavy purchases within Spain of clothing and also of the woolen blankets which the United States Commercial Company had been buying up as part of its economic warfare against the Axis.

In addition to all this timely and practical aid from the American Red Cross, we received notable special assistance from knitting and sewing circles which Mrs. Hayes and the other ladies of the Embassy conducted and which, through untiring collaboration of Spanish ladies and others from the Latin American missions at Madrid, produced hundreds of sweaters, socks, and undergarments for the refugees. And a supplementary gift from the American Catholic Bishops rendered it possible to furnish refugees with personal "comfort kits." Mention should likewise be made of the constant and sympathetic cooperation we had from the Spanish Red Cross and particularly from its active director, Count La Granja. On occasion, too, when we had to make representations at the Foreign Ministry, we were notably seconded by the Papal Nuncio and our Latin American colleagues.

Thanks to such support back home and at Madrid, our Embassy was enabled to discharge the responsibility it had assumed and in

[1] The President wrote me on January 6, 1943: "With regard to your efforts in connection with the refugee and internee problems, your subsequent telegraphic report to the Department of State, under date of December 24, is gratifying. I understand that you have since enlisted the cooperation of the American Red Cross in working out the details of this important problem."

February, 1943, to take over the care of the bulk of French refugees in Spain, whose number by this time reached 12,000.[1] Meanwhile neither we nor the British lost any time in seeking to counteract German pressure at the Spanish Foreign Office and to obtain from it the assurance and actions we wanted on behalf of the refugees. Count Jordana, I am sure, was favorably disposed from the outset, and so was the member of his staff whom he early designated as his representative in refugee and relief matters, Señor Baraibar. But the problem in that winter of 1942–1943 was quite as difficult for the Spanish Government as for the American Embassy—or for the refugees.

On the one hand, Spain, by harboring the French refugees, laid itself open to the charge of fostering on its own soil the recruitment of armed forces for the Allies against the Axis, and therefore of violating the laws of neutrality. On the other hand, Spain's facilities for housing and feeding such a large and sudden influx of refugees were thoroughly inadequate, and additional ones could not be provided overnight or within several months. Hence Miranda and other existing camps became horribly congested and insanitary, and the most disreputable provincial jails fairly bulged with the surplus. It took time, too, to settle jurisdictional disputes among the several ministries of Foreign Affairs, Army, and Gobernación (the Interior) and to get many different local officials to adopt and follow uniform policy and procedure. And there were always the Germans exhorting and protesting and threatening.

On January 14, in a conference with Count Jordana, I was glad to be able to thank him for numerous recent indications of the Spanish Government's progress with the refugee problem, particularly its transfer of women and children and some men from Miranda and various prisons to hotels and boarding houses, and its collaboration with the Spanish Red Cross in improving sanitary conditions in the refugee camps. On that occasion I received from the Foreign Minister assurance that he would expedite the admis-

---

[1] Inasmuch as the British promptly discouraged the French refugees from declaring themselves "Canadians," practically the whole number became charges of ours.

sion of our Red Cross supplies and of Mr. McDonald to Spain. Unfortunately, when an extraordinarily large shipment, containing some 6,650 cases of American Red Cross clothing, food, and medical supplies for refugees, arrived at Bilbao a month later, the Controller-General of the Spanish Customs stepped in and levied duties on it. Again I appealed to Count Jordana, and after considerable wrangling between him and the Controller and resultant delay, the whole shipment was released to us duty-free.

V

While we aimed at ensuring decent treatment and care of the multitude of French refugees in Spain, our primary aim was to get them out of Spain and on their way to North Africa. At various interviews with Count Jordana in January and the early part of February I countered the claims the Germans were making that these refugees should be regarded by the Spanish Government as belligerents and therefore should be either interned in Spain or sent back to France. I took the stand that refugees were only refugees and not belligerents, that Spain not only was under no obligation to return or intern them but would contravene international law and civilized practice if it should do so, and that any burden or danger to Spain on their account could best be removed by letting them pass freely, and as rapidly as possible, to North Africa. The Foreign Minister decided in our favor. He assured me that no refugees in Spain would be interned or expelled, and toward the end of February, in the face of angry German protests, he informed me that we might proceed with arrangements for evacuating French refugees from the Spanish port of Cadiz.

By this time the North African French Mission in Madrid was pretty well established. Through Mgr. Boyer-Mas, it was cooperating closely with Messrs. Bond and McDonald of our Embassy in the care of the French refugees, and the régime at Algiers which it represented was gradually assuming a large part of the expense involved. On March 31, while being advised of the allocation to us of another American relief fund of $100,000, I was notified that the French Banking Corporation in New York had been authorized to effect two transfers, one of $150,000 and the other of $100,000, to the Spanish Exchange Institute's account for refugee use in Spain by Colonel Malaise. On April 10 came word from Algiers that an additional $250,000 was being transferred to Malaise by the French, making a total of $500,000 when this transaction was completed.

As soon, therefore, as Count Jordana had assented to the evacuation of the French refugees, the French Mission, in concert with ourselves and the Allied authorities at Algiers, made arrangements for the departure, on March 8, of a first installment of some 1,400 men from their camps in the northern part of Spain by railway for Cadiz in the far south, where they would be met by French ships and transported to North Africa. But when all the complicated arrangements were complete, and on the very eve of the date set for moving this first installment, word came from the Foreign Office that Cadiz might not be used by us. The next morning, March 8, I hurried over to Count Jordana to find out what the trouble was. He was obviously in great distress. He insisted that the Spanish Government was not changing the policy it had defined to me regarding the refugees and was anxious to do everything in its power to aid their evacuation. Only, they couldn't leave from a Spanish port. And the reason for this, I elicited, was that the Germans had bluntly told Jordana they would sink any and all refugee ships which might enter or leave Spanish ports. He feared a serious incident. The ships might be sunk in Spanish territorial waters and some persons and countries would be sure to accuse Spain of connivance in the sinkings. He also referred to the recent German torpedoing (on February 24) of another Spanish ship, the *Monte Igueldo,* off the coast of Brazil. It was clearly a warning to Spain, and a warning which Spain, with its limited but vitally needed merchant marine, could not afford to ignore.

Nevertheless the Foreign Minister suggested a way out for us. Why not evacuate the refugees from Spain across the western border to a Portuguese harbor, such as Lisbon or Setubal, where our ships could pick them up with greater safety? Spain would readily grant the requisite exit visas, and he would talk with the Portuguese Ambassador and do everything else he could to help us obtain Portuguese cooperation. To my inquiry whether the Germans might not exert further, and even direct military, pressure on Spain, Jordana replied: "I can assure you that we have gone as far as we shall go and that in any case in which we are in the right Spain will positively resist pressure as well as aggression."

I had to see my friend, the Portuguese Ambassador, at once. Finding that he had gone to Portugal for a few days to visit his family and confer with Dr. Salazar, I took the Spanish plane at Madrid and flew down to Lisbon. There I enjoyed the hospitality of our American Minister to Portugal, Mr. Bert Fish, and had a good long talk with Dr. Pereira. The latter was quite understanding and sympathetic and agreed to seek Dr. Salazar's approval of the French refugees' passing through Portugal.

Some days later, when we were both back in Madrid, the Ambassador informed me that Count Jordana was strongly backing the proposal and that Dr. Salazar, if formally requested by the United States Government through Mr. Fish, would consent. There was some delay in obtaining from Washington the requisite instructions to our Legation at Lisbon, and more delay in the Legation's putting the request in the precise form desired by Dr. Salazar, and still more delay in settling upon Setubal as the embarkation point in Portugal. Eventually, however, the elaborate arrangements with both Spaniards and Portuguese for visas and railway trains, with the French for funds and foodstuffs, and with the British for transports and convoys, were complete and properly synchronized. On the morning of April 30, some 850 French refugees, all of them military men, crossed the Spanish-Portuguese frontier, and shortly after midnight they sailed from Setubal en route to the battlefield in Tunisia. Thenceforth, at stated intervals during the spring and summer of 1943, other contingents followed. Altogether, 16,000 Frenchmen, with Spain's active help, were transported to North Africa in the course of 1943 and incorporated with Allied armed forces.

Simultaneously, moreover, Count Jordana responded favorably

to British and other Allied representations concerning Polish, Dutch, and Belgian refugees, most of whom were soldiers or would-be soldiers. In the course of 1943, these were evacuated from Spain, under British auspices, *via* either Portugal or Gibraltar. And they too added to our fighting strength. The Poles, in particular, were destined to perform brilliant feats in our later Italian campaign.

At the end of March, 1943, Spain made an effort to stop the influx of more refugees by announcing the closing of the Spanish-French border, and rumors reached us that a few already across the frontier had been turned back and delivered to the Germans by Spanish local officials. The British Ambassador and I at once joined in protests to the Foreign Office, both verbal and written. The note I left with Count Jordana on March 29 read as follows:

I have the honor to acknowledge the receipt of the Ministry's Note Verbale of March 25, 1943, stating that the Spanish Government has ordered the complete closing of the Pyrenees frontier to those persons not in possession of legal documentation. I have transmitted the contents of this Note to my Government. This Embassy has been assured by the Foreign Office on a number of occasions that the Spanish Government would not return refugees of belligerent or occupied territories to the countries of their origin or to territory occupied by the enemy without their consent. I should like to be able to inform my Government promptly that this policy of the Spanish Government has not been modified in any degree. I avail myself, etc.

Count Jordana again responded favorably and took action which enabled me to inform the State Department: 'All local orders for the return of newly arrived refugees to France have been cancelled, and the Foreign Office has sent a note to the German Embassy placing sole responsibility on the Germans for keeping refugees from crossing the frontier. The note, in reply to the German contention that refugees can be extradited, vigorously maintains that, since Germany is carrying on a total war, refugees are entitled to be treated as escaped war prisoners.'

Considerably later, in the second half of June, 1943, the German Ambassador in Madrid renewed his protests against the facilities being given by Spain for the reception and evacuation of French military refugees. Count Jordana was impervious to them, however. We were most reliably informed that he told the German Ambassador he should not be bothered with such protests since it was Germany's inability to control France and to police its borders which rendered possible the presence of the refugees in Spain. Germany, he said, should not interfere with Spain's efforts to solve a problem which the Germans themselves had created. He also expressed indignation about an article in the German paper *Das Reich,* complaining about the help the Spanish authorities were giving us by aiding thousands of French military refugees to join our forces in North Africa.

VI

Amidst all our efforts in behalf of American airmen and French military refugees, we did not neglect the "stateless" and other civilian refugees whose plight was apt to be especially sorry. Some civilian refugees arrived with proper passports, which could be duly visaed for travel across Spain and on to Britain or America. But practically all had had harrowing experiences in escaping the Germans and getting over the rugged snow-clad ranges of the Pyrenees. I remember very well, for example, a young American woman, the wife of a French army officer. He had been captured and held prisoner by the Germans. Immediately after the German occupation of Vichy France in November, 1942, she, with her four-year-old daughter and a suitcase, made her way afoot day after day through the mountainous Pyrenees in intense cold and with almost nothing to eat. Once she got into Spain, she and the child were gallantly cared for by Spanish soldiers and Civil Guards, and the Embassy was able to assist them to Portugal and thence to the United States.[1]

But many, including practically all the Jewish "stateless," were without legal documentation, and few of these had any place to go

[1] She has since published a delightful and touching account of the French and Spanish experiences of herself and her little daughter in *Yours Is the Earth* by Margaret Vail (Philadelphia, Lippincott, 1944).

after arriving in Spain. The number that could be admitted to America or Britain was severely limited. Besides, in view of existing war conditions in the Mediterranean in 1942–1943, there was no possibility of arranging transportation for any of them to Palestine, and the knowledge that the Germans "planted" spies among them made the Allied authorities in North Africa very reluctant to admit them anywhere near our military operations without a most rigid "screening." Consequently, here in November, 1942, were upwards of 2,000 human beings, unable to leave Spain and lacking any citizenship which would entitle them to the governmental care and protection they so desperately needed.

In December, 1942, simultaneous with our establishment of Mr. Niles Bond's "refugee and relief section" in the Embassy and with our intervention at the Foreign Office in behalf of the French refugees, I discussed at length with Count Jordana and also with the peninsular representatives of the Joint Distribution Committee and the Friends' Service Committee, Dr. Schwartz and Mr. Connard, ways and means of caring most effectively for the "stateless" refugees. The Foreign Minister agreed to give special recognition and facilities to a joint office of the several American relief organizations, and the representatives of the latter agreed to form such a central office in Madrid under the direction of Mr. David Blickenstaff, an experienced social worker who was then attached to the Friends' organization in Portugal.

In January, 1943, the joint office was duly inaugurated, under the name of "Representation in Spain of American Relief Organizations." Temporarily housed in the Embassy, it soon secured convenient and commodious quarters of its own a block away, and, under Mr. Blickenstaff's guidance and in close liaison with Mr. Bond and myself, it rapidly expanded its staff and its highly beneficent services. At first its constituent members were the Jewish Joint Distribution Committee and the Friends' Service Committee, but later the National Catholic Welfare Council joined as a participating member. Each member contributed to the upkeep of the central office, whose staff was drawn from all; and the central office made separate accounting of relief funds to the several members. It is a source of special satisfaction to me that I, who had long been a co-chairman of the National Conference of Christians and Jews back home, could have an opportunity to promote in Spain this practical demonstration of sincere and successful cooperation, for important humanitarian ends, among American Protestants, Catholics, and Jews.

Two years afterwards, when I was about to leave Spain, Mr. Blickenstaff wrote me a letter which I particularly prize and which I may be pardoned for quoting:

> It is just two years ago that you arranged for my coming to Spain and obtained from the Spanish authorities their agreement to the carrying on of a program of assistance to stateless and other unprotected refugees. The setting up of this office and the fixing of policies to guide its work took place in those difficult months of early 1943 when thousands of unsorted and unclassified refugees were streaming across the Pyrenees and when the political (and military) situation . . . made identification, proper grouping and evacuation of refugees an extremely slow and cumbersome process. I cannot tell you how much your great interest and help was appreciated at that time. And throughout succeeding months, till now, in all things where it was necessary to our work, you have taken us into the confidence of the Embassy and given the facilities without which it would have been impossible to fulfil the purposes for which this office was established.

After all, however, it must be acknowledged, in simple justice, that had it not been for the friendly and pertinacious collaboration of Spain's Foreign Minister, Count Jordana, and his stout resistance to German pressure during an extremely difficult period, none of us Allied representatives in Spain could possibly have done the many things that were done in 1942–1943 to solve the complex refugee problem. Nor did the Foreign Minister merely await requests from us. In at least one important aspect of it he took the initiative. On March 18, 1943, he had his assistant, Señor Baraibar, inform Messrs. Bond and Blickenstaff that the Spanish Government was anxious to use its good offices to rescue as many Jews as possible from Nazi oppression and persecution and that it was ready to assert a fanciful Spanish "citizenship" for Sephardic Jews in German-occupied territories as a basis for asking the German

Government to free this group of Jews and let them join the other refugees in Spain. We were obliged to explain to the Foreign Office that there was no immediate prospect of our finding any place outside of Spain where "stateless" refugees might go, but that we hoped before too long we could find places for them and then, of course, the Sephardic refugees whom Spain was sponsoring could be included. With this understanding, Count Jordana managed shortly to have an initial group of three hundred Jews delivered by Germany to Spain. Eventually over a thousand Jews were freed from Nazi tyranny by direct intervention of the Spanish Government.

In a memorandum which I prepared for President Roosevelt on May 3, 1943, summarizing the current status of the refugee problem in Spain, I stated: "Early last week, 200 Poles (of military age) freely crossed the Portuguese frontier en route to North Africa, and at the end of last week 850 Frenchmen (likewise of military age) followed them. These are harbingers of something like mass emigration of refugees out of Spain. Great credit belongs to General Jordana, the Spanish Foreign Minister. He has responded finely to representations of myself and my British colleague and our friends the Papal Nuncio and the chiefs of Latin American missions here (including not least the Argentine), and has firmly resisted counter-representations of the Axis. He has had to convince the Caudillo and to overcome the opposition of important Falangist elements in the Government. But he has stood firm and adhered to a really constructive policy which, he assures me, has now full official sanction. This policy involves: (1) positive refusal to compel the return of any refugees to France or other countries from which they fled; (2) removal of refugees from prisons and internment camps as soon as provision can be made for housing and boarding them elsewhere; (3) evacuation of refugees from Spain as soon as visas can be secured and arrangements made for their transit through Portugal; (4) informal recognition of official representatives of the French North African regime so that these, in collaboration with our Embassy, may take immediate charge of caring for and evacuating the French refugees; (5) similar facilities to the British and other Embassies and Legations here for caring for and evacuating refugees of their respective nationalities; and (6) recognition of official agents of the Joint Distribution Committee, the Quakers, and the American and British Red Cross, and empowering them to dispense relief to refugees who have to remain in Spain because they have no other place to go."

"Of course," I went on, "the problem is a continuing one. For refugees will almost certainly continue to enter Spain as fast as we can get them out, and, at any given time, there will be thousands of them here awaiting clearance. Moreover, they will have to be clothed and housed and fed while they wait, and afterwards the cost of their transportation will have to be defrayed. So there will be continuing need for liberal financial aid from North Africa and from ourselves."

I concluded that memorandum of May 3 to the President by attributing our success with the Spanish Government in the matter of refugees "in large part to the policy we have been pursuing toward Spain. In spite of allegations to the contrary on the part of certain American journalists, I have never regarded our policy of respecting the neutrality and territorial integrity of Spain and of supplying it with petroleum and other products essential to its domestic economy as any sort of 'appeasement' to anti-democratic forces or as an instrument for strengthening and prolonging the life of the Franco Government. I have regarded it rather as in line with the principles of the Atlantic Charter and as an effective means of binding the Spanish *people* to us commercially and politically and thereby rendering them potential friends and allies of the United Nations instead of the Axis. This, I am convinced, is precisely what the policy is achieving. Our territorial guarantees and our petroleum supplies reassure and benefit the Spanish people at large, including Monarchists, and Republicans, and 'Moderates' of the present regime like Jordana, and all such know, even if the Falangist minority fail to acknowledge, that the reassurance and the benefit come from democratic America, not from Nazi Germany.

Jordana merely responds to that majority popular opinion in Spain which we are busily helping, by our policy, to form."

VII

I have now indicated a variety of facilities we were receiving from the Spanish Government in the spring of 1943, at a time when the Axis was still entrenched throughout Europe and seemingly invincible. These included non-internment and release of American and other Allied airmen, delivery to us of secret equipment on forced-landed planes, informal recognition of and collaboration with the French North African regime and its mission in Madrid, and reception and beginning of evacuation of thousands of "fighting French" and other refugees.

There was another, and extremely significant, facility which for some time could not be discussed or even mentioned. I refer to the spying we did on the Germans in France. The Allied High Command was vitally interested in getting continuously all the accurate information it possibly could about German troop dispositions and movements in France, about their fortifications and equipment, and also about the French "underground" and its potential collaboration with us. Such information was absolutely necessary to us, either if we were to be forewarned and prepared for a German invasion of the Iberian peninsula, or when, at a later date, we ourselves would want to attempt a sea-borne invasion of France with the greatest chance of success. Consequently, Madrid became in 1942–1943 a prime assembling and distributing center for secret intelligence. It was, indeed, an unexcelled "listening post."

Three agencies of ours engaged in this intelligence work: the Military Attaché's office, which reported to the War Department; the Naval Attaché's office, which reported to the Navy Department; and a local branch of General Donovan's Office of Strategic Services. The first was headed, from the spring of 1943, by an extraordinarily capable and experienced army officer, Colonel William D. Hohenthal, who had earlier been our Military Attaché in Berlin and was remarkably well posted about German military organization, strategy, and tactics. The second's chief, likewise from the spring of 1943, was Captain John Lusk,[1] an Annapolis man, notably efficient, discreet, and sane. Both had dependable and helpful staffs. Both were thoroughly cooperative with the Embassy. Both maintained close and friendly liaison with their counterparts in the British Embassy and other Allied missions. The Military Attaché [2] especially cultivated intimate relations with the French Mission, whose head at that time, Colonel Malaise, was himself a first-class intelligence officer.

Both the Military and the Naval Attaché, while naturally keeping in touch with Spanish military and naval authorities and reporting what would normally be reported about Spanish war preparedness, scrupulously refrained, in harmony with Embassy policy, from giving Spaniards any justification for suspecting that they were being spied upon by us or that we were plotting against their Government or their peace. To have done otherwise would not only have been in flat violation of the pledges made by President Roosevelt to General Franco. It would have made definite enemies of the Spanish Government and led inevitably to the denial to us of our principal means of ascertaining what went on in France. Rather, our intelligence services were directed squarely at espionage of our enemy, the Axis, and primarily at the Germans in France.

For this sort of espionage, we had excellent means and resources among the Allied airmen and the thousands of French refugees (many of them trained army officers) who streamed over the Pyrenees at the end of 1942 and during 1943, and were systematically interviewed and cross-examined by our people or by our French, British and other associates. Besides, there were the "chains" which the various intelligence services clandestinely formed and operated, through paid agents and the French resistance groups,

---

[1] Captain Lusk succeeded Captain White, a genial gentleman who had succeeded Commander Anderson but whose ill-health necessitated his retirement. Colonel Hohenthal had succeeded Colonel Dusenbury, who was transferred to London. See above, p. 21.

[2] Among Colonel Hohenthal's assistants, special mention should be made of Colonel Dorsey Stephens, Colonel Ebright, and Major Clark.

from the Spanish Pyrenean border far into France, even, in some instances, into the Low Countries and Germany itself.

The Spanish Government, with its own highly efficient secret service, was quite aware of what we were doing. It knew about our "chains" and about our "pumping" of refugees. It could easily have stopped, or at any rate gravely handicapped, our espionage against the Germans, and if the Spanish Government had been committed to the serving of Axis interests it would have done so. Yet it gave us a free hand with our "chains" and our "pumping", and actually abetted the latter by entrusting the refugees to us and thus affording us immediate and constant access to them. Colonel Malaise, I may add, learned a great deal of value to us direct from the Spanish secret service. The one thing for which the Spanish authorities closely watched us, and were ready to make trouble for us, was any evidence that we were allying ourselves with subversive elements within Spain or otherwise engaging in activities inimical to the existing Spanish regime.

There can be no doubt that information obtained from across the Pyrenees by our several intelligence agencies during 1943, and the facilities tacitly accorded them by the Spanish Government, were of inestimable advantage to our military authorities in planning and executing our subsequent successful landings in metropolitan France.

CHAPTER V

CROSS CURRENTS

I

Already in the spring of 1943, the trend in Spain was slowly but distinctly in our direction, and the Germans knew it. In January they had recalled von Stohrer as their Ambassador at Madrid because he failed to prevent Spanish acquiescence in our landings in North Africa. But von Moltke, who replaced him, presently discovered that a more menacing attitude on his part only served to bring out Spanish stubbornness and to quicken the trend he wanted to reverse. Late in March the disappointed von Moltke was stricken with a sudden fatal illness and died in Madrid. His successor, Dieckhoff, who had been the last Nazi Ambassador at Washington, reverted to milder tactics, but in the long run he too failed. It is an ironical footnote to the history of the period that I, who had expected a brief, if any, stay in Spain, should have outstayed three German Ambassadors.

In April, 1943, the Spanish Government sponsored a big celebration at Barcelona of the 450th anniversary of Columbus's return from his discovery of America. Departing from the usual Falange practice of giving a provocative Hispanidad complexion to such observances, Count Jordana urged that, as the official representative of the United States, I should participate in the celebration, along with the representatives of the other American Republics and the Portuguese Ambassador. I declined on the ground that I had already accepted an invitation to go to Sevilla, but I also felt that until we were quite sure of the newer trend, my attendance at an affair which had previously been identified with Hispanidad and the Falange might be misunderstood both in Spain and in America. As it turned out, I was very glad I did not go to Barcelona, for, while the Falange was kept in the background and kind things were said about the United States as well as about Portugal and Brazil, Count Jordana utilized the occasion to deliver a speech advocating a negotiated peace between the Axis and the United Nations. This speech naturally evoked much unfavorable criticism in the United States, where it was widely interpreted as a clumsy effort of the Spanish Foreign Minister to put out a "peace feeler" for Germany.

On May 10 Count Jordana sent for me and I had a long talk with him at the Foreign Office. He was much upset by what he described as "the large number of reports" reaching him and General Franco to the effect that numerous high officials in the United States, in response to the press campaign, were counseling violation of Spanish neutrality and sovereignty in contravention of assurances given Spain last November. He said he supposed it might be German propaganda aimed at creating trouble between Spain and the United States, but he wanted me to know that the Caudillo was seriously troubled and needed reassurance. I said I could fully reassure him. Only within the last few days I had had definite word from my Government that it intended no change of policy toward Spain and this policy certainly included the guarantees we had given on November 8. He thanked me profusely and said my statement would be most happily received by General Franco and would do great good in the present juncture of affairs.

The Foreign Minister went on to discuss his Barcelona speech. He feared, he said, it was being misinterpreted in the United States and was being attributed to German inspiration. This was simply and emphatically not true. He had expressed in the speech a purely *Spanish* attitude, the same as he had indicated to Mr. Myron Taylor as long ago as last September. Spain was *not* a cat's paw for Germany, and wouldn't be. Neither he nor General Franco had the naïveté to imagine that they could shorten the war or prevent its being fought through to victory for the Allies. Nevertheless the speech was in the record as a permanent reminder that Spain, like the Holy See, stood for peace, for a humanitarian peace, and might eventually, in happier days, be regarded as a bulwark of peace.

Further, he wished to emphasize that, while Spain was not a democracy like the United States, it was not totalitarian like Germany and, indeed, Nazi doctrines were repugnant to it. Internally, as well as externally, Spain was absolutely independent. It had no engagements whatsoever with Germany or with the Axis, and didn't intend to have any. It was firmly resolved to defend itself to the hilt against any and every outside power, and quite as forcefully against Germany and Italy as against the Allies or Russia. He wanted me to know, he said in conclusion, that he had always told me the truth without reservations, and that when he was called upon to do otherwise, or to suppress the truth, or to go back on what he had stated, he would no longer be Foreign Minister.

There was some indication at this time that General Franco might be contemplating a change in Spain's domestic régime in a liberal direction more consonant with Allied preferences. My British colleague was particularly hopeful that it might speedily eventuate in the restoration of a liberal monarchy, patterned after England's and presided over by Don Juan, who had been educated in England and had served in the British navy while Sir Samuel Hoare was First Lord of the Admiralty and whom he liked to refer to as "one of my boys." On March 1, 1943, General Franco took the unprecedented step of sponsoring and attending, with his cabinet and the entire diplomatic corps, a solemn requiem mass at the Escorial for "all the Kings of Spain." He also decreed the establishment of a pseudo-parliamentary body, a so-called Cortes, which was largely appointive rather than elective, but which included a considerable number of prominent Monarchists who were notoriously anti-Falangist. At the inaugural session of this Cortes, on March 17, the Caudillo, while still repudiating "liberalism" for Spain, admitted for the first time that it was not a universal evil but might well serve the needs of other countries.

Nevertheless, these March gestures of the Caudillo were a bit gusty and not lacking in ambiguity. It was widely and cynically remarked by Spaniards that his Mass for the Kings was really a requiem for the monarchy, and his speech to the Cortes was chiefly notable for its reference to the Bourbon dynasty as having ceased to exist and to the formerly ruling (Monarchist) classes as "decadent."

In April, at the time of the Columbus celebration at Barcelona, I went with my family to Sevilla for its unique and extraordinarily interesting observance of Holy Week, and we remained into the following week for the gala ball which the Duke of Alba gave in honor of his only daughter's début. At this we saw all the Spanish Monarchist élite, but not General Franco or any member of his Government or any Falangista. Two weeks later, as a kind of counter-demonstration, the Caudillo made a state tour through Andalucia attended by cheering crowds whom the Falange mobilized along the way.

Despite high hopes and a burst of activity on the part of Monarchists at this time, I was skeptical about any real desire or intention of General Franco to relinquish his authority. Curiously enough, the successful termination of the Allied military campaign in Tunisia and the final expulsion of the Axis from Africa, which occurred in May, considerably earlier than the Caudillo expected, seems to have had the paradoxical effect of convincing him that while he must speed up the reorientation of Spanish foreign policy favorable to the Allies, his own firm hand and that of the Falange were more than ever requisite for maintaining internal order and preventing revolutionary elements from utilizing our success as an occasion for rioting or revolt. At any rate, in June, when some twenty-five members of the Cortes signed a petition formally requesting him to restore the monarchy, he promptly deprived most of them of their offices and either jailed or exiled them.[1]

Already, on May 11, 1943, Count Jordana had given me the most positive assurances that Spain would not interfere in any way with whatever military operations we might choose to conduct in the Mediterranean or in Italy. It was then almost precisely a year

[1] These included Professor Valdecasas, of the University of Madrid, an early associate of José Antonio Primo de Rivera and co-founder of the Falange, and Manuel Halcón, chancellor of Hispanidad. Among the few who were not removed from office were the Duke of Alba, Ambassador in London; General Ponte, Captain-General of Sevilla; and Admiral Moreu, Chief of Staff of the Navy. Practically all the signatories were distinctly pro-Ally.

since I had come to Spain, and the developments of that year were quite encouraging. They demonstrated, it seemed to me, that Spain would not voluntarily join the Axis but that, on the contrary, it would offer all possible resistance to any attempted invasion by the Axis and was indeed disposed to grant more and more of our requests for facilities hurtful to the Axis in the war and helpful to the United Nations. I recognized, of course, that the Iberian peninsula was still a peculiarly strategic spot and that it would be more rather than less so as long as our European military operations were centered in the Mediterranean. Germans remained extremely active and assertive in Spain. They had friends and dupes within the country. And they still had, in nearby France, large and powerful armies together with numerous submarine and air bases which they might yet utilize to seize and occupy the Peninsula. The danger to us was by no means removed by our victory in Tunisia in May, 1943.

Nevertheless, we now felt much easier about Spain itself. If serious trouble should yet be caused us in the Peninsula, it would be by the Germans alone. For, in such an event we now had reason to believe that Spain would be on our side. In view of this easing of the situation, I obtained in May a year's extension of my leave of absence from Columbia University (until June 30, 1944). At the same time, I suggested to President Roosevelt and Secretary Hull the desirability of my making a brief trip home for consultation and renewed personal contact with officials in the State Department and other government agencies concerned with Spanish affairs, especially since my British colleague made similar trips to London twice a year. The suggestion was cordially accepted, and I would then have gone to Washington had not the Spanish Ambassador, Señor Cardenas, chosen the same time for a visit to Spain. Both our Government and the Spanish thought a bad impression might be conveyed to the public by the simultaneous departure of both Ambassadors from their posts. Afterwards I again proposed a visit home, but before I could get off, developments occurred which led me to withdraw the proposal. I was destined to remain continuously in the Peninsula for considerably over two years.

II

The developments to which I have just referred had to do less with the Spaniards than with the British and with "public opinion" in the United States. Indeed, throughout my entire sojourn in Spain, the Embassy was confronted with difficulties arising from a kind of three-sided struggle. First, we had to deal with a Spanish Government which at first was distinctly pro-Axis, and I am sure that our success on this front would have been more rapid and more complete if simultaneously we had not had to contend, second, with flanking movements in the British Embassy, and third, with sniping and sharp-shooting from the rear.

No one more than I and my colleagues in our Madrid Embassy recognized constantly the prime need of full and loyal Anglo-American cooperation for forwarding our joint war effort, and how especially needful it was to make the proper unified impression on Spaniards as well as upon our common enemies. Certainly the American Embassy at no time lacked the firm will to cooperate fully and loyally with our British colleagues. We invariably consulted them and in every conference put our cards, face up, on the table.

I don't mean to imply that there was not a good deal of real and effective cooperation on the British side. In fact, it was strikingly evident in the attitude of the British Military and Naval Attachés, the UKCC, and most of the staff of the British Embassy. It must be said, moreover, that the British Ambassador himself doubtless meant to be cooperative and at times, as the record in this book shows, was actually so. Personally I always found Sir Samuel Hoare interesting and got on well with him.

The trouble was that Sir Samuel Hoare was intent upon playing a lone hand and was seldom frank with us about his dealings with London or with the Spanish Foreign Office. His usual practice was to obtain information we had while withholding his from us, on the assumption apparently that it is more blessed to receive than to give, and then to make independent démarches at the Foreign Office and afterwards ask us to rubber stamp them. This procedure was no doubt natural and needful before the United States entered the war, but its retention after 1942 had disturbing effects. These were exemplified in the spring of 1943 in the matter of representation of the French North African regime in Spain,[1] and in that of the release of Allied internees.[2] There would be other examples as time went on. And while most members of the British Embassy might be quite out of sympathy with their chief in these matters, they naturally had to follow his orders.

It should be remembered, in this connection, that Sir Samuel had definite personal convictions concerning certain political readjustments which he deemed in Britain's long-term interests. He wanted, for all countries of western Europe, governments which would collaborate closely with Great Britain as in a British "sphere of influence," and to this end he wanted a monarchical restoration in Spain and a régime in France of only such Frenchmen as were habitually and vigorously pro-British. He told me he also wanted Morocco taken away from the French and Spanish and turned over to Anglo-American sponsorship, with emphasis on the "Anglo." How far these desires reflected his Government's views, I do not know. I only know that they colored his own attitude toward Spain and North African France and likewise toward the American Embassy in Madrid, which could not share them or cooperate as he wished in their attainment. I suspect that what chiefly nettled the British Ambassador with Count Jordana was the latter's failure to collaborate in restoring the Monarchy.

The British difficulty was local. Though at times it was annoying and troublesome, it could, with patience and adroitness, be overcome locally or, in a few instances, by informal and friendly interchanges between Washington and London.

III

The difficulty for us back home was at once more intangible and much more serious in possible consequences. It was the inflaming of public opinion in the United States against the Spanish

[1] See above, pp. 109–111.   [2] See above, pp. 102–103.

regime, with resulting public pressure on the State Department to break off all diplomatic and commercial relations with Spain.

This was not a question of persons. It was rather a question of the policy which the United States Government was pursuing toward Spain and which the Combined Chiefs of Staff of the Anglo-American armies and navies regarded as essential to Axis defeat. I was merely an agent of that policy; and any other agent of it in Spain could hardly have escaped criticism and denunciation by a noisy sector of "public opinion" in America.

I understood and thoroughly sympathized with the widespread repugnance throughout democratic America to General Franco's dictatorship with its Fascist trimmings and its earlier pro-Axis orientation. I likewise understood and appreciated the sympathy of the vast majority of American journalists and publicists, and of the American public at large, for the Spanish Republic which had been destroyed by armed force, and their hope and expectation that eventually it would be resurrected. It did seem to me, however, that the great majority of my countrymen, like my Government, would perceive the vitally strategic importance of the Iberian peninsula in the war, and the obvious need of subordinating a potential conflict with the existing Spanish regime to the actual and crucial conflict with Nazi Germany. As a matter of fact, the more sober and responsible journals in the United States did perceive it and refrained from making an issue of our "Spanish policy" or otherwise serving Axis interests in Spain.

Not so, however, with a group of journalists who compensated in noise and fury for what they lacked in numbers and knowledge. Their incessant campaign, which the State Department, by reason of the delicacy of the whole international situation, was unable or unwilling publicly to challenge, proved remarkably successful not only with the coterie of inveterate critics of every State Department policy but also with masses of ordinary Americans who honestly believed the stories circulated in the press and over the radio. In line with all these sensationalists were two major pressure and propagandist groups: first, Spanish Republican or Communist refugees, who wanted the United States to help them get back to power in

Spain; and second, American Communists and "fellow travelers" who took their cue, as usual, from Moscow.

I have no little sympathy for political refugees, including, of course, those from Spain, but however natural it may be for them to seek the sympathy and assistance of foreign nations, I don't believe they should be permitted to attack the Government and foreign policy of a country whose hospitality they enjoy, especially in the midst of a life-or-death struggle of that country. In the case of the Spanish refugees, they were especially listened to and reported because they were supposed (usually wrongly) to have "inside" knowledge of current events in Spain, and because what they said seemed to justify the common tendency in the United States to believe the worst of General Franco's Government both internally and in its foreign relations.

After all, to most Spanish exiles the defeat of Hitler was of secondary importance to the overthrow of Franco, while for Communists and their "fellow travelers" the full victory of Soviet Russia dictated the antecedent destruction of all "Fascists," particularly of the Franco régime. Hence what the two groups most wanted was an Allied intervention, direct or indirect, in Spain, regardless of what its effects might be on Allied military operations elsewhere or on the masses of the Spanish people. One group served factional Spanish interests, and the other, Russian. Neither was intent upon American or comprehensively Allied needs and purposes.

Throughout the spring of 1943, certain papers in the United States conducted an especially vituperative campaign against the Spanish Government and our own State Department. No hint they gave of any of the important facilities we were already obtaining from Spain for our war-effort against the Axis; only staccato and highly imaginative propagandist stories about Spain's supplying Germany with arms and food and Spanish tankers' fueling German submarines. And simultaneously appeared a rash of books and magazine articles of similarly tendentious character. Some of these articles the Germans deemed sufficiently serviceable for their purpose to translate into Spanish and distribute all over Spain.

A personal friend of mine in the State Department wrote me

at the end of February: "The virulent and almost invariably foun-dationless attacks upon the Department will have come to your attention, and these have been the opposite of helpful. Moreover, there is little we can do in the way of rebuttal for fear of exposing our entire position to the enemy and jeopardizing the tasks we have been directed to perform."

The State Department, unlike long-exiled Spaniards and super-heated publicists, was in a position to *know* what was really happen-ing in Spain and in Spanish-American relations and to appraise its relationship to our over-all war effort. But, unfortunately, in other important agencies of our Government, and even within the Depart-ment itself, there were individuals who had only a partial, if any, picture of what was really happening and who substituted for it the caricatures provided by these journalists. This was especially the case with an extremist element in the Office of War Information and also in the Board of Economic Warfare, although it must be said that the head of the former held his members in check and restrained them from playing their ambitious role of bull in the Spanish china shop. The BEW was less manageable and less con-sistent. Every little while it threw, or tried to throw, a "monkey-wrench" into the delicate mechanism of our extremely important economic warfare with the Axis in Spain, chiefly by withholding requisite export licenses.

In June I wrote in a personal letter:

I am a bit alarmed by what you suggest of the possible effects of the *PM* and similar campaigns on our more susceptible brethren in BEW. It is easy to jump to such a conclusion as that now the Tunisian campaign is over we should "get tough" with Spain. The fact is, however, that the Tunisian campaign can be but a prelude to still bigger and more critical campaigns in the Mediterranean area—Italy, the Balkans, France, et cetera—and that Spain's geographical relationship to this whole area renders its neutrality more rather than less strategically significant to us as time goes on. Besides, it's not merely a matter of Spain's formal "neutrality." It's a matter of making Spain's neutrality "benevolent" to us and utilizing its resources (its minerals, factories and shipping) for the Allied cause, while denying them to the Axis. Our chief weapon here is our economic program (including petroleum), and our second weapon is propaganda. If BEW will be reasonable and farsighted, I am sure we can gradually draw Spain into a practical economic alliance with us which may well prove extremely valuable in later stages of the war.

Of course I don't like the existing political regime in Spain. But, on the other hand, I have never liked, and still don't like, the existing political regime in Russia. Yet if we can have Russia as our ally, why not, and why not treat it as a true and great ally? And if we can have Spain as a benevolent neutral and economic ally, why not? We Americans have enough to do, I should think, to defeat and disarm Germany and Japan, without intervening in Russia and Spain and establishing by force of arms the sort of government which would be to our liking in these countries. I am quite convinced that the Spaniards can be relied upon to take care of Spain. The men of *PM* must be "men of little faith" or else of such superabundant faith as would "move mountains."

The State Department had already been gravely embarrassed by popular pressure inspired by the vociferous critics of our Spanish policy. "You cannot imagine," one of its officers wrote me in a personal letter on May 3, "the flood of correspondence that has poured in from all over the country." One result had been an increasing friction with the Board of Economic Warfare, which yielded more readily to the pressure, with consequent critical delay in meeting certain urgent requirements at Madrid.

IV

Early in March, 1943, at a time when our military situation in North Africa was still precarious and yet when Spain was reacting favorably to our requests for non-internment of Allied airmen, return of secret equipment on forced-landed planes, informal recognition of our French allies at Algiers, and free passage of thousands of French and other refugees, Count Jordana informed us that, unless we could make available a small quantity of 87-octane aviation gasoline, the Spanish commercial airlines would have to be discontinued. These airlines had previously operated on a store of Spanish aviation gasoline which had been saved from the Civil War. This was now almost exhausted, and the gasoline which we had been making available to Spain since early 1942 did not comprise any for aviation.

I at once passed on the request to Washington, with the Embassy's recommendation that it be promptly and favorably considered, and Sir Samuel Hoare expressed concurrence in an urgent telegram to London. We both recognized great advantages to the Allies in keeping the Iberia lines operating. The only other airlines then in Spain were a German line from Stuttgart, through Barcelona and Madrid, to Lisbon, and two Italian lines from Rome to Lisbon, the one *via* Madrid and the other *via* Sevilla. If the Spanish Iberia lines suspended service, everybody wanting quick passage between Lisbon and Barcelona, Madrid, or Sevilla, would have no choice but to use Axis planes; and we couldn't use them anyway.

On the other hand, the Iberia lines were of prime utility to us. The Madrid-Lisbon line was particularly valuable; our couriers used it constantly to make connections with the Pan-American transatlantic clippers. The importance of the Madrid-Sevilla-Tangier line was also apparent. It reduced transit time between our Embassy and the Legation at Tangier from two days to five hours. It seemed imperative to maintain this close contact because of the nearness of Allied forces to Tangier; and by maintaining the air service to Sevilla, we could ensure rapid communication with Gibraltar and thence with Algiers. Likewise, the Madrid-Barcelona line was frequently employed by our personnel to make rapid contact with our most important consular office in Spain and with an area which, because of its proximity to France, was of the greatest importance for our intelligence work. We were always given priority by Iberia, which was very helpful in emergencies.

Iberia had also once operated lines to the Canary and Balearic Islands but these, at the suggestion of our military authorities, had been discontinued at the time of our landings in North Africa. There were advantages to us in their resumption, for thereby we would be enabled to keep in touch with our two consulates in the Canaries and likewise with the Balearics which, it was rumored, the Germans might endeavor to occupy should we land in Sicily or Sardinia. Perceiving, however, the possible risk in the flight of neutral planes over our convoys and naval operations, we did not urge the reopening of the Canary and Balearic lines but only the maintenance of Iberia service on established routes in metropolitan Spain and to Lisbon and Tangier. Moreover, in passing on Count Jordana's request for the necessary aviation gasoline, we pointed out that only a very small quantity was needed, that the Spanish Government was perfectly willing for us to exercise rigid control of its shipment and use, and that we were sure we could utilize the opportunity to get rid of all German financial interests in the Iberia Company and to obtain control of Axis' passenger traffic between Europe and North Africa.

Our recommendation was wired to Washington on March 4, 1943, and repeated on March 15 and March 18. On this latter date the Under Secretary of the Spanish Foreign Office called in person at the Embassy to notify us that the Spanish stock of aviation gasoline was finally exhausted and that all Iberia flights were ceasing. On March 22 the Foreign Minister appealed anew and strongly to me for favorable action at Washington, and on the same day I cabled the Department: 'The Military and Naval Attachés and Colonel Hohenthal agree that the possible military advantages of acceding promptly to the Spanish request are considerable, while no military risk is involved. Sir Samuel Hoare concurs fully in the recommendation and is again today telegraphing urgently to London. I hope a prompt favorable decision can be reached.'

No answer from Washington; the State Department had divided counsels and was encountering difficulty with the BEW. Early in April, London informed Sir Samuel that the British were agreeable to making aviation gasoline available to Spain, and a few days later my Military Attaché received word from the War Department that the Joint Chiefs of Staff had also agreed and were urgently recommending the supply of 420 tons of aviation gasoline a month to Spain. Still no authorization from the State Department.

On April 30, the Department asked me to try to sell to Spain the transport planes which had landed in Spanish Morocco the previous November and which had since been interned at Madrid. To this I replied: 'It is futile for me to discuss with the Foreign

Minister any sale of American planes until I receive authorization to tell him that Spain can get some aviation gasoline. We are losing valuable time. Please expedite authorization.'

Still no reply, except another request from the Department on May 6 that I approach the Spanish Foreign Office, "within my own discretion and informally," regarding possible entrance into Spain of American commercial airlines. I accordingly "approached" Count Jordana, and reported that he evidenced much interest and said he would urge General Franco and the cabinet to agree to granting such rights. He again expressed hope that aviation gasoline would soon be made available because of its importance to Spain and especially now lest our continued withholding of it might be popularly interpreted as a change in our policy toward Spain. This would be difficult to understand, since the Spanish public was now well aware that Spain was orienting its foreign policy more and more toward the United Nations. I expressed the hope that the gasoline would be made available and said I would keep him informed.

Lapse of another month before the State Department and BEW came around to agree with the Embassy, the Joint Chiefs of Staff, and the British that Spain might import "limited quantities of aviation gasoline"—and then the approval was only "in principle." It was not until June 26—almost four months after our vitally important air communications within Spain and with Tangier and Lisbon had been cut off by enforced grounding of Iberia planes, and almost three months after our highest military authorities and the British had urged the supplying of requisite gasoline—that the State Department notified me of the specific conditions, "approved by the interested agencies of the American Government," under which aviation gasoline would be made available to Spain. Curiously enough, while the monthly allotment of 420 tons which the Joint Chiefs of Staff had recommended in April was cut to 320 tons, the conditions fell short of Embassy recommendations in that no provision was demanded for control of Axis passengers between Tangier and the mainland. This the Embassy insisted upon, on its own initiative, and got. The authorization of June 26 from the Department significantly indicated that the British had been very active in pressing for the approval of a program of aviation gasoline supply, and that therefore the outcome should be presented to the Spanish jointly by my British colleague and myself. It was.

The sorry and senseless delay in meeting an essentially military need of the Allies is explicable only in the light of the "public opinion" which had been inflamed by pressure groups in America more bent on warring on the Spanish Government (and embarrassing the State Department) than on putting the Axis to rout, and which rendered our responsible non-military officials extraordinarily timid. And I must confess to a feeling of shame that it required counter-pressure from the British finally to end the long delay.

V

But difficulty about aviation gasoline in the critical spring of 1943 was a minor difficulty compared with another which arose in the midst of it and which owed its origin and gravity to the same pressure politics back home. On April 19 I got the first wind of this new difficulty in an instruction from the State Department to halt the sailing of two Spanish tankers which were scheduled to load previously authorized allotments of ordinary petroleum in the Caribbean. I wired back that the tankers had already sailed. Then on April 27 the Department informed me it had agreed with the Board of Economic Warfare that, although the Chiefs of Staff and the British had not yet concurred, the total amount of all petroleum products henceforth to be made available to Spain should not exceed 100,000 tons each quarter-year, and it invited the Embassy's comments.

Embassy reaction was instantaneous and unanimous. The Counselor (Mr. Beaulac), the Commercial Attaché (Mr. Ackerman), the Military Attaché and indeed the whole staff recognized at once that we faced a crisis. In December, 1942, a petroleum program for Spain for the year 1943 had been carefully worked out and deliberately approved by the American and British military and naval authorities, the State Department, the British Foreign Office, the American Board of Economic Warfare, and the British Ministry of

Economic Warfare. It had set the total amount of petroleum products to be made available to Spain for the year at 541,000 tons, or 135,000 tons a quarter. Since then it had been functioning smoothly under the close and highly efficient supervision of Mr. Walter Smith and his Embassy corps of "oil observers." And, as I have explained at length in an earlier chapter, it had constituted our chief weapon in fighting the Axis in Spain and in bringing the Spanish Government into cooperation with us.

Now, at the end of April, 1943, suddenly and without prior consent of the Chiefs of Staff or of the British, the program was arbitrarily to be cut from 541,000 tons a year to 400,000 tons, with obvious grave injury to Spanish economy and, above all, to the Allied position in Spain. Our chief weapon was being turned into a sawed-off shotgun.

Washington received plenty of comment from the Embassy. We expressed our opinion along the following lines: 'The primary consideration when the 1943 program was under study was given to reaching a figure whereby Spanish economy would be permitted to function at a level sufficient—but only sufficient—to ensure the domestic production and distribution of the most essential commodities. There was a careful study made of quantities required for each component of Spanish economy. The sum of these requirements was then compared with the means of transportation, that is, Spanish tankers, and the net result was the program submitted by Mr. Smith in the despatch of last November, and subsequently approved by all American and British agencies concerned. No later developments have shown these calculations to be in error. We are convinced that supplies at the rate of 541,000 tons per year as agreed to in the program will be barely sufficient to meet minimum needs.

'The program, as it has been working out, has given us more favorable results than we anticipated late last year. In the political field, it has helped to strengthen elements in the Government favorable to us and has converted others to our side. It has been possible, as a result, to achieve many objectives which would have been extremely difficult otherwise, such as the acceptance of our guarantees at the time of the North African landing (if they had not been accepted, the soft underbelly of the Axis would not have been exposed for a long time), the determination by the Spanish to resist any Axis aggression, the release of all our military internees and of French military refugees, the return to us, uncompromised, of important secret military equipment, the consent to the establishment of a French North African mission. In the economic field, it has certainly expedited and heightened the success we have had in competing with and injuring the Axis. Public goodwill which extends from the lowest classes to the highest, except only among the Falange minority, who would like to see our petroleum program fail, has been created by it. The War Department has been informed by our military personnel that they now consider Spain a potential ally rather than a potential enemy.

'The program which was finally approved during Mr. Smith's visit to Washington last December was for 541,000 tons annually. This figure represents not more than 60 per cent of Spain's normal requirements. It is, in every respect, consonant with the policy which the Department has laid down and which governs the petroleum supply generally. Spain consumes the products allotted, and they are not benefiting our enemies directly or indirectly. Month-end stocks have been and will be kept within the agreed limit. Spanish tankers are carrying the products, and the authorities here are sufficiently aware of the world petroleum situation to know that ample supplies are available in the Caribbean.

'Furthermore, we are exploring the possibility of greater exploitation of Spanish economy to the advantage of our war effort. The carrying out of such a purpose might be seriously prejudiced by an arbitrary reduction of petroleum supplies to Spain, below the approved program. In view of all the foregoing, I see no reason for cutting this program down to 400,000 tons, or for modifying any of the detailed figures which were approved by State, BEW, and London after careful review last December. I request that this program be maintained.'

In a supplementary message I said I could not believe that the Spanish policy of the Department would be revised on the basis of popular misinformation about Spain (which partly derived from failure in the United States to make clear the advantages of that policy), instead of on the basis of the Embassy's careful evaluations (to which it was hoped the BEW had access) which demonstrated that Spain's neutrality had already been of great military assistance to us in conducting our operations in North Africa and promised in the future to be of still greater assistance to us. And in a personal appeal to the Secretary, I asked: "If no direct relation to Spain's present attitude is involved in the proposed reduction of petroleum supplies and if you agree that the Spanish attitude is improving steadily in our favor, how can such an arbitrary reduction be justified in view of the terms of the Atlantic Charter, including your policy, which has been continually impressed by me on the Spanish Government and the Spanish people, of not denying to any nation access to raw materials over which we have effective control?"

Secretary Hull, in a personal response, frankly confessed what the real reason was for arbitrarily cutting the petroleum program without the consent of either the Combined Chiefs of Staff or the British. To leave the program as it had been, he said, would not be viewed favorably by public opinion in the United States, and from his reading of my telegrams of recent date he imagined I might not be giving full weight to its importance; the criticism of the oil program for Spain was greater than that of any other matter of foreign policy coming under his direction, despite the care he used in following it.

'The weight and importance of public opinion in a democratic country like ours,' I rejoined, 'is quite well known to me. When much of that opinion, however, is so badly misinformed as it is about contemporary Spain, I doubt whether it should be the determinant of our Government's foreign policy in critical war times. It is actually an admission that our policy toward Spain has been wrong if we reduce the petroleum program by over a fourth below what was agreed to last December in order to cater to misinformed public opinion. Nor can I believe that such a reduction would at all satisfy the noisiest and most irresponsible makers of this misinformed public opinion; these aim at depriving Spain of any and all petroleum. On the other hand, I cannot bring myself to believe that the more enlightened and thoughtful segments of American public opinion, regardless of their attitude toward the present Spanish Government, wish to deny the people of Spain ready access to food-stuffs and other necessities of life that must be produced and transported with the aid of petroleum products.' I outlined the economic advantages to us of the existing oil program in Spain and pointed out that, whereas in Portugal our economic warfare with the Axis had been seriously impeded by the Portuguese Government's allocation of strategic materials between the opposing belligerents, the Spanish Government, thanks mainly to the oil program, was allowing us freely to utilize our resources in open-market competition with the Axis. 'From Spain we are now acquiring 100 per cent of its strontium output, 90 per cent of its fluorspar, and 75 per cent of its wolfram. Purchases by the Germans of woolen goods they greatly needed last winter were stopped by us. Our oil program is basic to our success.'

The British were even more concerned than I about the economic effects of a reduction in the petroleum program. America did not definitely require any Spanish commodities for itself; it was buying them to prevent the Axis from meeting its requirements. But Great Britain was positively dependent upon Spain for certain important commodities, notably iron and potash, and it was extremely anxious not to jeopardize the continuing unimpeded flow of these to England. Hence Sir Samuel Hoare zealously backed me up, and his appeals to London and to the British Embassy in Washington elicited immediate favorable response and correspondingly energetic representations to our authorities. Proportionately, I suppose, there were as many furious and voluble critics of our Spanish policy in Great Britain as in the United States, but the British Foreign Office did not let them swerve it from its central objective of knocking out Germany at the earliest possible moment.

Toward the end of May, 1943, I addressed a final appeal to the State Department substantially as follows: 'With reference to what seems to be the main reason for reducing the petroleum program, namely, an attempt to appease uninformed public opinion in the

United States, I do not in any sense discount the importance of public opinion. I do insist, however, that keeping this Axis-created
regime out of the war and bringing it progressively to the side of
the United Nations will eventually be adjudged by informed public
opinion as one of the outstanding diplomatic victories of the war
and one which, through ensuring Allied control of the Strait of
Gibraltar and of the Western Mediterranean, and through making
possible our landing in North Africa, may prove decisive in bringing
about the defeat of the Axis. I maintain, furthermore, that our success in Spain is capable of adequate explanation to the Congress of
the United States and to the American public. It is my hope that an
opportunity may be found by the President to discuss this matter
with Mr. Churchill before the latter's departure from the White
House.'

Simultaneously, I appealed direct to President Roosevelt for his
personal intervention in maintaining the petroleum program. He
must have acted quickly and decisively, doubtless in concert with
Mr. Churchill. At any rate, the tone and tenor of telegrams from the
State Department changed abruptly. On June 1 it requested
Mr. Walter Smith to come to Washington to discuss details of the
oil program for the second half of 1943, and on June 12 it notified
me there would be no change in the program as agreed to in December of 1942. We would continue to make available to Spain 541,000
tons of petroleum products from the Caribbean. Mr. Smith, during
his brief visit home, had a kind of love-feast with both the Department and the BEW. They approved his every recommendation, and
complimented him upon the efficiency with which our petroleum
control was functioning in Spain. The same month which witnessed
the happy termination of the difficulty about our general oil program witnessed also, as I have previously indicated, the end of the
difficulty about aviation gasoline for Iberia planes.

VI

June, 1943, was, indeed, an auspicious month. Allied armies had
just expelled the Axis from its last foothold in North Africa, and I
knew from a telegram I received from Washington that the Allies

would presently push their offensive across the Mediterranean into Sicily and the Italian mainland. Washington was plainly worried about possible action of Spain, as well as by the German armies in France, against our lengthening lines of communication in North Africa and against our new and necessarily heavy troop movements across the Atlantic and past Spanish Morocco. On the 17th I informed the Department: 'Count Jordana assures me he quite understands, and expects us to send reinforcements to North Africa. He reaffirms positively that no Spanish troops will be used offensively against us. Our guarantees continue to be accepted completely by General Franco and himself.'

There was considerable contemporaneous improvement in the attitude of the Spanish press and the Falange censorship toward us. Two outstanding Spanish publicists, Manuel Aznar and Manuel Halcón, were seemingly unhampered in conducting strongly pro-Ally campaigns. Leading dailies like *Ya* and *Madrid* in the capital, and *Vanguardia* and *Diario* in Barcelona, were now giving good publicity. Even the Falangist chief censor, Arias Salgado, told our Press Attaché that we would shortly perceive a general marked improvement in Spanish press, radio, and newsreels. On June 7 I was informed by the Foreign Minister that he had given careful study to the series of communications I had sent him about the press and that he hoped I had noticed during the past week a close approach to impartiality in it. This, he said, was the result of an agreement between himself and the Direction of Press and Propaganda, and it would be maintained despite protests already received from the Axis. He asked me to report to him any specific future statements in the Spanish press which we might deem unneutral or objectionable. He also expressed the hope that the changing attitude on the part of the Spanish press would be reflected in due course in a more friendly attitude of the American press toward Spain.

Actually there was a noticeable change during the previous week: an increase in news and photographs from United Nations sources; improvement in headlines; and a decrease in volume and less favorable presentation of Axis news. Separate reports from various consuls indicated that the press throughout the country had received instructions to present headlines and news in a more impartial manner, to cease comment on aerial bombardments, and to show Spanish opposition to Communism rather than to the Russian people.

Almost simultaneously the Under Secretary of Industry and Commerce broached to our Commercial Attaché the question of our supplying Spain with military equipment. He explained that Germany had recently been unable to pay for what it purchased in Spain by supplying goods needed for civilian uses and had offered to make up the difference with military equipment, and that an agreement by us to discuss Allied sale of this very equipment would relieve the Ministry of War from German pressure and might result in depriving the Germans of their remaining purchasing power in Spain. The suggestion had interesting possibilities which Mr. Beaulac and I, as well as Mr. Ackerman, readily perceived. We had no idea of recommending to our Government any actual sale of Allied military equipment to Spain, and we felt sure that a recommendation of the sort from any other source would, in existing circumstances, be flatly rejected. Nevertheless there were obvious advantages to us in agreeing to *discuss* the matter "in principle," and we so reported to the State Department on June 6, as did also the British Ambassador to London. We made it perfectly clear that "no commitment actually to furnish military equipment was involved."

A few other straws showed in that month of June how favorably the breezes were blowing. One was the refusal of the Spanish Government to accede to German demands for recovery of a cargo of rubber salvaged by Spanish fishermen from a German blockade-runner which, after a long and perilous run from the Far East, had been sunk by the British in the Bay of Biscay. Another was a promise of Count Jordana to reconsider the arrangements whereby, in order to avoid serious complications with the Axis, the French refugees were being evacuated *via* Portugal instead of direct from a Spanish port.

On June 15 I had the pleasure of receiving in my office an influential and distinguished Spaniard. He had been on General Franco's side in the Civil War but he had since been highly critical of the

Falange and notoriously pro-Ally. He had just come from a lengthy talk with the Caudillo, and he recounted it, in confidence, to me. General Franco had been sure, he said, that the Germans would win the war until they, with the Japanese, brought the United States into it. Then, for a time he had been doubtful, but now he was sure that sooner or later they must lose. Meanwhile, however, they remained a danger to Spain. According to reports reaching him, they had forty-two divisions in France, including some Panzer divisions. They might try to force their way through the Peninsula. As a military man himself, he thought, in their own interests, they should. But if they did try, he was resolved to resist, and the plan which had been worked out was for the Spanish forces to do their utmost to hold the line of the Ebro until they could get help from the Allies.

The time had come, I reasoned, for a new offensive in our Peninsular Campaign against the Axis. The situation was favorable. The Allies had just won a first-class victory in Tunisia. In Spain our economic warfare was going well. At Madrid our Embassy was an active and energetic unit, and we and the British were again in full cooperation. In the rear, back home, there was a temporary lull in the pot shots and sniping.

We would have a big celebration of the Fourth of July at the Embassy. The year before, in 1942, when we were dubiously feeling our way, we had restricted our invitations for the observance of the Fourth to the American colony in Madrid. This year of 1943, we had reason for greater assurance and we would invite Spanish intelligentsia, society and officialdom, along with the whole United Nations diplomatic corps, to our national celebration.

After the Fourth I would seek an interview with General Franco himself and talk frankly with him about a number of things.

CHAPTER VI

PROGRESS IN SPANISH NEUTRALITY

I

July, 1943, opened with a gala celebration of the "Fourth" at the Embassy. It was accompanied by two heavy thunder-showers with appropriate electrical discharges, but, as I wrote the President, "the reception symbolically reflected the changing public attitude here. Whereas two years ago no Spanish official was allowed to come, and whereas one year ago we invited none, this year we received not only the American colony and the Allied and neutral diplomatic corps, but also close to a thousand Spaniards, including Count and Countess Jordana and practically the whole Foreign Office, several other Cabinet ministers, Count Romanones (the old Liberal leader), the Bishop of Madrid, the Vice Rector of the University, and a pretty representative cross section of grandees, business and professional men, professors, artists, republicans, even some Falangistas!"

In the same letter to the President, I said: "Our landing in Sicily, which is being fully reported in the Spanish press, obviously gives the lie to Axis and Falange propaganda about the 'impregnability of the fortress of Europe' and amply confirms the Spanish Government's wisdom in keeping this country out of the war and orienting its foreign policy toward the United Nations. . . . The fly in the ointment is still the discrimination exercised against us by the Falange-controlled press, radio, and police. It has perceptibly lessened during the past month, but it is still sufficient to justify continuous bombardment of the Foreign Office with protesting notes and memoranda and personal letters. The trouble is not with the Foreign Office itself but rather with Franco's failure to make the Falange obey instructions of the Foreign Office; and my stream of protests is designed to provide Count Jordana with ammunition in his campaign with Franco. Military success for us in Sicily should clinch the argument."

Despite what we had been told the month before by Count Jordana and the Falangist press-chief, Arias Salgado, that they had reached an agreement and that we would at once see the result of it in an impartial attitude of the Spanish press and radio toward the belligerents, it was soon apparent that the Falange didn't know what impartiality was or that, if they did, they were not going to be honest about it either with the Foreign Minister or with me. A kind of indirect apology for the backsliding of the Falange censorship was implied in its vehement attack upon the American moving picture film "Inside Fascist Spain" and the photographs of scenes from it which appeared in copies of *Life* that arrived for distribution in Spain.

Indeed, these photographs led the Foreign Minister himself to address a *note verbale* to the Embassy, protesting against them and stating he did not understand why Spain was consistently represented in the United States as a Fascist country, when "this was notoriously untrue" and when "in various public statements of Spanish officials it had been repeatedly affirmed that the regime was not copied after any foreign system but was purely and exclusively Spanish." The *note verbale* afforded us a splendid opening for a frontal attack, not only upon the Spanish press censorship but also upon the Falange itself, its organization, attitude and methods. And we fully availed ourselves of the opening. Our reply, in quite undiplomatic language, pointed out that statements of the Foreign Minister and other high officials of the Government had in many cases been flouted and contradicted by the Falange, which was, after all, "the sole political party in Spain" and therefore part of the Government. The reply then itemized the respects in which the Falange so strikingly resembled the totalitarian regimes of Italy and Germany as to substantiate the practically universal belief abroad that Spain was "a Fascist country." [1] I heard nothing more, on this score, from the Foreign Office. I suspect that Count Jordana, who personally

[1] The pertinent passages of the reply have already been published in *Harper's Magazine*, for December, 1944, pp. 29–30.

had no love for the Falange, was not averse to having our indict-
ment of it in his "ready reference files."

On July 1, I remonstrated with Count Jordana, again in blunt
and quite undiplomatic language, about the continuing discrimination of the Falange censorship against us and in favor of the
Axis. I particularly called his attention to the recent appearance, in
the press all over the country, of a series of bold-faced pleas for the
"self-sufficiency of the fortress of Europe" and for Spain's selling all
its products to Germany. Did the Spanish Government wish, I
asked, to discontinue trade with the United States? If so, it must
wish to do without petroleum from the United States. The Foreign
Minister was greatly disturbed. Of course, Spain wanted to trade
with America. The Falange were making a lot of trouble. He would
appeal anew to the Caudillo.

On the evening of July 18, in company with my wife and the
Beaulacs and Miss Willis, I attended the Caudillo's customary
garden party in the mountain retreat at La Granja. The entire
diplomatic corps was present, and the supper, which was served out-
doors in the penetrating night air and close to the icy spray of the
fountains, was indeed a chilly affair. I admired the tactful valor of
the Turkish Minister's wife, who was the only barrier between me
and the German Ambassador and who devoted precisely the same
number of minutes of conversation to each of us.

I must say that I felt ill at ease on this occasion, not so much
because of my proximity to Herr Dieckhoff as because of a speech
the Caudillo had made the day before to the Falange. It was a bitter
speech, assailing both monarchists and republicans, and indeed all
groups except the Falange. It slammed the door shut against any
liberalizing of the domestic regime, and dismissed all criticism by
attributing it to "foreign propaganda and foreign machinations,"
which, in existing circumstances, could only refer to the Allies.
Moreover, one passage in the speech clearly implied that the recent
Allied successes in Tunisia and Sicily would enable Communist
Russia to extend its sway in North Africa.

The next day, July 19, I hastened to the Foreign Office and protested emphatically against these allegations and inferences. We

were not directly concerned, I said, with Spain's domestic politics, but we were greatly concerned that its foreign policy should be neutral, really and truly neutral. It was high time for the Chief of State to observe strict neutrality in word and deed and to compel the Falange to do likewise. I wished to say so direct to the Caudillo himself. Would the Foreign Minister arrange such a meeting at the earliest opportunity? He said he would, and in due course it was arranged for me to see General Franco.

Meanwhile, in accordance with instructions from Washington, and in order to permit the resumption of the Spanish commercial airlines, so vitally serviceable to the Allies, I presented to Count Jordana the conditions under which aviation gasoline would be made available. He accepted them without demur. There were four on which Washington insisted. First, the monthly importation of aviation gasoline would not exceed 320 metric tons a month, stocks at any one time would not exceed 640 tons, and the octane rating would not be over 87. Second, Spain would grant our Petroleum Attaché and his staff all necessary facilities for exercising effective supervision and control. Third, the aviation gasoline would be used by the Iberia Company for its customary commercial lines to Lisbon, Barcelona, Valencia, Sevilla, and Tangier, but not for any flight over enemy-occupied or enemy-controlled territory or for any other purpose unless specifically approved by the American and British Governments. Fourth, the Spanish Government would oust all Axis financial interests from the Iberia Company and make it strictly Spanish in ownership and management. This last, I may remark, was accomplished against energetic protests from Germany, which had previously held large blocks of stock in the Company.

Two other requests I communicated from Washington in connection with the aviation gasoline, though not, like the foregoing, as conditions. One was that the Spanish Government should try to arrange with the Germans for a direct airline between Spain and Switzerland to be freely operated by the Spanish or the Swiss or by both. The other was that it give favorable consideration to the grant of landing rights for American commercial airlines in Spain. Count Jordana acceded to both these requests. He failed, as we expected he would, to obtain German acquiescence in the first. The second, which required no Axis assent, he eventually acted upon, as I shall later show.

I went further than Washington in asking, upon my own initiative, that, as an added condition for our making aviation gasoline available to the Iberia Company, Spain should accord us control over the passenger traffic on the Company's line between Tangier and the mainland. The Axis had numerous agents at Tangier and throughout Spanish Morocco, who were spying on our military operations in North Africa, and had been making trips to Sevilla or Madrid to report to the German Embassy or Gestapo. If they were now permitted to come to the Peninsula, but not to return, we could check and halt Axis spying and influence in Morocco. The British, through their navicerts, already had means of controlling traffic by water; and although Sir Samuel Hoare was dubious about our ability to obtain Spain's assent to a similar air control by us, I decided to insist upon it. I so informed Count Jordana in a personal letter on July 22, 1943, and, to the surprise of our British friends, he came back with a most favorable response two days later. It took a little time to work out the details of the control and to put it in satisfactory operation, but by midsummer of 1943 we were enabled to strike a very serious blow at the Germans in Morocco.

II

Toward the end of July, the State Department wired me, in reply to my report of July 18 on General Franco's obnoxious speech of that date, that it was disturbed by his conceptions and his continued tolerance of the unneutral Falange party press in the face of current military developments. 'The vigorous tone of your June 22 note to Jordana has been read with satisfaction in the Department. It is not the intention of this Government to interfere in the internal affairs of Spain, as you have correctly observed. This Government's feeling is that the Spanish people themselves should determine Spain's definitive form of government, this being in exercise of "the right of all peoples to choose the form of government under which they shall live," as contemplated by the Atlantic Charter's point 3. We are, however, urgently interested in these matters: the activities of the Falange as they affect us directly, both in Spain and abroad; the tone of the Spanish press; the attitude of the Spanish Government and its officials toward the war.'

Before this reached me, I had my interview with General Franco on July 29 at the Pardo. I was with him an hour and forty minutes. The others present were Count Jordana and the official interpreter, Baron de las Torres. Inasmuch as it proved to be especially important in several respects, I shall here recount the whole conversation.

After reiterating the pledges the President had given about our respecting Spanish sovereignty and territorial integrity, and after emphasizing that though we were not concerned with Spain's internal affairs, we were very much concerned with its foreign policy, I said I felt that during my fifteen months in Spain there had been notable improvement in Spanish-American relations, especially in the economic and commercial fields. The improvement, however, had been slow and halting and had not sufficed to counteract the practically universal impression that the Spanish Government was pro-Axis and not, in fact, neutral. In view of the recent fall of Mussolini and collapse of Italian Fascism, it must now be clear to the Caudillo, as well as to us, that the United Nations were sure to win the war and that any Government which had not been sympathetic with them would find itself, sooner or later, in an intolerable position.

The Caudillo said he was not greatly surprised by the current situation in Italy. He had expected after our military successes in North Africa, and from his knowledge of the low state of Italian morale, that Italy would not be able to withstand us. But this didn't mean, in his judgment, that the war would end in the near future. Germany was still tough, and German morale high. I said I was not prophesying when the war would end, but he must admit that the offensive had now passed from the Axis to the United Nations. He nodded agreement.

There were three respects, I said, in which Spanish policy, in

Spain's own interest, should speedily be altered. *First,* the Spanish Government should abandon its ambiguous "non-belligerency," and in unequivocal terms declare its neutrality. The Caudillo said his policy was in fact one of neutrality. He was firmly determined that Spain should not participate in the war, but should be really neutral. However he didn't like the word "neutral," because it implied indifference, and Spain could not be indifferent to a struggle against Communism. I observed that whatever the word "neutral" might connote to him, the word "non-belligerent" could only remind the world at large of the policy which the now defeated and discredited Mussolini had followed. For Spain at this late date to imitate Italy, even in words, seemed thoroughly unrealistic and distinctly dangerous. To this, General Franco made no reply.

Second, I continued, if the Spanish Government meant to be really neutral, as he had just said it did, then the Falange as well as the Foreign Office should behave accordingly. The Foreign Office, under Count Jordana, was honestly trying, I believed, to pursue a policy of impartiality, but everyone knew that it was being constantly interfered with and thwarted by governmental agencies directed and controlled by the Falange. The Caudillo asked, what agencies? I mentioned the Ministry of the Party, the Vice-Secretariat of Popular Education, many of the Civil Governors, and agencies having to do with the postal service and the police. General Franco said that Count Jordana had brought this whole matter to his attention several times, and he supposed his resulting orders to the Falange were being obeyed. Was there not a big improvement, for example, in the press? I said there had been some improvement during the past two months, but it was sporadic and far from sufficient.

I then gave him a résumé of the discriminations and difficulties which we encountered from the Falange press censorship and the postal service. The Caudillo appeared to be greatly surprised. He said he was glad I had given him such detailed information. He would look into the situation at once. He was anxious there should be no discrimination by any of the government agencies between the two sets of belligerents. Democratic propaganda was sometimes peculiarly objectionable by reason of its criticism of Spain's domestic affairs. On this, I remarked that so long as the pro-Axis Falange played the central role in Spain's domestic affairs, these could not be divorced from Spain's foreign policy or spared from democratic criticism. He said he understood the significance of this remark and would give the matter early and serious consideration.

Third, the Spanish Government should withdraw its "Blue Division" from the German armies fighting the Russians. I understood, I said, Spain's repugnance to Communism and to any possible forceful intervention by Russia in Spanish affairs. But, conversely, I could see no reason why Spain should attempt a forceful intervention in Russian affairs. This was precisely what the Blue Division was doing. Further, there had been no Blue Division in 1939–1940 while Germany and Russia were in practical alliance. It had come into existence only in 1941 after Germany attacked Russia. Hence it suggested to outsiders that Spain was more interested in giving military support, even of a token nature, to Germany than in fighting Communism.

This was the first time, so far as I know, that any Allied protest had been made to General Franco against the Spanish "volunteers" on the Eastern Front. I had had no instruction from Washington to raise the question with him, and I anticipated that his reaction, to put it mildly, would be explosive. He surprised me by the calmness with which he replied. He said he would like to sketch the historical background of the current situation. The Spanish Civil War had involved a struggle within the country against Communist influences inspired and directed by Soviet agents, and so great and menacing were these influences that in the course of the Civil War he had signed the Anti-Comintern Pact with Germany and other Powers. Imagine his astonishment at learning, almost as soon as the Civil War was over, that Germany was making overtures to Russia and negotiating a kind of entente with its Communist regime. He protested to Hitler against such a violation of the Anti-Comintern Pact. He also protested to Mussolini, and approached England, France, and the Vatican about breaking up the new German-Russian association.

When Germany attacked Poland in September, 1939, he and all Spaniards were thoroughly sympathetic with Catholic Poland, and in its behalf he made strong representations to Italy and to the Vatican. As he watched Germany's allowing Communist Russia to appropriate a full half of Poland, he couldn't conceive of Spain's ever joining Germany under any circumstances. Then, when Finland was attacked by Russia, he explored the possibility of sending a volunteer Spanish division to help the Finns, and only the lack of needful armament and transport prevented its despatch. Finally, when Germany and Russia fell out, it became practicable to send Spanish volunteers to the Eastern Front. They were there, not to help Germany against us, but to show Spain's hostility to Communism, which it deemed the greatest menace in the world.

I said I was glad, as I was sure my Government would be, to have his explanation of the Blue Division, and I appreciated the historical reasons for it. Nevertheless I could not perceive any justification whatsoever for its continuing presence on the Eastern Front. It was actively and openly aiding Germany in a war of aggression against Russia. Russia had not attacked Germany. Germany attacked Russia. Germany patently had imperialistic designs and intended, if it possibly could, to annex extensive Russian territories. If the Caudillo opposed Russian intervention in Spain, how could he justify Spanish intervention in Russia? The matter was pressing. German power was waning, and Russian, waxing. Spain might soon be in a most embarrassing position. What would happen if Russia declared war on Spain? Russia was an ally of the United States and Great Britain. We all had to live with Russia now and in the future.

General Franco admitted that the situation was different from what it had been when the Blue Division first went to the East. The United States had since entered the war. There might still be some utility, he suggested, in keeping a few Spanish officers and men on the Eastern Front in order to obtain valuable information as to just what was happening there and within Germany. I said I should think he could get all such information through his Military Attaché at Berlin without having to maintain a division on the Eastern Front for the purpose.

In conversations of a year before, he had advanced a theory of "two wars," the one in Europe, and the other in the Pacific. Now he talked about "three wars." One was the war between the English-speaking countries on the one hand and Germany and Italy on the other; in this Spain was neutral, and indeed "benevolently" neutral toward us. The second was the Pacific War, and this was of prime importance. The Japanese must be defeated. They had never been touched below the surface by European civilization, and basically they were barbarians. They were the worst sort of imperialists. They intended to dominate China and the whole Far East and their recent pledge of independence for the Philippines was perfectly insincere. Spain had no liking for Japan, and would gladly cooperate with us in the Pacific War. But there was the third war, that against Communism. Unfortunately, the entire Continent of Europe was honeycombed with active and virulent Communist cells, by reason of a kind of decadence and breakdown of traditional civilization. As Communist Russia gradually got the better of the Germans, it would stir up and utilize for its own ends such cells in Italy and Germany and all the occupied countries, and thus manage in time to dominate the entire Continent.

I reminded him anew how arbitrary and impractical it was to divide into three or any other number of separate "wars" this World War for which the Axis was alone responsible. I asked him if the United States and Great Britain wouldn't be winning the war, as well as Russia. He said yes, but added that while we put great energy and enthusiasm into winning the war, we would both withdraw from the Continent and leave it to Russia when the present war was over. I said I must differ with him about this. We would continue to act jointly with Russia after, as well as during, the war. Besides, I had greater faith than he in Europe. No doubt there were groups of Communists, as there were of Fascists, in the countries he had mentioned, but there were also in them large numbers of people who didn't want any kind of totalitarianism. A choice didn't have to be made between Communism and Fascism. There was also Democracy, and I believed it would prove to be the eventual choice of the great majority of the masses of people everywhere.

In any event, I said, I couldn't see how one Spanish division on the Eastern Front was going to prevent the Communist triumph he predicted, or why he wanted to tie Spain's fortunes with Nazi Germany. Spain, after all, was an American even more than a European country. With this he expressed emphatic agreement. He said his greatest desire was for mutual understanding between Spain and the United States concerning Hispanic America, where the United States, he knew, had special economic, political, and strategic interests, and where Spain had its strongest ties of culture and blood. He hoped my Government did not think that *Hispanidad* had any political purposes or was directed in any way against the United States. I said that while recently, under Count Jordana, there had doubtless been improvement in this respect, the preceding Spanish Foreign Minister, Serrano Suñer, had certainly utilized *Hispanidad* to foster Falangist and anti-American activities. He said that if this had ever been the case, he deeply regretted it. It had certainly not been the case recently. He expressed satisfaction with our "good neighbor" policy toward Latin America and the hope that Spain might be included in it. There was no reason why the United States, Spain, and Hispanic America couldn't all work together in a kind of triangular relationship. He knew we had no thought of exercising any political sway over Hispanic America, and neither did Spain. Spain's interests there were purely cultural and sentimental.

I stated that this should reenforce what I had previously said. Throughout Hispanic America there was great repugnance to Nazi German imperialism, and Spain would be in closer step with its daughter-nations in the New World if it ceased to favor, or to appear to favor, Nazi Germany. Moreover, he must be aware that the large majority of Spaniards, as well as of Spanish Americans, were not pro-German. He said he thought this was true. Spain had owed some debt to Germany for assistance in the Civil War, but that debt had long since been amply repaid. He concluded the conversation by promising to give his most earnest attention to all the matters we had discussed.

III

I left the Pardo that July 29, 1943, feeling that I had cast a good bit of bread on the water, and wondering how much, if any, might return. I was not long in doubt. Five days later, on August 3, our Press Attaché was summoned to the office of the Falangist Vice-Secretary of Popular Education and told that General Franco had given orders that the Spanish press, radio, and newsreel services were to be placed on an impartial basis. Although during the ensuing month there were varying degrees of "obedience" to these orders, and some downright disobedience on the part of local officials and German-subsidized newspapers and one of the Spanish radios, I was able to send a generally favorable report to Washington. Discrimination against our news, pictures and press releases, against the advertising of our radio programs, and against the commercial sale of our propaganda magazines, had practically ceased. Three American newsmen were now broadcasting regularly from Madrid over our principal networks. Also as a result of my representations of July 29 and the ensuing directives of General Franco, Spanish newspapers as a whole were now publishing more news and illustrations of the United Nations than of the Axis. "I am glad," responded President Roosevelt on September 22, "that our position in the press is so much better."

Already, on August 7, the Office of War Information at Washington took cognizance of the improvement in a "propaganda directive for Spain," signed by Mr. Robert E. Sherwood, the chief of OWI's Overseas Branch. "1. Our policy towards Spain is to maintain and strengthen this flank of our supply line and to avoid all semblance of disorder in this important strategic quarter. 2. The United States does not propose to interfere in the internal affairs of Spain which are exclusively in the province of the Spanish people themselves. This is in accordance with point three of the Atlantic Charter which is the best reply to enemy propaganda to the effect that an Allied victory would bring Bolshevism to Spain and curtail Spain's independence. 3. We are aware of the larger measure of cooperation which we are receiving from the Spanish Government and expect that manifestations of unfriendliness to us and to other United Nations appearing in certain sections of the Spanish press and in the Falange will be further bridled and rapidly eliminated altogether by the Spanish Government."

General Franco must have given curbing instructions to Falangist leaders most inclined to combat us in deed or in word. At any rate from August onwards there was a notable lessening of Falange oratory, and one of the principal spokesmen of "the movement," who couldn't have been entirely silenced except by a major operation, began sounding a new note. His earlier denunciations of communism and praise of the "new order" were now subordinated to expounding the thesis that Falange was not an "ideology" nor a "platform," that it was purely Spanish and should not be confused with any foreign product like Fascism or Nazism, that its mission was simply patriotic and social, and that, above all, it was "adaptable."

Meanwhile, on August 1, two days after my interview with General Franco, Count Jordana departed from Madrid, with most of the Foreign Office, for a six-weeks' sojourn at the famous summer resort of San Sebastian, in the Basque country, close to the French border. This was reviving an old custom, which had been interrupted by the Civil War and the ensuing uncertainty of the world-war situation. It was significant, not only of Jordana's personal liking for San Sebastian, but also of a desire to show the world that Spain was getting back to normal and feeling secure about its Pyrenean border. The large majority of the diplomatic corps followed the Foreign Minister to San Sebastian and remained a month or more. Unfortunately, the United States Government had no consulate and no provision for a summer Embassy at San Sebastian. The best I could do, in the circumstances, was to alternate, during those six weeks, between a hotel-room in San Sebastian where I could be in periodic touch with the Foreign Minister, and the Embassy in Madrid, where our secretaries and code clerks were.

One of the ironies of the situation was the presence, in the same hotel with me at San Sebastian, of the German and Italian Ambassadors. The Italian held himself in dignified aloofness from the

Germán, but the German may have derived compensation from the court paid him by the Japanese Minister and the Vichy Ambassador. An official of the hotel offered to tap the German Ambassador's telephone wire for me, but I declined the offer. I couldn't imagine that he, any more than I, would transmit any real secrets by telephone. I soon found that my own telephone wire was tapped. Apparently the hotel official had been quite "impartial," and the German more responsive than I.

In my first conversation at San Sebastian with Count Jordana, on August 7, 1943, he expressed satisfaction with the discussion I had had, the week before, with the Caudillo, and said he was confident the suggestions I had made on that occasion would be acted upon. Already, General Franco had intervened personally with the Falange censorship to stop discrimination against us. Further, at the first auspicious moment we could expect a formal declaration of "neutrality," in place of the past "non-belligerency."

As for the Blue Division, Jordana said he had long believed that the sending of it to the Eastern Front was a mistake, and that it should be withdrawn. The Caudillo had been much impressed by what I had said to him on July 29, and had consulted the Supreme War Council, including the Ministers of Army, Marine, and Air and the Chiefs of Staff. They all agreed to a gradual withdrawal of the Division. This, however, would involve some delicate and painful negotiations with the Germans, which would soon be inaugurated but which would take time.

No publicity was given then, or for a long time afterwards, to the interview I had had with General Franco on July 29. I had, of course, immediately informed the State Department concerning it, and likewise my British colleague. I was sure we stood a better chance of getting prompt and favorable action on the proposals I had made to the Caudillo, by letting it appear that any such action was taken on Spain's own initiative, rather than as a result of pressure by us. It seemed to me that to give publicity to our representations in advance could only wound Spanish pride and alarm the Germans and elicit from them the heaviest counter-pressure.

Sir Samuel Hoare evidently thought differently. He was not only a diplomatist in Spain but a politician in England. He was about to make one of his regular trips home to meet fellow Members of Parliament and to reassure the British press and his own constituents concerning his forcefulness and successes in Spain. If Spain was to proclaim complete neutrality and withdraw the Blue Division, he might as well get public credit.

At any rate, the British Embassy announced about the middle of August that Sir Samuel was to have a momentous interview on the 20th with General Franco at the latter's summer residence near La Coruña. American as well as British newspaper correspondents were called in and given the text of "suggested despatches" they might send. Then Sir Samuel dramatically flew to La Coruña, while news of the flight and its "high significance" was broadcast by the BBC and carried widely in the world press. I saw him after his return to Madrid and just before he took off for England, and according to the version he gave me of his conversation with the Caudillo it covered almost exactly the same ground as mine of July 29, except that some mention of German agents was made and none of Hispanic America, and it was quite mild and friendly.

Immediately following Sir Samuel's arrival in England, however, the BBC and American, as well as British, newspaper men in London began transmitting detailed reports, which agreed substantially with what he had told me in Madrid, with one glaring exception. The publicity had it that the British Ambassador had *demanded* the withdrawal of the Blue Division, etc. This was not true. I am certain that no "demands" were made by Sir Samuel either at that time or subsequently.

Franco and Jordana were naturally annoyed at all this gratuitous publicity and distortion. On August 26 the latter expostulated to me about it. As a result of it, he said, the German Ambassador was protesting with extreme vigor, which did not lessen the practical difficulty of getting the Blue Division out of the German trenches and back across Germany. Moreover the gesture of withdrawing the Division had little advantage for Spain unless it appeared to be voluntary, and the British Ambassador, probably unwittingly, was now making it appear as forced. Hence, there would be added difficulty and perhaps delay. Count Jordana said he hoped I would have patience and understanding.

In commenting on this to Washington, I said that 'while it may possibly seem to be an effort on Jordana's part to drive a wedge between the British and ourselves, I have absolutely no reason to believe it is. The British Chargé here tells me that Jordana has made a similar protest direct to him, and that the publicity was "London's idea." '

At any rate, the net result of the episode was that Sir Samuel Hoare gained public credit, at least for the time being, for having been "tough" with General Franco, while Spanish compliance with the most important of my original proposals was delayed.

IV

In August, 1943, I presented a formal request to the Foreign Minister for landing rights for American commercial airlines in Spain, and received his assurance that he would submit it, with his endorsement, to General Franco and the Council of Ministers. At the end of the month, I also presented a formal request for the direct evacuation of the French refugees from a Spanish port, preferably Málaga. Simultaneously, Count Jordana raised with me the question of our supplying Spain with arms, a question which had previously been broached to appropriate Attachés of ours through the Ministries of Army and Commerce.[1] The Foreign Minister expressed doubt whether we would be willing to sell arms to Spain but emphasized that, if we should, it would enable Spain to stop importing arms from Germany and thereby to deprive the Germans of their chief purchasing power in Spain.

Washington had already informed me, in response to the earlier Spanish soundings, that the Joint Chiefs of Staff, after being consulted in the matter, deemed it inadvisable at this time to furnish Spain with military equipment. They perceived the possibility, however, that there might be developments which would render advisable the supplying of military equipment to the Spaniards, and they

[1] See above, p. 150.

accordingly proposed that the Spanish military authorities should keep our Military and Naval Attachés in Madrid informed of Spanish needs. This, of course, was an approval of the recommendation the Embassy had made,[1] and in accordance with it I told Count Jordana that, while we could make absolutely no commitments of any sort about actually supplying arms to Spain, our Military and Naval Attachés were authorized to discuss Spanish needs with the Ministries concerned. This, however, must have acted as a dash of cold water on the Spanish Government, for early in September I reported: 'A high official has informed us that negotiations for imports of German war materials to an estimated value of 500 million pesetas are being carried on in San Sebastian by the Ministry of Foreign Affairs with the Germans on behalf of the Spanish army. It seems evident that we were sounded out on the possibility of Spain's obtaining war materials in the United States out of a real desire to find an alternative to this arrangement, which, of course, greatly improves the Germans' economic position in Spain.' As events of the following winter were to disclose, I underestimated the effects of the German negotiations at San Sebastian in September, 1943.

Since the end of July we had been aware of secret British negotiations at Lisbon to obtain from Portugal Allied air and naval bases in the Azores. Neither we nor the British could overlook the very considerable possibility that as soon as these negotiations were successfully concluded and the Allies moved into the Azores, the Germans might take counter measures against Portugal and move across Spain. Here was, in prospect, a crisis comparable to the one we had faced in the Iberian Peninsula in November, 1942, when Allied armies first landed in North Africa.

The State Department and our military authorities were worried, and we were warned at Madrid to take extra precautions. I replied in a personal letter on September 8: "I have sent a secret circular letter to all of our Consulates in Spain reminding them of the Department's instruction, and directing them, should the emergency arise, to destroy at once all ultra-confidential materials and to have

[1] See above, p. 150.

the personnel depart as quickly as possible in the direction of Lisbon or Gibraltar, depending upon circumstances, and in the meantime to be sure that they keep in storage a sufficient reserve quantity of gasoline to supply their automobiles for such flight. I really do not think the emergency will arise. My guess is that the Germans are now so very heavily engaged on the eastern front and so fearful of what we may do in Italy, France, or the Balkans, that they will be unable or unwilling to risk a Spanish adventure. I am not losing sight, however, of the possibility or of the measures which we must take should the possibility become a reality."

The general military situation was becoming steadily more favorable for us and more threatening for the Germans. On August 17 we completed the conquest of Sicily. On the 23rd the Russians captured Kharkov. On the 24th Mr. Roosevelt and Mr. Churchill met at Quebec. On September 3 Allied forces crossed the Strait of Messina and began the invasion of the Italian mainland. On the 8th Italy, under Marshal Badoglio, surrendered "unconditionally." On September 26, Smolensk fell to the Russians and on October 1 Naples was taken by the Allies.

Meanwhile the Portuguese Ambassador in Madrid kept us informed about the progress of the Azores negotiations, which were concluded in early October, and about the resulting reaction of the Spanish Foreign Office. Dr. Salazar, the Portuguese Prime Minister, before publicly announcing the agreement with Great Britain, arranged a meeting with Count Jordana near the Spanish-Portuguese border on October 7. It lasted four hours and was attended only by the two ministers. The Spanish Ambassador to Portugal (Nicholas Franco) as well as the Portuguese Ambassador to Spain (Dr. Pereira) made the trip but did not participate in the discussion. On the way back to Madrid, Count Jordana told the latter he had stated to Dr. Salazar that Portugal's decision was wise and proper and would not disturb Portuguese-Spanish relations. Shortly afterwards Jordana further informed Pereira that the Caudillo had been consulted and perceived no reason why the Portuguese concession to the Allies should interfere with the Iberian bloc or with Spain's neutrality.

On October 12, 1943, the British Ambassador officially informed the Foreign Minister about the Anglo-Portuguese agreement regarding the Azores and reiterated Britain's guarantees to Spain. He immediately reported to me that the information was taken quite calmly and that he expected no difficulty with Spain. That same day, according to another report I had from the Portuguese Ambassador, Count Jordana called in the German Ambassador and told him that Spain remained loyal to the Iberian bloc and did not believe that the Portuguese action afforded any ground for bringing the war into the Peninsula. The German "listened to the message without reaction." In the evening, following a Columbus Day dinner, General Franco himself remarked to the Portuguese Ambassador that Portugal need not fear for her back door; "it will be guarded by Spain."

There were still large and powerful German forces along the French-Spanish border, but again they didn't move. By this time the German authorities knew only too well that any attempted invasion of the Peninsula would encounter resolute Spanish resistance, and that this would add immeasurably to their increasing difficulties elsewhere.

V

The "unconditional surrender" of Italy on September 8, 1943, had important repercussions in Spain and created several serious problems for us and also for the Spanish Government. The Fascist Italian Government had maintained a very large Embassy, with numerous auxiliary services, in Madrid, and a large number of consulates, cultural institutes, and agents throughout the country. Besides, there had long been in Spain a large number of Italian business men and workers, some of whom were strongly Fascist and others anti-Fascist.

Unfortunately for all concerned, the Italian "surrender" on September 8 proved more nominal than real. It was a surrender of Marshal Badoglio and the King, and of the main part of the Italian navy, but it couldn't be a surrender of the regions of Italy occupied by the Germans. And long after September 8, the Germans not only occupied all northern and central Italy (including Rome [1]) but also kept Mussolini at the head of a puppet Fascist government, newly labelled "Social Republican."

Hence, Italians in Spain were confronted with the question whether they should follow the King and Badoglio and go with the Allies, or stick by Mussolini and the Germans. The Italian Ambassador, Paulucci, hesitated little, if any. True, he had been a special confidant of Mussolini on foreign affairs during the early years of the Fascist regime and an admirer of certain internal reforms effected by that regime. In September, 1943, Mussolini called him by long-distance telephone at Madrid and begged him to accept the post of Foreign Minister in the "Social Republican Government" of North Italy—a plea urgently pressed in person by the German Ambassador in Madrid. Yet Paulucci, as a career man in the Italian Foreign Service, had served the King and various Liberal Governments before the advent of Fascism, and his loyalty to the King and his dislike for the Nazis now rose superior to pleas of Mussolini and Dieckhoff. He promptly aligned himself with us, and managed, through the exercise of notable tact and patience, to carry with him the large majority of his Embassy staff and of the Italian consulates and cultural institutes throughout Spain. Curiously enough, one of his chief lieutenants in the transition, the Italian most outspokenly anti-Fascist and pro-Ally and continuously most helpful to us, was Farinacci, consul at Sevilla, the son of that stridently Fascist collaborator with Mussolini.

Paulucci and his associates were gravely handicapped in September, 1943, and for some time afterwards, by having virtually no contact with the Government of Marshal Badoglio which they were supposed to represent, and by receiving only such news from Italy as the German-controlled radio dispensed. They had not only no instructions but no funds, and of this situation the Germans in Spain were quick to take advantage. They provided funds for Italians

[1] For a vivid account, by an American eye-witness, of the situation in the Italian capital during the German occupation from September, 1943, to June, 1944, see Jane Scrivener's *Inside Rome with the Germans* (New York, Macmillan, 1945).

who would desert Paulucci and follow Mussolini. They strove, with their propaganda, to convince both Italians and Spaniards that Badoglio and the King were fugitives and Allied puppets and that the only real government in Italy was Mussolini's.

Some of Paulucci's staff did leave him, and there was some trouble in various places outside Madrid. At Barcelona, where the Consul was lukewarm, to put it mildly, the Fascists gained the upper hand among the local Italian colony. At San Sebastian, the Consul, acting on the Ambassador's instructions, called in the Spanish police to prevent a Fascist Vice-Consul from taking possession of the Consulate. In Tangier, a crowd of Fascists, egged on by the Germans, staged a series of demonstrations outside the Italian consulate, which, however, remained loyal to the Royal Government. At Tetuan and at Málaga, the Consuls declared themselves for Mussolini, who presently named the latter, a certain Morreale, as his "Minister" to Spain. Such desertions, however, were the exception, not the rule. The main officials in the Italian Embassy, and most of the Italian Consuls in Spain, like Paulucci, adhered to the King and Badoglio, and were thoroughly cooperative with us.

Italian exigencies put new and heavy burdens on our Embassy's "Relief and Refugee Section," and the Secretary in charge, Mr. Niles Bond, rose handsomely to the occasion, as he had done in the earlier case of the French. There were thirteen or fourteen Italian merchant ships which had put into various Spanish ports in 1940 and whose crews now had to be cared for. Besides, a flotilla of Italian warships, on the way to surrender to the Allies, but being short of fuel, had recently put in at the Balearics. These included a cruiser and several destroyers, which carried, in addition to their own crews, at least 750 survivors of the battleship *Roma* which the Germans had sunk.

At the end of September, in harmony with the British Embassy, we reported: 'Daily the financial difficulties of the Italian representatives in Spain increase. Diplomatic and consular personnel have had no pay for five months. Current expenses for the crews of the fourteen ships average 350,000 pesetas a month, and, in addition, these ships owe debts amounting to 250,000 pesetas that must be paid prior to any possible departure. For supplying the warships in the Balearics and paying their crews, a million pesetas a month is needed. We urgently recommend authorization to advance to the Italian Ambassador the equivalent of 500,000 dollars for immediate emergency expenditures. Inasmuch as the Germans are liberally financing Italians who will cooperate with them, it is of the utmost urgency that funds should be available to the official Italian representation which is cooperating with us.' After somewhat protracted negotiations between Washington, London, Marshal Badoglio, and the Allied authorities at Algiers and in Italy, an arrangement was worked out whereby Great Britain and the United States jointly furnished necessary funds in the form of loans.

Meanwhile the State Department was naturally concerned lest the Spanish Government, on its own initiative or under German pressure, should recognize Mussolini's "Social Republican Government" and break off relations with the Royal Government which the Allies recognized. Consequently, on September 20, just after Count Jordana's return from San Sebastian, I raised with him, at the Foreign Office in Madrid, the question of Italian representation in Spain and also the question of the warships in the Balearics.

I reminded the Foreign Minister that, from the standpoint of my country and the other United Nations, one of the most significant developments within the past two weeks had been the armistice between our military authorities and the duly-constituted Italian authorities. The King of Italy and his Government, headed by Marshal Badoglio, were now functioning in southern Italy and cooperating in carrying the armistice into effect. My Government hoped that Spain would resist any pressure which Germany might seek to exert to obtain recognition of a puppet rebel government, which it was obviously trying to set up under the nominal leadership of Mussolini. It must appear to the Foreign Minister as well as to me that any fostering of schisms or civil war among the Italian people could only endanger the reestablishment of order throughout Europe. I should like some assurance that Spain would continue to recognize the Royal Italian Government and withhold recognition from any rival government which Mussolini and the Germans might attempt to create.

The Foreign Minister replied that no request had been made for Spanish recognition of any Italian government other than the Royal. Regardless of any such request being made in the future, Spain intended to adhere strictly to international law on the subject, and to continue to recognize only the government which was legally constituted in Italy, which was clearly the Royal Government that had accredited the present Italian Ambassador to Spain. He said he had given instructions to all Spanish Consuls in Italy to observe strict neutrality, and to the Civil Governors in Spain to suppress Fascist demonstrations. He would not permit Spain to be used as a battleground for Italians.

Then referring to the Italian warships, I said that, according to my information, they had put into the Balearics after the Armistice in order to obtain fuel to enable them to proceed on their way. Apparently no fuel had been available, and the Spanish local authorities had indicated that the ships would be interned. There was a fundamental question, I pointed out, whether the ships should be regarded as belligerent or non-belligerent. If they were the latter, they most certainly should not be interned at all, but should be allowed to proceed whenever they could. If, however, the Spanish Government held them to be belligerent, they should be supplied, under the Hague Convention of 1907, with fuel necessary to carry them to their nearest home port, and should be allowed 24 hours, or an exceptional 48 hours, after the fuel was available, in which to depart. The 24- or 48-hour rule about fueling, I said, clearly presupposed the existence of a fuel supply, and the framers of the pertinent 19th Article of the Hague Convention obviously did not have in mind a case of inability of the neutral power to supply fuel. It was certainly inequitable to invoke the 24- or 48-hour rule against the ships, which could not obtain fuel through no fault of theirs. Our petroleum attachés, I suggested, would gladly cooperate with the Spanish authorities in remedying the situation and seeing to it that requisite fuel was made available. In the meantime, I hoped that orders for internment would be held in abeyance.

The Foreign Minister said that his own information about the matter was as yet sketchy and incomplete but according to it the warships had put into the Balearics not so much to obtain fuel for continuing a voyage as to seek a safe haven. Three destroyers had already been scuttled by their officers, and this caused him to suspect that the others did not really wish to leave the Balearics but would prefer to be interned. He suggested it might be to our advantage to have them interned. I dissented, and expressed doubt about the accuracy of his information. He said he would investigate further and determine the juridical status of the ships as soon as possible. On the whole matter he believed we could reach an amicable agreement.

VI

The month of October, 1943, abounded in evidence that General Franco had taken seriously my conversation with him on July 29 and that his Government was orienting its foreign policy decidedly toward the English-speaking countries and especially toward the United States. Already in September, in a speech at La Coruña, he significantly affirmed that "Spain's future, like her past, is on the seas and toward the Americas."

Then, on October 1—the "Day of the Caudillo"—his customary reception of the diplomatic corps and the staffs of the several Spanish Ministries at the Oriente Palace in Madrid partook of quite a different character from previous ones. The year before he wore a Falange uniform. This year he wore the uniform of an Admiral of the Fleet. The year before he received representatives of the Falange and of numerous Falangist auxiliaries. This year none such was received. The year before he was noticeably cordial to Axis diplomats. This year he greeted them only perfunctorily. The German and Italian Ambassadors did not speak, and while the latter was cordially welcomed by myself and all the Allied and neutral diplomats, the former was almost completely isolated.

The address which the Caudillo delivered on that day contained the formal declaration of Spain's "neutrality." He uttered the word, and never afterwards did we hear of "non-belligerency" or have cause to wonder what it meant.

The address, as a whole, clearly represented an effort to draw closer to the democracies. The Caudillo reiterated that Falange was not a program or an ideology. It would modify its policies without hesitation or fear in order to meet changing conditions. The regime, he said, was essentially Spanish and was not to be identified with any foreign system. Speaking in general terms of the Falange and the Falange Youth, he remarked that "the hour for changing the guard approaches." Most of the address was devoted to a review of the regime's accomplishments, principally along economic and social lines. The need for land reform was discussed at some length. Appeals for support were made in turn to capital, labor, and agriculture, especially the farm worker. There was no reference to the Axis, and no prediction concerning the length of the war. There was, as everybody expected, an attack upon communism and a stressing of the future menace from it in a post-war Europe, disorganized and impoverished. But the chief attack was leveled at the "Spanish exiles" as having been the moral, if not material, authors of the 1934 revolt in Asturias and of the death, during the Civil War, of "13 bishops, 5,255 priests, 2,669 monks, and 112 nuns." The Caudillo charged the exiles with having brought Soviet commissars to Spain, and with conducting more recently a defamatory campaign throughout the American nations. They were trying, he said, to embroil Spain in the war so that they could profit by resulting disturbance within the country. Spain, however, was determined to stay out of the war.

At about the same time, I received a Note from the Foreign Minister informing us that General Franco and the Council of Ministers had agreed to our request for the evacuation of French refugees direct from Spain, instead of by the indirect and complicated route through Portugal which had been used since March, and that we might utilize the port of Málaga for the purpose. This good news we immediately communicated to the British Embassy and the French Mission. The latter at once arranged for rail transportation of groups of the French fighting men from their several camps in northern Spain to Málaga and for lodging them in the big bullring in this city while awaiting shipment to North Africa, while the British made the necessary arrangements for sea transport and convoys. A first contingent of some 1,200 men got off safely from Málaga on October 21, and a second on October 26. Thenceforth the trips across Spain and the embarkations proceeded with regularity and despatch. By the end of the year, the total number of Frenchmen arriving in North Africa from Spain reached the figure of 20,000.

In October, too, the French Mission in Madrid was strengthened by the arrival of additional staff and of a new chief, with the rank of Minister, in the person of M. Jacques Truelle, a career diplomat who had been Counselor of the French Embassy in Washington and French Minister to Rumania. The Minister was cordially received by Count Jordana, as well as by the Spanish Under Secretary, Sr. Pan de Soraluce, and he brought friendly letters from General de Gaulle and the French Minister of Foreign Affairs at Algiers.

The Germans did not take at all kindly to these developments. Failing to obtain any satisfaction from the Spanish Foreign Office or from General Franco, and evidently unable to carry into effect their threats to sink the refugee ships leaving Málaga, they resorted to the cheap expedient of hiring Falange gangsters to demonstrate against the French Mission in Madrid and to assault some of the French refugees in Barcelona. I called these cowardly activities to Count Jordana's attention in a Memorandum which I left with him on November 5. It had, I may add, the desired results.

We also made progress, in October, 1943, with negotiations concerning the Italian questions which had come to the fore in September. While the British concentrated on seeking the release of the Italian merchant ships, the American Embassy pushed for the release of the Italian warships. The juridical basis for the latter was laid in a Note which I submitted personally to Count Jordana on October 22 and which was supported by a supplementary Note of the Italian Ambassador. The Foreign Minister told me he would refer the Notes to a special committee of legal experts in his office who were already studying the question and he imagined a way could be found of meeting our wishes without doing violence to recognized principles of international law. He also reaffirmed the determination of the Spanish Government to maintain friendly relations with the Royal Italian Government and not to recognize the new Mussolini regime.

In connection with Italian affairs, I very frankly told Count Jordana that, since the Italian surrender on September 8 and as a result of our subsequent contacts with the Italian Embassy and Consulates in Spain, we had obtained a good deal of detailed information about what Germans, as well as Italians, had done on Spanish soil against Allied military and naval operations outside, particularly regarding sabotage around Gibraltar and espionage in Spanish Morocco. It was not a pretty picture, and regardless of whether the Spanish Government was privy to it, it was bound to be most damaging to Spain's reputation abroad, and it clearly called for immediate and drastic correctives on the part of the Government. Axis agents should be subjected to much closer surveillance, and those implicated in espionage and sabotage should be unceremoniously expelled. This should particularly apply to Spanish Morocco, where no Axis agent could be engaged in anything but sabotage or espionage. The Foreign Minister disavowed any complicity of the Spanish Government with illegal activities of Axis agents and said he was sure such activities were as harmful to Spain as to us. He promised to act on any complaints we could substantiate with specific facts.

Progress was likewise noticeable in the withdrawal of the Blue Division from the Eastern Front. The British Military Attaché learned from the Spanish Chief of Staff on October 15 that the Spaniards had reached an agreement with the Germans for its withdrawal, and that the Division had begun moving back from the Front on October 12. Members of it who might freely volunteer to stay would enter a foreign legion under exclusively German command, but the remainder would return to Spain.

The Foreign Minister told me at the end of the month that the entire Division was then being reassembled behind the lines at Königsberg, preparatory to its transportation home as rapidly as rail facilities would permit. To date four contingents of about 600 men each had arrived at San Sebastian. The Spanish Government, he stated, wanted the whole Division home and would seek to discourage any of its members from remaining with the Germans, although "a few," he admitted, might remain "either because they were fanatical or because they were irresponsible." To my plea that Spain, in its own interests, should give publicity to the withdrawal of the Blue Division, he replied that I could not imagine the trouble he had already had with the Germans about the matter, and that publicity now would but add to the trouble and probably lead the Germans to put new obstacles in the way of the return of further contingents.

Two weeks later, our own Military Attaché learned from a reliable source within the Spanish Army that 4,000 out of an estimated total of 12,000 in the Division were already repatriated, and that the rest were expected back within the next five weeks, and that stories of new recruitments for the Division were quite false. The figure of 4,000 was confirmed by our intelligence services which kept careful tab on comings and goings by rail across the frontier. We did get information that the extremist element in the Falange tried to drum up recruits for the "German Foreign Legion," and there was a tendency, especially in the foreign press, to confuse this with regular army recruiting for the "Spanish Foreign Legion" in Spanish Morocco. We confidently expected, as I wrote to the President, that "all the Spanish boys will be out of the trenches in Russia well before Christmas."

The time was auspicious, I reasoned, for pressing the Spanish Government to adopt a less intransigent attitude toward Russia and the Soviet Union. I had broached the matter, in general terms, in my conversation with the Caudillo on July 29. I would now follow it up in greater detail and with specific recommendations through a personal letter to the Foreign Minister. So, on October 21, I addressed to him such a letter. It was written on my own initiative and without any instruction or authorization from Washington. I made it clear therefore that the communication was "personal and confidential." Count Jordana's lengthy reply of October 29, in which he very fully exposed his Government's intense feeling about Russian Communism, was similarly marked "personal and confidential."

The reply was hardly satisfactory, from my standpoint. It didn't really answer the questions I had asked, or squarely face the fundamental issues involved. Yet it was no "slap in the face" and it enabled the Foreign Minister to "get a good deal out of his system"—a good deal which conditioned the thinking of many Spaniards and which foreign critics should at least be aware of. I prepared a rejoinder, but in view of certain unfortunate developments in our relations with Spain in early November, I did not send it to Count Jordana until considerably later. When finally it was sent, it evoked a sympathetic response.[1]

In the midst of this personal correspondence with Count Jordana about Russia, I appealed to him, likewise on my own initiative and in a strictly personal way, in behalf of certain Spanish exiles, whom, according to stories then current in Allied countries, the Germans had seized in France and turned over to the Spanish authorities for early execution. I recognized fully, I told him, that the matter was one of internal policy and one therefore exclusively for the Spanish Government to determine and that my Government would not wish to offer any advice about it. Nevertheless, I said, I must express a grave personal fear lest the shaping of the course for a better relationship between our countries would be materially prejudiced by Spain's accepting the men in question from Germany and putting them to death. In such an event there would be no bound to the public indignation in the United States, not necessarily because of sympathy for what the men stood for or had done in the past, but because they were executed long after their alleged crimes and after having been handed over by the Germans. The Foreign Minister greatly relieved me by denying quite categorically that the Germans had offered, or Spain had requested them, to turn over any Spanish exiles. None of the men in question, so far as he knew or had heard,

[1] Main parts of the correspondence, which must have been obtained from the files of the State Department, were later published in the article, "How We Dealt with Spain," by Ernest K. Lindley and Edward Weintal, in *Harper's Magazine*, Vol. 190 (December, 1944), pp. 23–33.

were in Spain or on the way hither. He and General Franco didn't want the men in question and wouldn't accept them from the Germans.

In turn, Count Jordana made a personal plea to me in October, 1943, to help arrange clipper passage for his young son, Don Rafael Jordana, on a first trip, half-business and half-educational, to the United States. The young man was a delightful person, a student in the foreign-service school, and almost notoriously pro-American. He was eager to see something of the country he admired, and his father was equally eager that he should. I gladly complied with the request, and in due course young Jordana made the trip.

VII

I have explained in an earlier chapter that one of our most important activities in Spain during 1942 and 1943, probably *the* most important, was our economic warfare with the Axis, particularly the program of "preemptive buying," conducted jointly by the USCC and UKCC in close relationship with the American and British Embassies, and aimed at depriving the enemy of strategic war materials which he needed. The program proved eminently successful, first because Spain maintained an "open market" and afforded us the same freedom to buy as it afforded the Germans, and second because we had greater financial resources than the Germans and were able, therefore, to outbid and outbuy them. Thanks to our "overpricing" of certain commodities, such as petroleum products,[1] which Spain imported from the dollar or sterling areas, we managed to accumulate more pesetas with which to purchase Spanish goods than could the Germans through their exports to Spain.

By October of 1943 the economic battle in Spain seemed to be just about won by us. Already, in the early spring of 1943, we had driven the Germans out of the market for sheepskins, rabbit skins, woolen textiles, and fleece-lined gloves. Henceforth we had the satis-

---

[1] On petroleum, for instance, we fixed a price double the market price, in order to obtain more pesetas for our preemptive buying of Spanish commodities.

faction of knowing that we didn't have to spend any more of our money on these articles and yet that they were not going to save Nazi soldiers from shivering and freezing on the bleak Russian plains. Certain commodities we continued to buy in Spain for our own needs, for example, mercury, fluorspar, and strontium.

By far the biggest item of our expenditure, however, was for wolfram. This was the commodity which the Germans most desperately wanted from Spain (and Portugal) and on the purchase of which they concentrated their available financial resources. If only they could get the precious wolfram, they would do without anything else and let their soldiers suffer from the cold in Russia.

Until July, 1943, the battle for Spanish wolfram raged fierce and furious between the Germans and ourselves. But then the financial strain proved too great for the Germans. They no longer had the means for competing with us in the open market and were obliged to fall back on the relatively small output of the few mines they owned outright and on what they could pick up clandestinely. This enabled us in August to reduce drastically our purchases of wolfram and the prices we paid for it. Whereas, during the first seven months of 1943, we had purchased an average of 112 tons a month at a cost of 243 pesetas a kilo, we bought during the last five months of the year an average of 63 tons a month at a cost of 86 pesetas a kilo.

Altogether, according to careful estimates of the U.S.C.C., the amount of wolfram sold in Spain during the first eleven months of 1943 was 3,743 tons, of which the Allies bought 2,563 tons and the Germans 1,180. This total of 1,180 tons for the Germans consisted of 701 tons which they obtained in the open market, 309 tons from mines they owned, and 170 tons which they procured clandestinely.

It should be borne in mind, moreover, that foreign purchase of wolfram in Spain did not automatically lead to its export. Before any could be exported, the purchaser had to pay the Spanish Government a heavy "production tax" and obtain an "export license." The immediate cause of the Germans' quitting the open market in July, 1943, was their inability to raise some eight million pesetas required to pay the tax on accumulated stocks for which they held export licenses but which they couldn't remove from Spain without paying the tax. The total export licenses issued by the Spanish Ministry of Industry and Commerce, during the year 1943, were for 3,003 tons of wolfram: 690 tons, or 23 per cent, to the Germans; and 2,313 tons, or 77 per cent, to the Allies.

In October, 1943, with the tide running so generally favorable for us in Spain, it naturally occurred alike to the State Department and to the Embassy that the time was auspicious for persuading the Spanish Government to halt wolfram exports to Germany altogether and thus to give the *coup de grace* to our adversary in the economic warfare. There was no difference between our people in Washington and our staff in Madrid about the desirability or the timeliness of such a move. But we in Madrid had a closer and clearer, and, I believe, a more realistic, view of the practical obstacles in the way. We were optimistic about the chances of surmounting the obstacles, but we were pretty well convinced that the best and quickest way of surmounting them lay in the economic domain through some sort of reciprocal trade arrangement.

In wolfram Spain had a huge "vested interest." It was providing extraordinarily large revenues for the Government Treasury, handsome profits for many hundreds of mine-owners and middle-men, and employment and a living for thousands of Spanish workingmen. Moreover, the high competitive prices paid for it by foreigners were ensuring to Spain favorable balances in dollars and sterling and also in Reichsmarks, with which she could purchase not only petroleum, wheat, cotton and other needed products from the New World but also arms and machinery and other desiderata which the Allies didn't supply but the Germans did. The Spaniards were quite aware that shutting the Germans out of the wolfram market, without obtaining economic compensation, would be equivalent to killing the goose that laid the golden egg. If the Germans couldn't get wolfram from Spain, the Allies, who didn't really need it, would at once stop buying it. A panic would follow the boom. And how then could Spain meet her requirements for foreign imports of petroleum, wheat, fertilizer, machinery, and arms?

Some sort of answer to this basic economic question had to be ready, we felt, simultaneously with any request for an embargo on wolfram exports to Germany, that is, if we were to get prompt and favorable action on the request. Consequently, the Embassy officials most directly concerned, particularly the Commercial Attaché (Mr. Ackerman), the Counselor (Mr. Beaulac), and the First Secretaries in liaison with the USCC (Messrs. Butterworth and Harrington), gave much thought, in the latter part of September and throughout October, to the formulation of proposals which might be acceptable both to the Allied Governments and to the Spanish and would thereby induce the latter to break off remaining commercial relations with Germany. The British, who shared equally with us in the conduct and costs of the existing program of "preclusive buying," and who, besides, were peculiarly dependent upon Spain for certain commodities, such as iron, potash, and citrus fruits, also gave a good deal of thought to the problem, both in conjunction with us and independently.

The British Government, doubtless on the advice of its Embassy in Madrid, notified our Government, in September, that after carefully reviewing the situation, it was reluctant to upset existing arrangements or to pursue a more severe economic policy toward Spain. A month later, the British reiterated and emphasized their satisfaction with the economic status quo.

Thus, Washington should have been fully aware—as we were in Madrid—that the British were not likely to go along with us in making any new economic "demands" on Spain. In Madrid we therefore recognized that the early cessation of Spanish wolfram exports to Germany would involve the working out, in advance, of a comprehensive plan which would be persuasive not only with the Spanish Government but also with the British.

On October 26, we presented to Washington the Embassy's considered recommendations for just such a plan. We made clear that it was intended merely as a possible outline for detailed negotiations which might lead to considerable modifications in it and that we awaited Washington's reaction before discussing it with the British or with the Spaniards. We felt, however, that we should lose no time in preparing the Spanish Government to give serious

attention to whatever representations we might presently be authorized to make concerning wolfram and commercial arrangements in
general.

Wherefore, on October 22, just before submitting our specific
recommendations to Washington, I had a preliminary conversation
with Count Jordana in which, after stressing the imminence of
Allied victory, I pointed out the desirability of Spain's putting its
merchant marine more at our disposition and curtailing its export
of strategic materials, including wolfram, to the Axis. The gist of
my argument was contained in a personal memorandum which I
left with him. This read as follows:

There is no longer room for reasonable doubt concerning the outcome of the war. Complete victory for the United Nations can be
clearly predicted. There is reasonable doubt only concerning the time
which may elapse before that complete victory is achieved.

The increasingly powerful blows being delivered against Germany
and Japan by the United Nations are directed at shortening the war
as much as possible. The Government of the United States will do
everything within its power to shorten the war. It will do nothing
which might lengthen the war.

As the war progresses, and Germany's military, political and industrial strength declines, the United States is obliged from time to
time to review its trade not only with Spain but with other countries
of the world in order to insure that no portion of such trade is
operating, directly or indirectly, to help Germany and thereby to prolong the war.

As the war effort of the United States increases, the expenditure
of materials of all kinds increases correspondingly. The bulk of the
American armies have not yet entered into action, but they will enter
into action soon, and expenditure of materials in the total war against
Germany and Japan will increase correspondingly. All such materials
will be used for the purpose of ending the war in the shortest
possible time. This rule applies to petroleum products as well as to
all other products.

The Government of the United States has continued to trade with
Spain within the limits made possible by the war effort, and has
supplied Spain not only with commodities which hitherto could be
freely spared, but also with commodities of which there has been a
scarcity in the United States.

Spain, on its part, has supplied the United States with surplus Spanish products. While products having little or no wartime value to the United States have been transported in Spanish ships, little or none of the strategic materials purchased have been so transported.

The economies of the United States and its allies are directed at winning the war in the shortest possible time. It follows therefore that no products can be made available by the United States unless their export contributes in the greatest possible degree to shortening the war.

In accordance with this policy, the Government of the United States expects that, in return for products made available by the United States to Spain, the Spanish Government will undertake to insure not only that such products are transported to Spain in Spanish ships, and thereafter are not utilized in the benefit of the enemies of the United States, directly or indirectly, but that products which Spain makes available in exchange will be transported promptly to the United States in Spanish vessels, whenever the Government of the United States so requests.

As a result of trade between Spain, on the one hand, and the United States, other American countries, and Great Britain, on the other hand, Spanish economy has experienced a substantial improvement. So far as concerns petroleum, Spain is in an especially favored position and has had available for its use an even larger percentage of its normal imports of petroleum products than American countries actively associated with the United States in the war against Germany and Japan.

The maintenance and improvement of Spanish economy, made possible principally as a result of trade with the democracies, has, on the other hand, made it possible for Spain to continue to produce and transport to Germany and to German-occupied territory quantities of foodstuffs and other materials, including strategic materials of war.

Since the United States can not be expected to continue to carry on trade with any country if such trade directly or indirectly assists the enemy, it is obvious that the Spanish Government, if it desires to continue trade with the United States, should take steps to reduce its trade with Germany, especially its trade in foodstuffs and strategic materials.

The Foreign Minister gave close attention to what I said on that October 22, and from remarks he made I gathered the impression that both he and the Minister of Industry and Commerce

(Señor Carceller) rather expected us to present some specific proposals and were prepared to give them at least "sympathetic consideration." There seemed to be a fairly good prospect of getting Spain to meet our wishes about wolfram, as already in October it was meeting so many of our other wishes: declaration of neutrality instead of non-belligerency; withdrawal of the Blue Division; cessation of most of the discrimination against the United States and Great Britain in press and radio; grant of Allied control over travel of Axis nationals between peninsular Spain and Spanish Morocco; direct evacuation of French refugees; withholding of recognition of the new Mussolini regime; Spanish backing of Portugal's concession of military bases in the Azores. And progress was being made in current negotiations regarding Italian warships and merchant vessels, Axis agents, and landing rights for American commercial airlines in Spain.

But then, at the very end of October, occurred an event which suddenly halted the progress we were making and produced a succession of unfortunate consequences during several months thereafter. I refer to the so-called "Laurel Incident."

VIII

On October 25, 1943, we received word that the Office of War Information had picked up radio broadcasts from Tokio and Berlin praising the Spanish Government for having sent a congratulatory message to José P. Laurel, a former judge in the Philippines who was now a collaborationist with the Japanese and whom the latter had just placed at the head of their puppet "government" in the islands. How could Spain thus recognize an essentially Japanese regime in the Philippines? Would we investigate the truth or falsity of the broadcasts and report at once to Washington?

Our first reaction at Madrid was one of complete disbelief. It seemed so obvious to us that here was just another example of Axis propaganda calculated to disturb Spanish-American relations, and that it would prove to be quite as unfounded as dozens of other canards which we had previously been asked to investigate and report upon. As recently as July 29 General Franco had voiced to me, in no uncertain terms, his hostility to the Japanese and his sympathy with us in our war against them;[1] and Count Jordana had since repeated and emphasized those words. There had been no indication in the Spanish press or radio of any "Laurel message" or anything else which could be interpreted as contradicting what the Caudillo and his Foreign Minister had told me. Moreover, we knew, and supposed most Spaniards knew, that Laurel had been notoriously anti-Spanish as well as anti-American, while Señor Quezón, the president of the Philippine Commonwealth which we recognized, had been partial to Spanish culture as well as a loyal ally of the United States.

Confident that the Spanish Foreign Office couldn't have sent a "congratulatory message" to Laurel, I didn't bother to go myself to Count Jordana about it, but instead had the Embassy Counselor, Mr. Beaulac, make a presumably perfunctory call on the Under Secretary, Pan de Soraluce, in order to obtain the expected official denial of the story. Imagine his amazement, and mine on his return, to discover that such a message had indeed been sent. Pan de Soraluce explained to Beaulac that it had been a natural and courteous acknowledgement of a cordial personal telegram from Laurel reflecting the long and intimate cultural relationship between Spain and the people of the Philippines, and that it did not signify any recognition then or in the future of Laurel's "Philippine Republic" by Spain.

In discussing the matter with the Under Secretary, Beaulac took a properly vigorous stand—and Beaulac was always vigorous. He said he was sure our Government could not accept as valid the Foreign Office's explanation of the telegram. In all his experience he knew of no precedent for the sending of such a message by one government to another which it did not recognize or plan to recognize. The long and intimate relationship of Spain with the Philippine people and Spain's determination not to recognize the so-called "Philippine Republic" were overwhelming reasons why no reply should have been made to the original telegram from Laurel. By

[1] See above, p. 161.

replying to it, Spain had given Japan very valuable propaganda material and, whether consciously or unconsciously, support for its military and political plans in the Far East. Further, it plainly violated what General Franco had said on July 29. The United States Government must take a most serious view of the matter.

That afternoon I wired the Department a full report, and expressed the opinion that I should present to Count Jordana personally a very strong Note along the lines of Beaulac's conversation. 'Please inform me at the earliest possible moment if the Department wishes me to prepare such a Note or would prefer itself to supply the text. It is my idea that the Note should inquire whether there is any intention on Spain's part of granting recognition to the so-called "Philippine Republic." A prompt reply would be insisf ed upon, with the thought that both my Note and the reply shou'd be published by our Government.'

Two days later I submitted to the Department for its approval a stiff draft of the proposed Note. This crossed a telegram from the Department, affirming its 'very serious view of the matter,' and continuing: 'Before issuing any instructions the Department naturally desires to consult with appropriate departments of the Government, but will communicate with you as soon as possible. Please take no further action nor have any further conversations with the Foreign Minister on your initiative on any subject until instructions are received from the Department.'

Five days later, with still no further word from Washington, I wired in this tenor: 'It is my hope, as I am sure it must be the Department's, to use the incident of Jordana's message to Laurel to improve our position in Spain and to bring further deterioration in the Axis position here and elsewhere. I am concerned over the continued delay in receiving instructions concerning this incident. We have a number of very important matters pending with the Spanish Government concerning which I am anxious to talk with Jordana at the earliest possible moment and I suggest that my relations with him be not interrupted any longer. Our objective in this whole affair should be to utilize the incident in order to promote the interests of the United States rather than to punish Jordana.

I request prompt instructions concerning the delivery of the Note transmitted in my previous telegram, since I believe it adequately meets the situation.' The Department answered on November 3, indicating that I might resume relations with the Spanish Foreign Minister but 'not take any initiative regarding the Laurel telegram.'

Certainly, the sending of the message to Laurel was an egregious blunder on the part of Count Jordana, or of whatever other Spanish official was really responsible for it. It was so very stupid, and so utterly indefensible.

We learned afterwards that none of the officials of the Spanish Foreign Office who would normally have been consulted—the Under Secretary, the Chief of the Division of Overseas Affairs, the Protocol Section, or the Legal Advisers—had known anything about the message, or that it was contemplated, until after it had been sent. I can't be sure, but I have some reason to believe that it was prepared by a minor official who had certain financial interests in the Philippines which he imagined the telegram might serve to protect, and that it was slipped in for signing or initialing by the Minister without the latter's grasping what it was, or what its implications. Naturally, Count Jordana, as Foreign Minister, had to assume responsibility, but his reiterated insistence that he, and only he, was responsible, gave me the impression that, for some personal reason or from a misplaced sense of chivalry, he was shielding a "lame duck" in the Foreign Office or in General Franco's entourage.

At any rate, Count Jordana undertook, immediately after Beaulac's interview with Pan de Soraluce on October 26, to undo the harm done with our Government. In accordance with the Minister's instructions, the Spanish Ambassador in Washington, Señor Cardenas, besieged the State Department on October 29 and 30 with "explanations" and "assurances." He registered 'a firm denial of any intention or desire on the part of Jordana or the Spanish Government to recognize the Laurel regime or the "independence" of the so-called "Philippine Republic," or to act in any manner contrary to the good relations between the United States and Spain.' At the same time he offered to put all this in a written memorandum which might serve as the basis for a public statement and for the "liquidation of the affair."

The State Department was unwilling, however, that the affair should be "liquidated." It would not accept Ambassador Cardenas's memorandum or indicate what sort of statement it would accept, and for several days it treated the Spanish Ambassador with scant courtesy.[1] It imagined that thereby it was "softening up" the Spaniards and preparing them to accede to new and peremptory "demands." In this, it was undoubtedly backed by the bulk of American public opinion, which had naturally been incensed by the message to Laurel and which, lacking any word of explanation from the Department, called for a "show down" with Spain.

Some persons within the Department may have thought of utilizing the Laurel Incident for an open break with Spain. At any rate, the incident was discussed "on the highest military level," where it was pointed out, however, that 'Allied war plans did not contemplate entry into Europe by way of Spain, and that it was important to avoid any trouble which might require a diversion of Allied strength, and to see that no untoward incident should disturb the Spanish status quo in one direction or another.'

Despite this caution from our highest military authorities, and without bothering either to consult its own Embassy in Madrid or, what was much more important, to ensure British cooperation, the Department instructed me on November 6 to request of the Spanish Government (a) *a complete and immediate embargo on wolfram exports to all destinations, without any quid pro quo*, and (b), in conjunction with the British Ambassador, *the removal of German agents from Tangier*. Four days later a high official of the Department informed Ambassador Cardenas that, to clear up the Laurel Incident, Spain should forthwith grant "an embargo on the export of wolfram, release of Italian warships and merchant ships, expulsion of German agents from Tangier, and landing rights for American planes." The telegram informing me of these "demands" went

[1] This is detailed, apparently from sources within the State Department, in the article by Ernest K. Lindley and Edward Weintal, "How We Dealt with Spain," in *Harper's Magazine*, Vol. 190 (December, 1944), pp. 27-28.

on to remark: 'The difficulties you have stressed regarding an embargo on wolfram are understood by the Department, but the Department deems these very difficulties and the critical need of the enemy for wolfram to make urgently desirable the securing of a complete embargo from Spain at this time.'

I had already cabled the Department that the British Ambassador's 'last instruction from London was to refrain from acting at present about Tangier' and that he thought I should not act until after he did.

In a long conversation with the Foreign Minister on November 10, I made a plea, in accordance with the Department's instructions, for a complete and immediate embargo by Spain on wolfram exports and also for early favorable action on pending requests, particularly for release of Italian warships and merchant vessels and for landing rights for American commercial airlines. An incidental remark of the Minister that "the British Ambassador deemed it more important to give attention to the Italian merchant vessels than to the warships," gave additional indication that the British, as well as the Spaniards, might not fall in with our "demands" quite as readily as the Department was assuming. While Count Jordana was polite about the wolfram demand, and asked me for a written memorandum on the subject, he stated over and over again that until the Laurel Incident was liquidated and the United States Government showed a friendly disposition, we could not expect Spain to deal with pending questions affecting us. It was unfair to blame Spain for a "minor fault." When the incident was liquidated, we could be sure that Spain would redouble its sincere cooperation with us.

In vain, I stressed the justifiably excited state of public opinion in the United States and the need of allaying it through prompt action which only Spain could take by granting our requests. The Foreign Minister's rejoinder was that there was also a public opinion in Spain, which was greatly exercised by the belief that the United States was taking unfair advantage of a trivial episode and might be entertaining sinister intentions toward Spain. He did not need to assure me, he said, but he would reiterate that he personally was anxious and determined to meet all our reasonable requests. But he could not do so if General Franco and the Council of Ministers felt that the United States was holding a pistol at his head.

So the end result of the Laurel Incident was not to hasten Spanish compliance with our desires, but rather to delay it and to bring on a crisis in Spanish-American relations. This was primarily because the significance and expected consequences of the incident were regarded very differently by the State Department in Washington (and public opinion in America) and by the Spanish Government in Madrid. The Department chose to interpret it as a clear and deliberate insult to the United States, a currying of favor with Japan as well as with Germany, and as affording the occasion and the justification for "getting tough" with Spain and frightening it into speedy yielding to some pretty stiff "demands."

On the other hand, the Spanish Government, especially the Spanish Foreign Office, while admitting that a "blunder" had been committed, insisted it was not deliberate and should not be construed as a pro-Japanese or anti-American gesture. Failing to understand, in spite of our best explanations, how the American Government could take the incident so seriously, and deeply offended in its pride by the studied coolness of the Department toward the Spanish Ambassador in Washington, the Spanish Government concluded that we were utilizing the incident for ulterior purposes, that we were making impossible demands preparatory to attacking Spain or at least intervening in its internal affairs. And, of course, German propaganda worked overtime to confirm the Spaniards in this conclusion.

Hence ensued a serious and protracted strain, not only between the Spanish and American Governments, but within the Spanish Government between Count Jordana and some of his colleagues who took to criticizing the "failure" of his pro-Allied policies. In the circumstances, both Jordana's and our moral influence with the Spanish Government were gravely weakened, and the numerous important negotiations, which in October, 1943, on the eve of the Laurel Incident, had been going so well, now took a turn for the worse and for several months afterwards were rendered extremely difficult and largely fruitless.

CHAPTER VII

THE WOLFRAM CRISIS

I

I have explained in preceding chapters how essential to the Nazi war-machine was the steel-hardening tungsten derived from wolfram ore, and how central in the Allied program of economic warfare in the Iberian Peninsula was our preemptive buying of this ore.[1] Germany, unlike the United States, had no wolfram of its own. It had to import it in order to continue waging war. Conceivably, it might obtain it from Russia, or from Japan. But practically, only a few tons at a time could be brought, and then most hazardously, by an occasional submarine or other blockade-runner from the Far East to Europe; and the Russian military success before Stalingrad in January, 1943, decisively removed the possibility of getting wolfram from that quarter. Consequently, Germany became almost wholly dependent on one remaining source of supply of the precious mineral—the Iberian Peninsula. Here, the chief producer was Portugal; the secondary, Spain.

In the last chapter I have further indicated how by August, 1943, through our superior financial resources and the free competition permitted by the Spanish Government, we had driven the Germans out of the open wolfram market in Spain and limited their supply to the produce of the few mines they owned in the country besides what they could send out from previously accumulated stocks. The next step, which we all clearly envisaged, would be to persuade the Spanish Government to withhold export licenses and thus impose a practical embargo on Germany's getting any more wolfram from Spain. To this end, we submitted a tentative plan to Washington on October 26, 1943, and I made a preliminary approach to the Spanish Foreign Minister on October 22.[2]

[1] See above, pp. 83–86. [2] See above, pp. 183–187.

Very unfortunately, in my opinion, the immediately ensuing Laurel Incident served to interrupt the logical development of negotiations, to transfer the initiative from Madrid to Washington, and, instead of proceeding along economic lines (as the Embassy urged), to make it appear that we were "demanding" a quick complete wolfram embargo, along with other and unrelated things, as a kind of political penalty for the Foreign Minister's message to Laurel.

We had, at Madrid, the greatest sympathy for, and fully shared, the "righteous indignation" which possessed American public opinion and the State Department over the Laurel Incident. I think, however, that, being on the spot, we saw the incident in perspective, and appreciated that it was an exception to, rather than the rule of, Spanish behavior toward us. And we doubted whether "indignation," no matter how "righteous," was the most statesmanlike accompaniment of such complex and realistic negotiations as persuading Spain to embargo wolfram exports to Germany.

The State Department, in instructing me on November 6, 1943, to request of the Spanish Government "a complete and immediate embargo," must have acted impulsively and without thinking the matter through. The instruction said I was to make the request "on any grounds you wish" except that I was not to indicate "that the United States contemplates any material quid pro quo."

I obeyed instructions, of course, and duly made the request on November 10. We didn't have to be reminded anew by the Foreign Minister—we already were well aware—that the wolfram business was a cornerstone of current Spanish economy, and that immediately to abolish it, as the proposed embargo practically demanded, would encounter strenuous opposition, not only of numerous private citizens in Spain, business men and workers, but also of the Ministers of Finance, Industry and Commerce, War, Navy, and Air. The Spanish State was collecting large revenues from the production of wolfram; and from its sale to Germany it was deriving the means which enabled it to import machinery and arms that it wanted but could not get from us.

Moreover, we were aware that the Germans, after having been

driven out of the open wolfram market in August, were now, in November, back in it again. They had accumulated, in the meantime, enough pesetas to permit them to reenter into financial competition with us, and the prices of wolfram were again soaring. Two methods the Germans had employed to replenish their coffers in Spain. One was to take advantage of Spain's recall of the Blue Division. This had, of course, very unpleasant implications for Germany, both political and military. Yet Germany wanted wolfram even more than it wanted the Blue Division, and in consenting to release the latter, it drove a hard bargain for the former. It insisted upon squaring its bill for the "volunteer" aid it had given General Franco during the Spanish Civil War, with Spain's bill for the "volunteer" Blue Division, and the sizable difference, in Germany's favor, it expected to devote to wolfram purchases in Spain.

The second method of the Germans was to step up their exports to Spain. Despite their own needs and shortages, they increased the quantities of war materials and industrial machinery they had been sending. In the winter of 1943–1944 they even sent considerable amounts of foodstuffs, including wheat, barley, and potatoes. In the single month of January, 1944, as much as 20,000 tons of wheat arrived in Spain from Germany! Already, in November, 1943, with finances restored, the Germans could resume large-scale buying of wolfram from Spain.

This newer development made it all the more needful for us to put a stop to the wolfram business in Spain—and all the more difficult. For it was not merely that the Germans were benefiting. Spain was benefiting also, and the more brisk the business, the bigger the benefits. Certain extremists would have had us make our request for a wolfram embargo in the form of an ultimatum, and, on Spain's non-compliance with it, would have had Allied armed forces invade the country and seize the wolfram mines. Any such solution, however, was definitely and categorically ruled out by the President and our highest military authorities. These held that we had enough to do on our central fronts without undertaking dubious diversions on the side.

How, then, to get the desired and needed wolfram embargo?

When I simply asked for it on November 10, the Foreign Minister requested a written memorandum. What should I say in it? I knew that it would be passed around in the Cabinet, and that if it were to receive serious consideration from Count Jordana's vitally concerned colleagues, it must be couched in terms of Spanish interest as well as of our own. But how to do this, in the face of the Department's crisp instruction not to suggest or discuss any quid pro quo?

The night after I verbally presented the bald request to the Foreign Minister, Mr. Beaulac (our Counselor), Mr. Ackerman (our Commercial Attaché), and I stayed up late, drafting a reasoned telegram for the Department. It went off to Washington the next day, November 11, and because it was basic and represented the best collective thought of the Embassy on the whole question of tactics, it is here summarized:

If we demonstrate that an embargo on wolfram exports will be to Spanish interest, it is believed that such an embargo will be imposed by the Spanish Government. This would result in certain immediate, serious disadvantages to Spain, such as these: (1) immediate loss to Spain of her main source of sterling and dollar exchange; (2) immediate loss of revenue derived from export tax on wolfram; (3) opposition from wolfram producers, some of whom have depended for many years mainly on export trade in this commodity; (4) opposition from Germans, of course; (5) opposition from Spanish armed forces. Badly needed arms are being obtained from Germany since no other source is available. In exchange for these arms, Germany hopes to obtain wolfram from Spain.

Considering these factors, we should be in a position to show that Spain would gain certain advantages through such an embargo which would outweigh the obvious disadvantages, some of which are indicated above. Three possible ways of demonstrating this are:

I. A reasoned plan for inducing the imposition of an embargo on wolfram exports by the Spanish Government, such as the one presented by us on October 26.[1] Certain advantages would accrue to Spain under this plan, but what it offers is small compared with the cost to us of continued purchases of wolfram. The plan, we believe, is economically sound, and constitutes a reasonable basis of discussion with the Spanish authorities.

II. The main advantage which Spain derives from her economic

[1] See above, p. 184.

relations with the United States is the supply of petroleum. In order to continue receiving supplies of petroleum, Spain may be expected to make great sacrifices, if necessary. Petroleum supplies cannot be obtained from any other source in adequate quantity and are vital to Spain's national economy. Should Spain have to decide between losing petroleum supplies or placing an embargo on the export of wolfram, the decision would probably be to protect its source of petroleum supplies.

However, we should not *threaten* Spain with reducing or cutting off the supply of petroleum. Our economic relations with Spain to date have been based entirely on mutual interest and cooperation. So far this policy has been successful, and in this case it should not be abandoned without further trial.

In the past the Germans have made liberal use of threats toward Spain. These threats have been instinctively resisted by Spain, and even while German military prospects seemed exceedingly bright to them, the Spaniards have tended to come closer to us. This aspect of German policy in Spain has not been successful. Germany now has an intelligent and able Ambassador in Spain, who is employing persuasive methods. We must take care not to assume the earlier German role.

As an alternative to *threatening,* we could present the Spaniards with a *fait accompli,* explainable on reasonable grounds and associated later with the wolfram question. Reduction or interruption of petroleum supplies to Spain without previous warning would be such a *fait accompli.* The ground for this step has already been prepared by the Embassy. It has been made clear that due to the expanding war effort of the United Nations, petroleum products are no longer a surplus commodity, that we can consume all the petroleum products we can produce, that the terrific consumption of petroleum products, due to expansion of united war effort on an unprecedented and gigantic scale, is depleting rapidly valuable reserves, and that it is a definite sacrifice to make such products available.

III. We would recommend the following tactics:

A. Offer to the Spaniards a reasoned plan, such as outlined in I above;

B. If this is not successful after a reasonable length of time, interrupt shipments of petroleum with sensible and courteous explanation as in II above;

C. Then make clear to the Spaniards gradually that only in return for some advantage, such as an embargo on wolfram exports, commensurate with sacrifice involved, can petroleum products be made available to them.

In our opinion there is an excellent chance of these tactics succeeding.

In view of its secret nature, this plan has not been discussed outside the Embassy. If the Department approves, however, it is suggested that it take the matter up with the British Government, and that I be authorized to discuss it with the British Ambassador here in strictest confidence.

The Department's response, on November 15, was disappointing to us. While expressing approval of our proposals "in principle," it indicated that there was as yet no agreement at Washington, or with the British, about any details. I was not to await any such agreement or any approved program, for "we must proceed rapidly." *After* we got the embargo, we might consider some quid pro quo. Meanwhile the Department would consult the British, and I should confer with Sir Samuel Hoare, but if prompt instructions were not received by my British colleague, authorizing him to concur in the course of action, it was nevertheless desired by the Department that I press the Spanish Government for a wolfram embargo, leaving the quid pro quo (should such prove indispensable) for subsequent consideration by London and Washington.

On receipt of this message the next day, I had a conference with Sir Samuel. Its upshot I reported to the Department: 'The British Ambassador emphasizes he has had no instructions about any wolfram embargo. He expresses grave concern lest, if Portugal doesn't also agree to the proposed embargo, more rather than less wolfram will be obtained by the Germans.'

This Portuguese angle of the matter we had already called to the Department's attention. 'It should be appreciated that the Germans procure considerably greater amounts of wolfram from Portugal than from Spain and that consequently an exclusively Spanish embargo would not suffice. As long as wolfram continues to be bought at attractive prices, every device will be employed to smuggle the embargoed Spanish product into Portugal, and the strategic position of the chief Spanish mines close to the frontier will render it difficult or impossible for the Spanish authorities to prevent the movement of wolfram to Portugal. It is estimated by our experts that the minimum flow across the border, with Portuguese prices at present levels, would be a hundred tons a month, whereas the estimate of actual present German acquisitions in Spain is sixty tons a month. Inquiry has already been made by Spanish officials as to whether we expect to request the Portuguese to embargo wolfram exports. We shall, of course, press for the embargo in Spain, as instructed, but we believe that without parallel action in Portugal it would probably result in a boomerang, giving Germany more wolfram from the Peninsula as a whole than she is now receiving.'

To this, the Department replied, on November 17, that the Portuguese angle was being considered and appropriate representations were contemplated "at the proper time," though the Spanish Government was not to be so informed. No further illumination from Washington on the subject for almost two months, and then, on January 6, 1944, we were told that the question of a wolfram embargo in Portugal would be taken up at an appropriate time, though, for reasons of a secret nature, action there would have to be indefinitely postponed.

The "secret reasons," we learned from Lisbon, were that the State Department had been pushing Portugal, since before requesting any Spanish wolfram embargo, to grant to the United States the same sort of military and air bases in the Azores which it had granted to the British, and that until this was settled the Department didn't want to raise any complicating wolfram question with Portugal. As a matter of fact, negotiations for the Azores bases hung fire for months and months. I know nothing about them in any detail, but I suspect that the Portuguese were not unmindful that by protracting them they could stave off any threatened collapse of their own wolfram boom. At any rate, we didn't press the Portuguese, as we did the Spaniards, for a wolfram embargo, and all through the critical six-month period with the latter, from November, 1943, to May, 1944, Portugal continued sending wolfram to Germany.

Nor were the British prepared to cooperate with us in seeking a wolfram embargo from Spain. London had clearly stated to Washington in September and again in October, 1943, before the State

Department made its independent demand for the embargo, that the British Government would be averse to any change in the existing economic policy toward Spain.[1] Spain had become a valuable source of supply for several important raw materials which Britain needed, most notably iron ore and pyrites. This did not mean, London explained, that every opportunity should not be taken to obtain supplies from Spain on more favorable terms and to persuade the Spanish Government to allow less to go to the Axis, but it was the expressed belief of the British Government that these results were more likely to be achieved by maintaining the present economic policy than by turning to one of pressure.

Apparently the British were not consulted when the State Department decided to apply pressure and impulsively set out to demand a wolfram embargo from Spain. It was only afterwards, on November 15, that the Department informed us it "would consult the British." Whatever this consultation was, it produced no helpful results. The British Ambassador in Madrid was left for over a month with no indication whatsoever that Britain would support our request. A long instruction to him from London on December 20, while dealing with a number of pending matters, made no suggestion that he discuss wolfram with the Spaniards. On the contrary, it evidenced satisfaction with the existing wolfram situation by remarking that the Spaniards, in deference to our representations and despite the resumption of German exports to Spain, were keeping exports of Spanish wolfram to Germany down to a low level.

II

I believe Spain might have been persuaded to embargo all wolfram exports in the early winter of 1943–1944, if in advance Washington had appreciated the practical difficulties in the way and had concerted a comprehensive plan for overcoming them. As it was, however, the British were left out of account, as were also the Portuguese, and the Americans had little tangible to offer Spain in the place of the very real benefits it derived from exporting

[1] See above, p. 184.

wolfram. All we could do was to refer to "public opinion" in the United States, to hold out vague hopes—or fears—for the future, and to reassert that we simply must have an embargo complete and at once. And this while the Spaniards perceived that the British were not insisting, and that in the case of Portugal we were not insisting.

The Spanish rather naturally concluded either that we were bluffing or that we had some ulterior political or military purposes. In the former case, they could afford to procrastinate; in the latter they might play the British against us. In any event, they were not going readily to surrender the wolfram-bird in their own hand for a bird which might be in a distant bush.

Our Embassy at Madrid, I know, did the very best it could in the circumstances. The written memorandum which we prepared for the Foreign Minister, as he had requested on November 10, 1943, was, if I may say so, quite masterful. It was mainly the work of our Commercial Attaché, Mr. Ralph Ackerman, who managed to couch it in terms of Spanish as well as of American economic interest and still to get into it a maximum of demand on Spain with a minimum of offer from the United States. It was framed, too, with a view to exciting Spanish curiosity and leading to detailed negotiations.

I handed the memorandum to Count Jordana on November 18, 1943, and during ensuing weeks I repeatedly pressed him for a response. Besides, Mr. Beaulac argued our case with the Under Secretary, Pan de Soraluce, and other officials in the Foreign Office. And Mr. Ackerman had numerous lengthy conversations about it with the Minister of Industry and Commerce, Carceller, with his Under Secretary, and with the liaison officer between Industry and Foreign Affairs, Señor Iturralde (who had been Spanish Commercial Attaché in London). On November 30, for example, the last-named, in answer to a query of Ackerman's, said the two Ministries, and likewise the Treasury, were very much aware of the Memorandum and were giving it most careful attention, for it obviously involved fundamental considerations of policy. One was the effect of a wolfram embargo on public finances. Another was its effect on

Spain's neutrality. Carceller was troubled by the former; Jordana, by the latter.

To such objections of the Spaniards, Ackerman replied with the greatest possible persuasiveness—and Ackerman was always persuasive. Moreover, Beaulac and I did our best to remove what appeared to be the chief stumbling block at the Foreign Office, by emphatically denying that a wolfram embargo would be a breach of Spanish neutrality. The significance of an embargo was purely internal and no foreign country had the right to object to it. If Germany should object that this particular embargo was in fact discriminatory, Spain could point out that in 1940 and 1941 it had permitted its olive oil to be exported to Germany and Italy but to none of the United Nations. That had been discriminatory, and we were asking nothing like it in the present instance.

On December 1, the Foreign Minister told me he was not seeking to delay a reply to our wolfram request, but in view of its many-sided importance and the technical questions it posed for a variety of Government agencies, he had felt obliged to seek the advice of Cabinet colleagues and their experts and must await reports from them before making answer. He was anxious, he said, that a decision should be reached which would not (1) impair Spanish economy, or (2) impair relations between Spain and the United States.

III

Meanwhile, some progress was made with other matters. On November 18 we were informed that the Council of Ministers, on the recommendation of Count Jordana, had approved our request for landing rights for American commercial airlines,[1] and proposed to create a special commission, under the chairmanship of Sr. Gomez Navarro of the Foreign Office, which, in conjunction with representatives of the Embassy, would arrange details concerning routes and airfields, number and type of planes, etc. As our representatives I named First Secretary George Haering and Captain John Lusk.

[1] See above, pp. 142, 167.

Detailed negotiations were at once inaugurated, and proceeded smoothly for the next month or so. They were halted only by indecision at Washington as to what specifically we wanted, and by the gradually overspreading wolfram crisis.

Also there was progress about the Italian ships. The Foreign Office agreed in November to release all the merchant vessels except two, which Spain wished to retain as compensation for two Spanish ships that Italian submarines had sunk earlier in the war. This seemed to my British colleague, and to the British Admiralty, an eminently fair arrangement and they agreed to it, as did also, in time, our Government. Within a month, six of the eleven vessels in question were actually delivered to the Allies, and the rest would have duly followed had it not been for delay in implementing the agreement about Spain's retaining the two ships, and for the increasing absorption of everybody in the wolfram crisis.

The Italian warships were a harder nut to crack. But even here we felt we had a good chance of success. The Foreign Minister indicated to me on December 9 that his legal advisers were carefully studying the case in international law which we had presented for their release in our Note of October 12, and that some justification could be found for Spain's not interning them. Simultaneously Beaulac learned, in the strictest confidence, that the report of the advisers, then about ready, was likely to be favorable to us. I am pretty sure we could have obtained the release of the Italian warships that winter, had it not been that, for some strange reason I have never fathomed, Sir Samuel Hoare was not interested in them and didn't back us up, and that this matter, like so many others, was engulfed by wolfram.

Sir Samuel concentrated on the merchant vessels and on German agents; and in requesting Spain to close the German Consulate at Tangier, he naturally took the lead. Great Britain was a party, as the United States was not, to all the complicated international conventions concerning Tangier and, as such, had a better case than we in international law for protesting the existence of a German consulate there. On these matters, I, of course, seconded his efforts at the Foreign Office, and we had reason to believe that the Spanish

Foreign Office held no brief for German agents in Tangier or any-where else.

Indeed, there would have been relatively little trouble or delay, I am sure, in Spain's meeting all the "new demands" the State Department made on it on November 6, 1943,[1] had it not been for the wolfram matter. The others were in a fair way to settlement before the "demands" were made.

Another matter our Embassy was particularly interested in at the time. We wanted new office quarters for the Chancery whose personnel had been steadily and rapidly increasing during the previous year, to such an extent as to preclude its being possibly accommodated any longer as a unit on the third floor of the Embassy residence. Already we were outgrowing some four apartments we had temporarily rented outside. Now it happened that the Ministry of Education was utilizing, as a Falange annex to the University of Madrid, a commodious building close to the Embassy. It was a building which in the days of the Monarchy had been erected by an American corporation, the "International Institute for Girls," and employed as a joint school and dormitory for Spanish young women and for visiting undergraduates from women's colleges in America. Its American Board of Trustees, headed by Dr. William A. Neilson, had then leased it to the Spanish Ministry of Education and in that way, after the Civil War, it had come under Falangist control. I cast longing glances at it, shortly after my first arrival in Madrid, as possible quarters for the Embassy's press section, but it took over a year to obtain the consent of the Trustees in America, and by the time this was forthcoming our press section was located in the smaller but more appropriate "Byne house." [2]

But now, what about the "International Institute" for our sprawling, overgrown Chancery? I tackled the Foreign Minister in mid-December, 1943, and boldly asked him to get the Falangist educational people to quit the building and turn it over to us. His response was unexpectedly sympathetic, and in all probability we would presently have been in possession of the Institute had not wolfram here again intervened.

[1] See above, p. 191.   [2] See above, pp. 75, 76.

It was at this time, moreover, that I was resuming my personal correspondence with Count Jordana about Russia and eliciting from him a conciliatory expression of Spain's attitude toward our Eastern ally.[1] Simultaneously, too, the Foreign Office "re-recognized" the Polish Minister in Madrid, and resumed the interchange of official diplomatic notes with him.

Also, the evacuation of our airmen and of the French and other refugees continued in regular, orderly fashion. It was one thing which suffered no interruption or impairment during the wolfram crisis.

When our chief consular officers from all parts of Spain assembled in Madrid, at the end of November, 1943, for their annual conference, the tone throughout the Embassy was one of hopeful optimism. The Laurel Incident seemed to have dropped into the background, and Spain appeared to be taking steps to comply with our pending requests. Even the wolfram matter, despite an obvious stacking of cards against us, might be susceptible of satisfactory settlement—if only the Spaniards would promptly accept our Memorandum of November 18 as a basis for negotiation, and if Washington would give us some latitude about a quid pro quo.

IV

By mid-December, however, we were reaching an impasse about the proposed wolfram embargo. On one hand, the Spanish Government, supported by British indifference to our proposal, was procrastinating. On the other hand, the State Department, yielding to the extremist press in the United States, was more insistent than ever that we must get the embargo at once. All sorts of wild stories were being published at the time fostering a most suspicious, and even malicious, attitude toward Spain. I can't suppose that everybody in the State Department was "taken in" by this propaganda, but apparently enough were to harass the Embassy with complaints and to prevent the adoption of a realistic plan for obtaining the desired embargo.

[1] See the correspondence, previously cited, in *Harper's Magazine* for December, 1944.

There was special uproar, for example, over a so-called "Valencia Incident." The actual facts about it, as I explained in a report to the Department, were that two Falange youngsters, aged 19 and 22 respectively, misbehaved in the Valencia Consulate at 6 p.m. on Saturday, December 18, by pulling down some of our propaganda pictures and making unseemly remarks. On Monday, December 20, I called in person on Count Jordana, and received from him an apology and assurances that the two youths were being brought to Madrid and would be punished and that everything possible would be done to prevent a recurrence of similar incidents. While I was at the Foreign Ministry, two high Falange officials at the behest of the Party Minister were calling at the Embassy and giving to Mr. Beaulac a like apology and like assurances. On Tuesday, December 21, the Civil Governor of Valencia paid a similar visit to Mr. Galbraith (our Consul there), and the newspapers published an account of the offending youngsters and their consequent expulsion from the Falange.

The current state of mind in the United States, as whipped up by the extremist press, was not conducive to sanity or success in the difficult wolfram negotiations at Madrid. And any attempt to provide American popular opinion with some first-hand objective facts about the Spanish situation, such as the veteran *New York Times* correspondent, Mr. Harold Denny, tried to do in a series of articles in December and January, was immediately countered by the extremists with virulent attacks upon the author as an "appeaser" and "Fascist" and with a fresh torrent of propagandist tales about "pro-Axis Spain." The Spanish Government was well aware of all this and naturally interpreted it as reflecting a conscious American purpose to utilize our wolfram demand for ulterior purposes.

With a crisis imminent, I put up the whole wolfram problem anew to the Department in a telegram which a number of us in the Embassy jointly drafted and which went off in the latter part of December, 1943.

From latest conversations with the British Embassy, [we said in substance], it is quite clear that the British Ambassador and the key members of his staff are not in favor of embarking on any drastic course of action for obtaining an embargo on wolfram or, for that matter, any of the other desiderata under current discussion with the Spanish Government. They state that they have the backing of London in this. They are now looking to Spain as a source of supply as well as an area of economic warfare.

It is equally clear here that the Spaniards have every intention of employing delaying tactics in the matter of an embargo on wolfram. During the past few months the Germans have greatly improved their financial position, and have been supplying Spain with increased quantities of chemicals, coal, machinery, military equipment and miscellaneous products. The Spanish Government policy, in these circumstances, will be to reap the benefit of the wolfram boom so long as there is no effective severance of communications between Spain and German-controlled France.

If our Government hopes to force an early issue, we must be prepared to offer to the Spanish Government substantial and definite compensatory advantages. If these are rejected or there is undue delay in reaching a decision, economic pressure should be employed. Without doubt the Spaniards would accede to our demand under duress. Benefits would be lessened, however, by an increase in smuggling, both over the French border and over the Portuguese border (unless Portugal also embargoes wolfram exports).

London and Washington should in any case reach agreement on the policy and procedure to be followed in this matter of joint concern and should determine just how far both governments are prepared to go: (1) regarding the offer of compensating advantages to the Spaniards in return for an embargo on wolfram; and (2) regarding sanctions to be applied in event of failure of the first offer.

We shall continue to press the Spanish Government for a reply to the request already submitted. Meanwhile, we hope consideration will be given by Washington and London as to whether economic sanctions should be applied at some point with the approval of the Combined Chiefs of Staff.

In a supplementary telegram on the same day, I added that, during my first discussions of the proposed wolfram embargo with the Foreign Minister, as well as in my memorandum of November 18, I had intimated a possibility of interrupting the supplies of petroleum. Under suitable conditions, therefore, I was not averse to the exercise in a decisive way of our economic strength in Spain. Nevertheless, I urged that, should this become necessary, it be concurred in jointly by the United States and the British, and that steps be taken to bring Portugal into the wolfram program. Moreover, if and when it was agreed to apply sanctions to Spain by the British Government, the Department of State, and the Combined Chiefs of Staff, I hoped that the reasons for such action would be chosen with care and that the Madrid Embassy would receive advance notice so that it might efficiently do its part to obtain the broad objectives contemplated at that time.

The report of a conversation I had with Sir Samuel Hoare on December 28 rounds out the picture of the situation as it stood at the end of 1943: I asked the Ambassador if he would go along with us in pressing for an embargo on wolfram. He replied he would second our request, but he was opposed to sanctions. Sanctions should be invoked, if at all, to obtain broad benefits and not in connection with specific matters. He recalled only too vividly, he said, the unfortunate consequences of the sanctions which had been imposed on Italy at the time of the Ethiopian affair. He believed a threat to employ sanctions was of more value than the sanctions themselves. He also believed, he said, that neither the United States nor Great Britain would impose sanctions on Portugal, and unless a wolfram embargo was obtained in Portugal it would be useless to obtain one in Spain. He thought we were now getting a great deal from Spain, such as the actual withdrawal of the Blue Division and a big improvement in the Spanish press. In his opinion the expulsion of German agents from around Gibraltar was more urgently important than a wolfram embargo.

The British Embassy, I concluded, evidently opposed our employing economic pressure on Spain for any purpose for some time to come. On this, as I reported to Washington, I had an open mind, while inclining to the view that in order to oblige Spain to comply with certain of our requests some form of economic pressure might eventually be required.

The weapon in our hands was petroleum. It had seemed to me too big a weapon to discharge over minor issues. For these, Spain's mere knowledge that we possessed it had usually sufficed. But for what was now a major issue, I was prepared to use it to the full, and so indicated on December 22.

At the same time I was quite aware that such drastic procedure might be dangerous without concurrence of our highest military authorities, and would certainly be ineffectual without British acquiescence and support. It was with this latter consideration in mind that I talked with Sir Samuel Hoare on December 28, and my report of his dubious and dampening reaction was intended to stir Washington into pressing the button at London.

The new year of 1944 opened inauspiciously. On January 3, I had an extraordinarily unsatisfactory conversation with Count Jordana at the Foreign Office. He appeared greatly troubled and depressed, and I gathered from his attitude and from several remarks he dropped that German propaganda, combined with *PM* and similar extremist propaganda in America, had been seriously alarming the Spanish Government and disposing influential members of it to give less attention to our requests than to those of the German Ambassador.

To my complaints about the inordinate delay in replying to our wolfram memorandum of November 18 and to our note of October 12 about the Italian warships, the Minister rejoined with complaints about "too much pressure from the United States." The more we got, the more we asked, he said. There was a limit. Spain had to keep a few trumps in her own hand. If she was going to preserve a genuine neutrality and stay out of the war, she had to give to both sides, and not merely to one. An embargo on wolfram would mean a break with Germany, because Germany simply wouldn't tolerate it. As for the warships, political considerations would have to be controlling inasmuch as there was not a good case in international law for releasing them; and he hadn't wished to put in writing a decision that would be adverse to us.

Moreover, when I queried the Minister about radio broadcasts from Rome and Berlin reporting that Spain had recognized Morreale, the renegade Italian ex-consul at Málaga, as an agent of the Mussolini puppet government, he admitted that this was true. In response to my protest that this was a violation of assurances he had previously given me, he apologized, I thought very lamely, on the ground that while Spain would not "recognize" the Mussolini regime either *de jure* or *de facto,* it must have "informal relations" with it for the protection of Spanish interests in North Italy.

V

That whole conversation on January 3 was most painful. Spain was obviously yielding to German pressure and procrastinating with us. We would have to exert strong counter-pressure, and not merely by words. The next day, I cabled a full report to the State Department, and also advised it that in my judgment the time had come to seek the approval of our highest military authorities and of the British for a suspension of petroleum shipments to Spain. The Department replied on January 8: 'We fully approve the line you took with Jordana. Your recommendation has been read with interest and is receiving careful consideration. You will be further communicated with in the near future.'

While awaiting the Department's action, I had several conferences with the British Ambassador. He was still dubious about economic sanctions, and argued that if they were applied at all it should not be until after we had effected a successful military landing in France and removed the possibility of a German counterstroke across the Pyrenees into Spain. I argued, on the other hand, that, in order to be of the greatest utility to our war effort, the sanctions should precede any landing of ours in France, especially since their direct effects would not be immediately felt, and the sooner we could cut off wolfram from Germany the better.

I don't know, of course, just what passed, on the subject, between Washington and London, or between the British Foreign Office and the British Embassy in Madrid. I do know that Sir Samuel Hoare changed his attitude shortly after the middle of January. Quite aside from possible instructions to him from London, he was doubtless moved by two remarkable discoveries which we made in Spain at this time and which clinched the argument for immediate application of sanctions. One was the alleged grant to Germany by the Spanish Treasury of a credit of some 425 million pesetas, the greater part of which, according to the Minister of

Industry and Commerce, could be devoted to the purchase of wolfram. The other was a deal, about to be consummated, whereby the owners of the largest wolfram mine in Spain, the "Santa Comba," would sell its entire product, about 120 tons a month, to the Germans.

In the midst of these disclosures, Sir Samuel agreed to a line of action which I recommended to Washington on January 18, and which he presumably recommended at the same time to London. It called for a suspension of petroleum shipments to Spain during the month of February, without publicity and without prior explanation to the Spanish Government. Our thought was that Mr. Smith, our Petroleum Attaché, would simply notify the Spanish Commissioner, General Roldán, of the "inability" of our oil people in the Caribbean to supply the Spanish tankers on their next scheduled date for loading in the Caribbean, February 11–12. Then, when the Foreign Office asked us why, we would merely explain at first that petroleum was extremely precious to the Allies for their war-effort. Later, Mr. Smith would notify General Roldán of our continuing "inability" to supply Spanish tankers on the remaining scheduled dates in February, the 21st and 22nd. By this time, we calculated, the Spanish Government would be getting the "jitters," and the Foreign Office would be prepared to heed our requests and hasten favorable action upon them. Whereupon, petroleum shipments would be quietly resumed, as if nothing had happened. No ultimata, and no publicity. Only quiet, and, we believed, most effective pressure. Meanwhile, the USCC and UKCC would undertake to head off the Santa Comba deal, and the British Ambassador and I would keep pressing Count Jordana.

With this plan, the Department promptly concurred; and we proceeded to put it into effect. I wired Washington on January 22 that Roldán was notified by Smith this morning that authorization cannot be given for tanker loadings on February 11–12; no reasons assigned; because Roldán didn't seem surprised, Smith had impression he must have had some previous inkling of the decision.

As we had expected, the Foreign Minister at once sent for me. He inquired as to the reason for the suspension of the February

11–12 loadings and expressed deep concern. He said the economic situation in Spain would become very serious should the loadings on February 21–22 be also suspended. I informed him our instructions did not convey reasons for the suspension.

On January 27, I saw Count Jordana again and found him in a much more conciliatory mood. Replying to my emphatic protests against the recent wolfram deals, he said it was true that the Germans had pressed Spain for settlement of old financial accounts, but the information from the Minister of Industry and Commerce was erroneous. The Spanish Government had merely agreed that a sum was owing Germany, but it still had to determine how Germany might spend it in Spain. There was nothing in the agreement or other commitment which earmarked any part of the sum for wolfram purchases. He understood that the British and American commercial companies were still purchasing wolfram, and the Spanish Government was resolved to see that most of it went to the United Nations. Insofar as the Santa Comba mine was concerned, he had just assured the British Ambassador that no step would be taken to let the Germans have any of its production pending the conclusion of current negotiations. I seized this opportunity to ask for assurances that until we reached a mutually satisfactory settlement no export licenses would be issued to the Germans for any wolfram.

The Minister said he would do everything in his power to comply with this request and also to furnish me forthwith with a detailed reply to the memorandum of November 18. He must again remind me, he remarked, that there were important private interests in Spain, as doubtless there were in most countries, which would strive to block a settlement in order that they might continue to line their own pockets. To which, I observed that Spain must now have reached a point where national interests should take precedence over private interests and that, while I did not wholly sympathize with the utilitarian philosophy, I thought there was a good deal of truth in Jeremy Bentham's slogan about "the greatest good for the greatest number."

On the next day, January 28, we received authorization from

the Department to notify the competent Spanish authorities that petroleum loadings for February 21–22 were suspended. Mr. Smith so notified General Roldán at once. Our plan was proceeding into its second stage.

At this point, however, a complication arose. The publicity which the British Ambassador and I wished to avoid broke around us in earnest. The BBC began and continued for two weeks a series of broadcasts attacking the Spanish regime of General Franco and asserting that the Allies had shut off petroleum supplies because it was pro-Axis and not meeting our "demands." Sir Samuel was much upset, but seemed to derive a bit of consolation from advices from London that the "leak" which started the BBC off had occurred in Washington. At any rate, the press in both our countries eagerly seized upon the "disclosures" of the BBC and bombarded our respective Governments with questions which shortly brought official statements from Sir Anthony Eden in England and Mr. Cordell Hull in America. They said "yes," the Allies were dissatisfied with Spain's failure to redress our grievances about wolfram, Italian ships, and German agents, and had accordingly suspended all petroleum shipments to Spain. This, of course, was a signal for the extremist press to swing into full action with vitriolic attacks on General Franco and vehement demands for rupture of relations with his Government and even for armed intervention in Spain.

Both the British and American Embassies in Madrid at once appreciated that this publicity which poured into Spain over the radio would hinder rather than help the attainment of our objectives. It could only antagonize the Government with which we had to deal, and reenforce Spanish stubbornness against yielding to "foreign pressure." Both Sir Samuel and I besought our Governments to give no countenance to the campaign and to prevent official agencies from participating in it. I must say that in this respect my British colleague was less successful than I. For while the OWI immediately imposed silence on short-wave broadcasts from America to Spain, the BBC remained full of noise and fury— greatly to Sir Samuel's annoyance and chagrin.

When I next saw the Foreign Minister, on the evening of January 29, his surprise and pain over the suspension of petroleum shipments seemed mild compared with his anger at the publicity. Our people, he said, had no comprehension of Spanish mentality. Attacks from abroad simply aroused resentment and stubbornness. In the present instance they only helped the Germans and deterred a settlement with us. Spain could not, and would not, act under advertised duress. Would I appeal to my Government about the publicity? I did so, and was able to inform Count Jordana on February 3 that Washington thoroughly disapproved of the publicity and intended to deal with Spain through usual diplomatic channels and not over the radio.

On February 3, the Foreign Minister proposed a "plan" for the settlement of pending questions, which, with certain modifications, I reported, the next day, to the State Department: Agreement would be made in advance by the Ministry of Foreign Affairs to (1) prompt release of the Italian warships; (2) prompt release of all but two Italian merchant vessels, which Spain might retain under terms to be agreed upon; (3) pending the outcome of negotiations looking toward an embargo on wolfram, licenses for wolfram exports to Germany would be withheld for at least one month; (4) suppression of the German Consulate in Tangier and expulsion of German espionage and sabotage agents from Spanish Morocco and Tangier, coupled with energetic suppression of espionage and sabotage activities by the Germans in peninsular Spain, and expulsion of agents engaged in such activities; (5) withdrawal from Germany and German-occupied territory of all remaining Spanish soldiers. Following receipt of assurances from the Minister for Foreign Affairs that these arrangements would be carried out, a statement would be made by the Secretary of State, possibly in reply to a question at a press conference. We would then resume shipments of petroleum to Spain.

To this I added that it should be made clear to the Minister that such shipments would probably again be suspended if the commitments were not carried out satisfactorily, or if no satisfactory wolfram agreement was reached, and he should be warned that if they were suspended again the resulting situation would be more serious than that existing at present.

To the whole foregoing "plan" the British Embassy agreed, and I urgently requested Washington's consideration of it. Its acceptance would have served the immediate ends which the British Ambassador and I had in view in recommending, on January 18, the suspension of petroleum shipments for the month of February. We were getting favorable action on all pending questions, except wolfram, and on this the Spaniards were now well aware that we held the trump card.

On February 5, the Foreign Office suggested as a basis for wolfram negotiations that Spain might limit its export of the ore for the year 1944 to perhaps 720 tons, this figure to include 300 tons which had gone to Germany in January. The total amount might be allocated by half- or quarter-years, so that, by counting in the first half-year the 300 tons already exported, only 60 more tons would go to Germany before July 1, and 60 tons a month thereafter. The British Embassy, to which the suggestion was also offered, thought it promised a "drastic limitation" which might be acceptable to us, and I so reported to Washington.

VI

Back came the answer, on February 9, that Jordana's "plan" of February 3 was "unacceptable" and that Washington would insist on an "immediate and complete embargo." And, by way of reenforcing the State Department's resolve, I was instructed two days later to tell the Foreign Minister and the British Ambassador that the United States Government would not resume tanker loadings until a complete and permanent wolfram embargo was imposed, although, perhaps out of deference to the British, it might agree to a compromise on the Italian warships.

So the suspension of petroleum shipments, originally proposed by us for a month, was to be extended indefinitely, as was likewise the wolfram crisis. Spain immediately tightened its already severe restrictions on the use of gasoline, so as to make its small stock on hand last as long as possible. Passenger cars and motorcycles completely disappeared, except as they operated with "gasogeno" contraptions. The number of taxicabs and trucks was reduced by half. Most buses were laid up, and all fishing vessels and farm tractors. Quotas for public works were slashed by over two-thirds.

The Foreign Missions in Spain and the highest officials of the Spanish Government continued to use automobiles and to suffer relatively little inconvenience. The British and ourselves could bring in gasoline from Lisbon or Gibraltar, and the Germans obligingly shared with Axis friends the extra supplies which were imported direct from Germany. Where the shoe pinched hardest was among the Spanish working people—the farmers, the fishermen, the taxi drivers, the truckmen, the chauffeurs. I couldn't help wondering if the persons in America who posed as the greatest "friends of labor" and shouted the loudest for "getting tough with Spain," ever gave a thought to the effects of the actions they demanded upon the Spanish workers.

Following receipt, on February 9, of the Department's rejection of Jordana's plan and its insistence on a complete wolfram embargo, I had a most disturbing conversation with Sir Samuel Hoare, with results which I duly reported to Washington: 'Hoare informs me that the British Government's attitude diverges sharply from ours in the matter of insisting on a total embargo. He emphasizes that in accordance with instructions from his Government he could not sustain with the Foreign Minister any insistence on an "embargo" but would eventually have to admit that Great Britain was prepared to accept a "drastic limitation." It seems absolutely essential, for obvious and imperative reasons, that our two Governments, which embarked jointly upon the present course of action, should maintain a united front until a solution satisfactory to both Governments is attained. I therefore ask that most urgent action be taken so that both Hoare and I will receive the same instructions. I feel I must also again mention the fact that the course on which we are now embarked is not without danger, and it is disturbing that the attitude of the two Allied Governments should be so divergent as to indicate that we may not be proceeding with the full approval of the Combined Chiefs of Staff.'

When I waited upon the Foreign Minister, on February 15, to

acquaint him with our rejection of his proposals and our insistence on the total wolfram embargo, he kept me in conversation two hours and a half straight and had me come back for two hours more in the evening. Backwards and forwards we discussed the wolfram problem, until Count Jordana finally observed that we would never again need to revert to the pros and cons—they had now been completely exhausted. He immensely regretted, he said, to be obliged to go back to the Council of Ministers with what was virtually an ultimatum from us, and he was very pessimistic about the outcome. One remark of his, in the course of the lengthy conversation, tended to confirm my fears about the effects of the divided counsels between ourselves and the British. "The British Ambassador and the British Commercial Attaché [Ellis-Rees]," the Minister said, "had repeatedly stated that the wolfram question was not a closed matter and that the Allied object was to arrive at a *limitation* on the exports to Germany, rather than at a complete embargo."

A week later, February 21–23, Jordana, on his own initiative, made a new proposal, for a "drastic limitation" on wolfram exports in 1944 "to as low, say, as ten percent of the exports in 1943." According to the Minister's figures, the exports in 1943 had totalled 3,100 tons. Ten per cent of this would be 310 tons and inasmuch as 300 tons had already gone out in January, 1944, only ten tons would go during the remainder of the year. Here, it appeared to me as well as to Sir Samuel Hoare, was the basis for a settlement. Spain would save its face by calling it a "drastic limitation," while we would obtain a practical embargo.

On February 28, Count Jordana confirmed the ten per-cent proposal, explaining, however, that his figures for 1943 exports had been questioned by Carceller (the Minister of Industry and Commerce) and were probably too low. Nevertheless, whatever the excess was, it could be distributed over the whole year, and inasmuch as there was no question about the 300 tons which had gone to Germany in January, no more need go before July 1. Arrangements for the second half of 1944 could be made later on the ten per cent basis, when the exact figures for 1943 were available and agreed to.

Meanwhile the Department had wired me that, "on British representations," it would recede from its demand for a permanent embargo and insist only on a six-months' embargo, but this must be "from the date of final agreement with Spain." Consequently I had to tell Jordana that we couldn't accept his latest proposal for an embargo until July 1; it would have to extend to six months from the present, that is, until at least September 1. Jordana said he was not authorized to agree to this, and therefore would have to consult the Cabinet anew—a prospect which he gave indication of dreading.

His premonition was justified. I don't know just what happened at the Cabinet meeting, but according to stories we heard afterwards, Carceller gave no support to Jordana, and others attacked him for being too yielding. At this very time, moreover, the Portuguese Minister of Finance made a visit to Spain, ostensibly for personal reasons, but it would be strange if he didn't see his Spanish colleague and point out that Portugal was granting us no embargo. Simultaneously, too, the Soviet controlled press and radio emitted a particularly virulent lot of lies about Spain, which *PM* dutifully repeated, and which could not have helped us at the Cabinet meeting.

On March 7, 1944, Count Jordana had the unpleasant task of informing me of his defeat in the Council of Ministers. The Council had refused to approve of a continuing embargo until September. More than that, it had withdrawn authorization of the ten per cent proposal. It did want a settlement, however, and for this purpose it had set up a special inter-departmental committee of experts, headed by the Under Secretary of the Foreign Office, Pan de Soraluce, and including representatives of the Ministry of Industry and Commerce.

We soon became aware of friction between Jordana and Carceller. The latter expressed contempt for his colleague's alleged lack of business sense, and gave the impression that he wanted to force him out of the Cabinet. Carceller made direct overtures to the British and to ourselves, indicating that he had an "inside track" with General Franco and that consequently we should negotiate with him rather than with the Foreign Minister. He explained that

as Minister of Industry and Commerce he had earlier promised the
Germans export licenses for 209 tons of wolfram in addition to the
300 tons they had obtained in January. If we would agree to let
the 209 tons go before September 1, he could guarantee us an
embargo on everything else.

The Foreign Minister, on his side, made still another proposal
on March 11. It was, he said, "the very last and maximum concession." Spain would limit wolfram exports, for the year, to 600
tons: 300 tons had gone to Germany in January; no more would
go until June; 60 would go in June; and 240 from July through
December at the rate of 40 a month.

Meanwhile the special Spanish committee of experts, headed by
Pan de Soraluce, began holding meetings which were attended by
Mr. Ackerman from our Embassy, and Mr. Ellis-Rees from the
British. It, too, refused to consider an outright embargo and con-
fined itself to slight variants of the "limitations" proposed by Jor-
dana or Carceller.

VII

The situation in the latter part of March was, indeed, very
complicated. The Spaniards, despite the protracted petroleum famine from which they increasingly suffered, were a unit against meeting our wishes for a permanent or long-term embargo on wolfram,
although they were obviously divided on the extent of the "limitation" they might offer. And, while the State Department (and our
Embassy) was still insisting on an embargo, the British made it
clear to us (and more or less so to the Spaniards) that they wanted
an early settlement and would be willing to accept a mere limitation.
They inclined to favor Carceller's proposal.

We had reached the stage in the wolfram crisis where the immediate issue was really between London and Washington. If the latter
could prevail over the former, then we still stood a good chance of
maintaining the suspension of petroleum shipments until Spain was
forced to agree to a total wolfram embargo. If, on the other hand,
London could prevail over Washington, then we would have to

effect a retreat and a compromise with whatever grace we might be able to command.

The British Ambassador pressed me for a compromise on March 21. At the same time the British Foreign Office indicated to the State Department its willingness to concede to Spain leave to export 100 tons of wolfram to Germany within the next few months, and another 209 tons subsequently. The British argued at length some such compromise on the grounds that they were in constant and urgent need of iron and potash which Spain might deny them if the crisis continued; that Britain lacked pesetas for continuing indefinitely the preemptive purchase of wolfram; and that a friendly, rather than an enforced, agreement with Spain would be the best guarantee against future smuggling of wolfram.

In response to this pressure from London, the Department executed a minor retreat. It instructed me on March 24 to seek an embargo until August 1 instead of September 1. The next day, its retreat was more marked. I could agree to an embargo until July 1, and an export of 209 tons of wolfram afterwards.

On March 30, Sir Samuel Hoare told me that London was not at all satisfied with the extent of Washington's retreat. It must go still farther, and Mr. Churchill was making a personal appeal to Mr. Roosevelt not to insist on an embargo until July 1, but to agree to Spain's exporting 209 tons of wolfram at the rate of 50 a month. Sir Samuel added that personally he didn't think we should reject an earlier proposal of the Spanish Wolfram Committee for exporting 450 tons, in addition to the 300 exported in January.

A few days later, the Department notified me that, "because of the Prime Minister's appeal to the President," an agreement had been reached between Washington and London, whereby we would still insist on an embargo until July 1 but would agree to Spain's sending to Germany 50 tons a month during the second half-year. But this "agreement" proved not to be an agreement. The instructions which Sir Samuel received from London about it contained a provision which was not in mine, that the British reserved the right to urge Washington, if necessary, to accept token shipments before July 1. I wired the Department on April 7: 'It is perfectly evident that there is still no real meeting of minds between London and Washington and that until there is I cannot expect full support from Hoare in the future any more than in the past.'

The next day Count Jordana put up a new proposal to me, which in one respect was well within the authorization now accorded me by the Department. It was to limit exports after July 1 to 40 tons a month instead of 50—a total of 240 tons instead of 300. The fly in the ointment was that we agree to "token" shipment of 60 tons prior to July 1:—15 tons in April, 20 in May, and 25 in June. In the discussion, he admitted a possibility of whittling the 60 tons down to 45 by cutting out an April shipment. Three days later he informed me he had the Cabinet's approval of this proposal. It was distinctly more favorable than what the British had recommended, and I so reported to Washington.

The State Department was not satisfied. Mr. Cordell Hull made a strong personal plea to the British Ambassador in Washington, Lord Halifax, for Britain's standing firm with us for an embargo until July 1. London rejected the plea and supported Jordana's proposal for export of 60 tons before July 1, and 240 tons thereafter. Whereupon, on April 17, Mr. Hull, much piqued, and unusually deferential to "public opinion," told Lord Halifax that the British might conclude a separate agreement with Spain, in which case they could take over from us the supplying of petroleum to Spain. I must say that our Embassy was shocked by the news. Mr. Hull could not have thought through the implications and consequences of the course he was now proposing.

On April 22 Mr. Churchill appealed anew to Mr. Roosevelt, but the State Department still held out for an embargo until July first. On the 24th I made a strenuous protest to Count Jordana against a threatened lifting of the temporary embargo which had been in effect since January, and obtained from him a promise to resubmit to the Council of Ministers our proposal for a continuation of this embargo until July 1 and a limitation of subsequent exports to 50 tons a month.

On the next day, April 25, Mr. Churchill made yet another

approach to the President, indicating to him that unless the United States went along with Great Britain, the latter would conclude an independent agreement with Spain and furnish the petroleum, thereby advertising to the world a cleavage between the English-speaking Allies. The result was a capitulation of the State Department.

On the 26th and 27th I had two revealing conferences with my British colleague, the significance of which may best be indicated by quotations from the memorandum I made of them on the 27th.

I told Sir Samuel Hoare yesterday that I thought there was still a chance of our persuading the Spanish Government to reach a prompt agreement with us on the basis of the renewed proposal I had made on the 24th to Jordana, who had promised to resubmit it to the Cabinet and to inform me of the result as soon as possible. I also said that if the reply was unfavorable I would ask Jordana to arrange an interview for me with Franco. I was sure the existing embargo could meanwhile be maintained and thus carried into May.

Hoare said that a good deal of water had gone over the dam since my conversation on the 24th with Jordana. On the 25th he had received a number of telegrams from London and Washington, explaining that our two Governments had finally reached an agreement to accept the Jordana proposal of April 8th. In reply to my query as to whether he had definite instructions on the matter, he replied that he had, and he outlined them as follows:

We would try to reach an agreement whereby there could be exported to Germany 40 tons of wolfram between now and June 30. If the Spaniards objected to this, we might increase the allowable export to 60 tons between now and June 30, and then 40 tons monthly could be exported thereafter.

I told Hoare that instructions were just coming in to me, but they were not as yet fully decoded. He said he thought I should seek an interview with the Foreign Minister at the earliest possible moment and inform him of the proposal on which agreement had been reached between the British and American Governments. I replied it would seem preferable for me to await a summons from the Foreign Minister and to ascertain whether or not he had been able to obtain authorization from the Spanish Government to conclude an agreement along the lines of the proposal made by me on the 24th. At any rate, I was not in a position to seek an interview with the Foreign Minister until I knew precisely what my latest instructions were.

Just before I left the British Ambassador, Beaulac transmitted to me a telephone message he had just received from Mr. James Dunn in Washington. I told Hoare about it and said it reenforced my conviction that, until the whole matter was clarified further, neither of us should confer with the Foreign Minister. Hoare seemed to be in agreement with this and said he was going home to keep certain engagements he had made there. We separated at 7:15 p.m.

I saw Hoare again this morning. He said that, following our conversation of yesterday afternoon, Jordana had asked to see him and he had therefore called on the Foreign Minister, who appeared greatly agitated at the prospect of facing the Council of Ministers at an adjourned meeting this morning. Jordana wanted some assurance that a wolfram agreement would be quickly reached. Hoare said he told Jordana he had no communication to make, but hoped the Council of Ministers would delay taking any step by which the reaching of an agreement might be imperilled. He counselled him to take Franco aside before the meeting and point out to him the desirability of avoiding discussion of the matter in the Council and of postponing for a week any decision. Hoare said he further told Jordana that he believed Washington and London were disposed, with cooperation of the Spanish Government, to reach an agreement within the next very few days; and, since little difference remained between Spain and the Allies, this should be easy. The British Ambassador said the Minister seemed to be heartened and better prepared to meet the Council of Ministers.

The Spanish Foreign Minister was doubtless "heartened" by this coup of the British Ambassador. But I was not. Sir Samuel had effectually removed any possibility that the Council of Ministers or General Franco might yet yield to renewed American representations for a wolfram embargo until July 1. The only question left for discussion was whether Spain would limit its exports, prior to July 1, to 60 tons or to 40.

I saw Count Jordana on the evening of April 28th and said I was authorized by my Government to reach an agreement with him if Spain would limit its wolfram exports to 20 tons for May and 20 tons for June, and to 40 a month thereafter. He argued at length for 60, or at least 45, tons' export before July 1, but I insisted that the absolute limit was 40, and he finally consented to seek authority to agree to this limit.

The next morning, April 29th, the Foreign Minister informed me he had the needful authority. Consequently, we proceeded on the spot to arrange the terms of a general agreement which were confirmed shortly after by an exchange of letters between Count Jordana and myself and between him and the British Ambassador. The wolfram crisis, at long last, was past.

VIII

The agreement which thus terminated the crisis at the end of April, 1944, provided not only for a drastic limitation of wolfram shipments to Germany "and German occupied territory" and for the resumption of petroleum shipments from America, but also for the release of all but two of the Italian merchant vessels, the submission of the question of the Italian warships to future arbitration, and the closure of the German Consulate at Tangier and expulsion of German agents engaged in sabotage or espionage.

Two questions remained to be settled between ourselves and the British. One was about the nature of the publicity to be given to the agreement. The other was about the supplying of petroleum. On the latter, I informed the Department on April 27th that Hoare cheerfully assumed that the oil shipments, when resumed, would come from British sources and be under British control, while I assumed they would be our special business in the future as in the past and I had told him so. If oil control should pass from American to British hands, any incentive for the British to act jointly with us would disappear, and we would lose basic influence and power not only with the Spanish Government but with the Spanish people.

The Department already thought better of the somewhat impulsive suggestion of Mr. Hull to Lord Halifax that the British might take over the oil control, which, after all, had been predicated on the assumption that Britain alone would make an agreement with Spain. Now that we had joined—and even led—Britain in arranging the final settlement, there was no reason why we should surrender the oil control, and every reason why we should retain it. On May 5 the Department wired me that, according to the British Embassy in Washington, the British Embassy in Madrid had been instructed by cable that the status quo ante on petroleum had been restored. Nevertheless the British sent a "Petroleum Attaché" of their own to Spain, and it took a month or more of pressure on Sir Samuel Hoare at Madrid and on the Foreign Office in London to establish the position of the British Petroleum Attaché as subordinate to that of Mr. Walter Smith and to restore full American direction of the petroleum program.

The question of publicity was resolved more speedily, but, from the standpoint of our Embassy, less satisfactorily. Count Jordana, on the eve of the conclusion of the agreement, had earnestly requested that the American, British, and Spanish Governments collaborate in preparing and in publishing simultaneously a brief official communiqué which should outline the terms of the agreement and express acceptance and appreciation of it. The British agreed to such a procedure, but Mr. Hull notified me on April 28 that, "because of the situation here," he must include in any press release a statement to the effect that we had arrived at this settlement at the request of the British Government whose supply situation in Spain differs from ours.

At Madrid, we thought this a big mistake, for reasons which I set forth in a personal plea to the Secretary on April 29:

I fail to see the necessity for regarding this diplomatic victory as a diplomatic defeat and for giving all the credit to Britain for the considerable achievement resulting from American efforts and initiative. While doubtless we could have achieved more with full British support, still the achievement is notable. While obtaining a complete embargo for three months, we have in fact limited exports of wolfram to Germany during the last 11 months of 1944 to 280 tons, so spaced as to make it almost certain that most of this will never actually be shipped.

I am quite aware that in certain sectors of American public opinion there is a strong feeling against Spain. But from my own examination of the American press, I am convinced that the feeling against Spain has been heightened by systematic propaganda of persons and groups more intent on advancing their own interests and ideologies than in supporting our war effort, and who, in order to advance those ideologies and interests, do not hesitate to jeopardize the war effort.

Our Government, it seems to me, has failed in the opportunities which it has possessed to present the other side of the Spanish picture in order that our people might judge fairly, in the light of real facts, on what advantageous basis, from the point of view of our country, our relations with Spain now rest.

It is very seriously recommended that in any statement which the Department may issue, it present our agreements with Spain on wolfram and the other important matters as an outstanding accomplishment of the United States Government, which, in fact, they are, and that the State Department should reserve for itself full share of the credit for this accomplishment.

Mr. Hull courteously but definitely rejected our plea. 'I appreciate the sincerity and scope of your comments,' he cabled on May 1, 'and in no way do I wish to detract from the results you have obtained. But a compromise with Spain will not be popular, and the fact that it is favorable to us will not allay all criticism. Without detracting from what you have accomplished, I feel I must inform our people that it was at British insistence that we accepted a settlement on a basis short of what we wanted.' The Secretary so acted. I think it was to the delight of my British colleague in Madrid, as it was to the temporary embarrassment of our relations with Spaniards.

The OWI, letting itself go in the realm of prophecy, at once issued instruction to its propaganda "outposts" in all neutral countries to follow up "the facts" about our agreement with Spain with a "hammering" of the dissatisfaction of the American people with it and the unfavorable press reaction in the United States. This curious instruction brought an immediate protest from our Ambassador to Turkey, Mr. Steinhardt. 'Any emphasis placed by OWI on American dissatisfaction with the action taken by the Spaniards will unquestionably cause the Turks to feel that, having discontinued chrome shipments to Germany, they need be in no hurry to make substantial reductions in export of other strategic materials.'

Nor did the press reaction in the United States prove to be just what the OWI prophesied. To be sure, *PM* and Walter Winchell (and the Moscow radio) assailed the agreement, but I can't imagine any kind of agreement with the Spanish Government which they wouldn't have assailed. On the other hand, there was a surprising amount of favorable comment in important American newspapers. For instance, the *Baltimore Sun* said, on May 3: ". . . Bargaining is never easy and it never produces perfect results. But the terms of the new agreement with Spain, published yesterday, show that the main objective has been all but achieved. Spain's shipments of wolfram to Germany are to be reduced to a mere trickle. . . . We can be hard, but not too hard. For the most part we have to depend upon the appreciation, by the neutrals themselves, of the changed position of the opposing powers."

Similarly, the *New York Times* commented on May 3: "Coming on top of Turkey's suspension of chrome exports to Germany, the Spanish cut in tungsten ore shipments represents a new body blow to the German armament industry, in urgent need of both. This blow must be all the more painful because, while Turkey is an ally of Great Britain, Spain has been regarded as an ally of Germany. . . . Once again it has been demonstrated that power is its own best propaganda, able to overcome many ideological differences. But it is also a tribute to the skill and patience of Allied diplomacy that the present result could be brought about without the outright break with Franco urged by a minority which seems to hold that the more enemies the better."

If our State Department (and the OWI) depreciated the significance of our diplomatic victory in Spain, the German Foreign Office didn't. We were confidentially shown, on May 4, a telegram from the Spanish Ambassador in Berlin, reporting that he had just been called to Ribbentrop's office, where the German Under Secretary, "pale with rage," protested in the most violent language against Spain's agreement with the United States and Great Britain. We knew, too, that simultaneously the German Ambassador in Madrid lodged emphatic and angry protests with Count Jordana and also with General Franco.

Nevertheless, the Spanish Government proceeded calmly, and with reasonable despatch, to implement the agreement. On May 6 the Foreign Minister informed me that he was serving written notice on the Germans to quit Tangier, and on the 16th—which happened to be the second anniversary of my arrival in Spain—the swastika shield was ceremoniously removed from the German Consulate.

As for the wolfram part of the agreement, the Spaniards gave us every facility for seeing that it was scrupulously observed and that smuggling was prevented or, if detected, was heavily penalized. Even back in March, 1944, while the temporary embargo was in effect, the Spanish authorities collaborated with an energetic young Embassy officer, Mr. Robert Brandin, whom we detailed, with several of our secret intelligence agents, to keep close watch at the Spanish-French border on illicit movements of wolfram. This watch was intensified in May and systematically extended to all wolfram producing and transport areas.

Smuggling had long been practiced as a fine art in Spain. Amid our grim discussions of ways and means of discovering and combatting the smuggling of wolfram—or of petroleum—we were reminded by one of our staff of a despatch which James Russell Lowell had written to the State Department, A.D. 1878, when he was our Minister in Spain. Opening with solemn formality, it went on to describe an "ingenious" device of a certain M. Fourcarde for smuggling petroleum into Madrid without paying the city entrance-tax.

To this end, [Lowell wrote], M. Fourcarde established his storehouses in the suburbs, and then hiring all the leanest and least mammalian women that could be found, he made good all their physical defects with tin cases filled with petroleum thus giving them what Dr. Johnson would have called the pictorial proportions of Juno. Doubtless he blasphemed the unwise parsimony of Nature in denying to women in general the multitudinous breasts displayed by certain Hindu idols. For some time these seeming milky mothers passed without question into the unsuspecting city and supplied thousands of households with that cheap enlightenment which cynics say is worse than none. Meanwhile M. Fourcarde's pockets swelled in exact proportion to the quaker breastworks of the improvised wetnurses. Could he only have bethought him in time of the *ne quid nimis.* But one fatal day he sent in a damsel whose contours aroused in one of the guardians at the gates the same emotions as those of Maritornes in the bosom of the carrier. With the playful gallantry of a superior he tapped the object of his admiration and—it tinkled. He had "struck oil" unawares. Love shook his wings and fled; Duty entered frowning; and M. Fourcarde's perambulating wells suddenly went dry.

With a gentleman so ingenious the Spanish Government is perhaps justified in being on its guard. Even charity has eyes and ears.

I have the honor to be, Very respectfully, Your obedient servant,
J. R. LOWELL.

In May, 1944, Spain exported the agreed-to twenty tons of wolfram to Germany. It was the first that had gone since January. But when our agents at the border got track of the Germans' smuggling out a few additional tons in May, Spain volunteered to deny to Germany the twenty tons promised for June. Hence from the end of January to the beginning of July, 1944, the Germans obtained from Spain only 28 or 30 tons of the indispensable mineral, and by the latter date our successful landings in Normandy and our heavy bombing of French railways rendered practically inoperative any further bulk shipments to Germany from the Iberian Peninsula. To all intents and purposes, therefore, we did have an almost complete Spanish embargo from January onwards.

This is all the more significant in view of the fact that Portugal continued freely to ship relatively large quotas of wolfram to Germany until June,[1] that Spain until this date received large and important imports from Germany, and that Germany, with plenty of available funds, accumulated in Spain at least 1,300 tons of wolfram which it was not allowed to export. If one adds to the 28 or 30 tons exported from Spain in May the 300 tons which had been exported in January, one gets a total of 328 or 330 tons for the entire year of 1944, as compared with at least 1,200 tons for the year 1943.

Moreover, we and the British were now relieved of the need of

[1] Portugal shipped at least 600 tons to Germany in the first five months of 1944.

spending vast new sums of money on the preemptive purchase of Spanish wolfram. Until the final conclusion of our agreement with Spain at the end of April, we had felt obliged to maintain our competitive buying against the Germans, and down to this time, from the start of such buying in the spring of 1942, we had purchased, altogether, 21,860 tons. From the first of May we could stop buying, and the USCC could prepare to leave Spain and the job it had done so long and so well.

IX

It was natural for the British and particularly for Sir Samuel Hoare to take public credit for the concessions and favors Spain gave us in the spring of 1944. Immediately after the conclusion of the agreement, Sir Samuel flew to England; and Mr. Churchill, in a speech before the House of Commons in May, bestowed fulsome praise upon Spain and General Franco. The effect of this was heightened within Spain by the noticeable contrast between it and the official pronouncement at Washington which indicated that our Government was ashamed of the wolfram agreement and "blamed" the British for it. Our peculiar reluctance to take credit for an important accomplishment which, in conception and broad execution, was principally the result of American initiative and effort, and which was actually achieved in the face of considerable British skepticism and resistance, made it all the easier for the British to take the credit without being challenged.

Certainly Sir Samuel Hoare was quite willing to exploit, for British ends, the widespread impression that, whereas I and my Government had sought to be "tough" with Spain, he and his Government had arranged a fine and mutually advantageous compromise. He flew back to Spain at the end of May, not as hitherto by British plane to Lisbon and thence by Spanish plane to Madrid, but by a very special British plane direct to Madrid. To add to the sensation, he was accompanied by Viscount Knollys, the head of British commercial aviation. The two shortly arranged with the Spanish Government for a weekly British air service between London and Madrid via Lisbon. Likewise, the British concluded an important commercial agreement with Spain, ensuring England not only an increase of iron and potash but also the whole surplus of Spain's citrus fruits.

Spaniards, however, do not lack a sense of humor—or respect for material and moral strength. And I soon perceived that the Foreign Office, and indeed the whole Spanish Government, were quite as ready to extend facilities to us as to our Ally. A week before Sir Samuel's return to Madrid, I resumed negotiations with Count Jordana for the grant of landing rights to American commercial airlines, which had been in abeyance since November when we obtained the rights "in principle." It was now agreed that a technical commission should come over from the United States in July to work out preliminary details with the Spanish commission which had previously been created under the chairmanship of Sr. Gomez Navarro.[1]

Likewise, we resumed negotiations for the removal of the Falange from the "International Institute," which we wanted for our Embassy Chancery. For a time the Minister of Education procrastinated, but the Foreign Minister, after carrying the matter to the Caudillo, finally arranged for us to take possession of the building on July 1.

Meanwhile a change occurred in our Embassy's administration. In March, 1944, in the midst of the wolfram crisis, word came from Washington that our Counselor, Willard Beaulac, was to go as American Ambassador to Paraguay. It filled me with very mingled emotions. On the one hand, I was immensely pleased by the promotion and recognition thus accorded him, which I knew was fully merited. On the other hand, I intensely regretted losing, as my first assistant, a man who had been constantly at my side ever since I arrived in Spain and whom I greatly liked as a friend and highly respected as a wise and forceful adviser. We had a party for him and his wife at the Embassy on March 25, attended by our entire official staff and our Latin-American colleagues, and marked by both congratulations to the guests of honor and regrets for ourselves.

[1] See above, pp. 202–203.

A few days later, Mrs. Beaulac, in company with my wife, who for personal and family reasons wished to make a brief trip home, departed from Madrid for Lisbon, and thence by clipper to the United States.

Beaulac himself stayed on in Madrid until May, after the end of the wolfram crisis and the conclusion of our agreement with Spain. He did so, in part because I wanted and needed his experienced familiar hand in those difficult negotiations, and in part because he had much to do in arranging for the removal of his family and goods to faraway Paraguay.

I must say that the State Department invariably took special pains to provide us, from its depleted roster of Foreign Service Officers, with an exceptionally competent staff in Spain. We were indeed fortunate that in April it selected as Beaulac's successor at Madrid Mr. W. Walton Butterworth. Butterworth, native of New Orleans, graduate of Princeton, Rhodes Scholar at Oxford, and Foreign Service Officer in a variety of posts in England, Canada, and the Far East, had been serving since the spring of 1942 as chief of the USCC for the Iberian peninsula, both Portugal and Spain, and hence he possessed a veteran's knowledge of a most important aspect of Spanish-American relations. At the time of his appointment as Counselor of the Madrid Embassy, he was in Lisbon. Shortly afterwards, he came up to Madrid, and early in May he formally took over from Beaulac. He was destined to remain throughout the last year of my mission in Spain and to carry over into my successor's. He proved to be an outstanding person in every way, vigorous, conscientious, intelligent, clever. Whatever success attended my three years' mission in Spain must be attributed in no slight degree to the wise counsel I had during the first two years from Willard Beaulac and during the third year from Walton Butterworth.

The protracted wolfram crisis had been tiring. When it was past, and Beaulac was preparing finally to leave for America, I decided I would take a brief vacation with my daughter (Mary Elizabeth) and accompany him by a roundabout route to Lisbon. We started off on May 7 and stopped the first night at Salamanca, where we walked about the marvellous plaza (the loveliest in all Spain) and visited the venerable university (comparable in age with Paris and Oxford). The next day we took a vile road past the picturesque castle of Ciudad Rodrigo, over the Portuguese border, and on through the smiling countryside of northern Portugal to Oporto. Here we remained two nights, inspecting the beautifully situated "second city" of Portugal, sampling its famous "port wines," and enjoying the hospitality of the local American consul. From Oporto, we proceeded southward, visiting and being deeply impressed by the fine old halls of the University of Coimbra, and staying over night in the attractive resort of Busaco. Followed two days at Lisbon, where we talked with Ambassador Norweb and met various members of his staff. In taking leave of Beaulac at Lisbon, I couldn't repress a mistiness of the eye. He had shared so intimately in all the cares and worries—and incidental humors—of our critical period in Spain.

My return to Spain was timed so as to enable me to be present at an exchange of wounded war prisoners at Barcelona, scheduled for May 17. As the result of negotiations with the Spanish and the Swiss, it had been arranged for the simultaneous arrival of two Red Cross ships, one bringing some 1,500 German wounded prisoners from the United States, and the other, a like number of British and American prisoners from the German-occupied port of Marseille, and for an ensuing departure of the ships after their passengers had been transferred from one to the other.

So Mary Elizabeth and I left Lisbon on May 13; and after halting to inspect the ancient Roman monuments at Mérida, and stopping overnight in the *parador* at Oropesa, we reached Madrid on Sunday, the 14th. We intended to go on to Barcelona on Tuesday, the 16th, in the Embassy plane, but the weather was so bad for flying that our competent and trusty pilot, Lieutenant John Emmanuel, advised us to go by train instead. For the exchange of prisoners, a considerable number of officials made the trip to Barcelona: the Swiss Minister; representatives of the Spanish Foreign Office and Red Cross; the German Ambassador and some of his staff; several secretaries from the British Embassy; and, for the

Americans, besides myself, Mr. Niles Bond, our "Relief" officer, and Colonel Sharp, our Military Attaché.[1]

I was present at the exchange on the dock at Barcelona on May 17. It was a most moving experience. The German boys looked so gloomy and downcast. It was obvious they expected no joyful homecoming. The American and British boys, on the other hand, were so very cheerful and even gay. Some of them were badly wounded—legs or arms gone, occasionally both; terrible injuries to body or face. Yet as I passed among the American stretcher cases, as among those able to walk, and personally greeted each one, I encountered only typically American smiles and jokes. They were very mindful of one another and of the fellows they had left behind in German prison camps. In these they had been half-starved, though they said they had had decent medical and surgical attention.

The Spanish authorities, on whom devolved the actual management of the transfer, displayed remarkable efficiency and the utmost courtesy. They provided a small army of helpful Spanish Red Cross nurses, and special boxes of chocolate, fruit, soap, etc., for the exchanged prisoners. On the next day the Allied representatives were entertained at luncheon by the Spanish local officials—Captain-General, Civil and Military Governors, Mayor, etc. That night Mary Elizabeth and I left Barcelona by train, and arrived in Madrid on the morning of May 19, just in time to meet Mrs. Hayes at the airport on her return from America.

A tragic event of the exchange of war prisoners was the death of Arthur Yencken, the Counselor of the British Embassy and at the moment, by reason of the Ambassador's absence in England, its Chargé d'Affaires. Despite the very bad weather and the warnings at the airport, he had insisted, at the last moment, on attempting to fly to Barcelona. The plane crashed in the fog-swept mountains, and Yencken and his pilot were instantly killed. We had, of course, seen much of the British Counselor and his hospitable wife, both

[1] We were having at about this time a considerable shift in personnel at the Embassy. Colonel Sharp succeeded Colonel Hohenthal, who had been called to the War Department in Washington and who, like Beaulac, had been a tower of strength to us in difficult days.

officially and socially, and in his untimely passing we all felt a sense of personal loss.

It remains to say a few words concerning American participation in the "Barcelona Fair" in the spring of 1944. Barcelona, as the commercial capital of Spain, had long held an annual "sample fair," at which foreigners as well as Spaniards exhibited samples of manufactured and other products which they wished to sell in the country. The series of these fairs had been interrupted by the Civil War from 1936 to 1939, and when the series was resumed the international war deterred most overseas foreign countries, especially the United States, from participating.

There were, however, numerous Spanish representatives of American business concerns, such as Ford, General Motors, Chrysler, General Electric, Westinghouse, Remington Rand, Tel. and Tel., Baldwin Locomotives, Singer Sewing Machines, Shoe Machinery, etc., who constituted the main constituency of the "American Chamber of Commerce" with headquarters in Barcelona and a flourishing branch in Madrid. These, of course, were particularly anxious to reestablish the profitable business they had once done in Spain, and to this end they urged both our Embassy and the authorities at Washington to expedite requisite exports from the United States and to display samples of them at the Barcelona Fair. We had repeatedly to point out to these Spanish friends of ours that, on account of the war in which we were engaged, most of the commodities they wanted were in extremely short supply in the United States or were not being produced at all. They argued, nevertheless, that it would be excellent advertising for us, as well as for themselves, if we could bring over and exhibit at Barcelona some "samples" of our latest industrial and mechanical developments which would stimulate Spaniards to buy from us after the war was over and our products were generally available.

The Embassy had recommended to Washington in the winter of 1942–1943 a "token" participation of the United States in the 1943 Fair, for propaganda purposes. That was a time when normal avenues of propaganda and advertising were largely closed to us. The Spanish Government was still "non-belligerent," and Spanish imports were almost exclusively from Axis sources. The Spanish press, as a whole, was pro-Axis in tone, and so were the local radio broadcasts. Relatively few American motion pictures were publicly shown, and none of our war pictures. The Embassy then thought that the Barcelona Fair could be utilized as a means for telling our story to large numbers of Spaniards, provided the exhibits were dignified, representative, and well presented, especially inasmuch as what was displayed at Barcelona could subsequently be displayed at local fairs in other Spanish cities. The Swiss specialized in this sort of thing. Why also shouldn't we?

However, our recommendation was then rejected. And we understood and appreciated the reasons. There was, at that time, no agency in the United States equipped and able to take charge of the matter. There was a complete absorption in war production, with rigid control, for purely domestic consumption, of all other production. There was a grave problem of sea transportation.

A year later, in the winter of 1943–1944 the Embassy recommended to Washington that we *not* participate in the Fair scheduled for June, 1944. We had no evidence of any loosening, in the meantime, of wartime restrictions on the export of goods in which Spaniards were most interested, and we no longer felt a need of utilizing the Fair for propaganda purposes. By this time, we had access to the masses (and classes) of Spaniards, for the telling of "our story," through the press, through local broadcasting, through a vastly increased circulation of OWI releases, and through the motion picture theatres, which now showed many more American films than any other country's and a considerable number of our war scenes.

Again, our recommendation was rejected—this time in the opposite direction. Washington, chiefly on OWI prompting, ruled that the United States would participate in the Barcelona Fair of June, 1944, and I was instructed to notify the Spanish Government accordingly. As it turned out, very few samples of American industry were actually made available and shipped to Spain—a quite unrepresentative job-lot—and most of the exhibit was confined to photographs, placards, and books supplied by OWI. Amusingly enough, even this brought a flood of molten lava from certain readily eruptive journals; and certain American publishing houses righteously refused to let any of their books be displayed in "Franco Spain" "alongside of Axis exhibits"—as if the Fair were for Fascists and Nazis rather than for Spaniards.

As a matter of fact, none of the Axis countries had any exhibit at the Barcelona Fair of 1944. The only foreign countries which did participate, besides the United States, were Switzerland, Sweden, and Chile.

As the official representative of a participating nation, I went to Barcelona, as did also the Swiss Minister and the Chilean Ambassador, for the opening of the Fair on June 10, 1944. We were wined and dined, paid military honors, given front seats at the ceremonies, and conducted by guards of honor throughout the spacious and really interesting exhibition-buildings. The gentlemen of the American Chamber of Commerce, being good Spaniards as well as decidedly pro-Ally, had done wonders, with true Spanish art-sense, to make our sparse exhibit appear attractive, and our book display did make a big hit with the crowds. But in comparison with the extensive and truly magnificent industrial exhibit of the Swiss, ours was indeed pitiful.

I tarried in Barcelona for another annual meeting and dinner of our American Chamber of Commerce—my third, and the largest yet—and also for a gala night showing which it sponsored of an American feature film, and for a reception tendered by our Consulate General. Then, on June 13–14, my wife and I, in company with First Secretary George Haering and his wife, motored pleasantly along the Mediterranean through Tarragona, Benicarló, and Valencia, and thence back to Madrid.

With the wolfram crisis a thing of the past, Spain's neutrality was now becoming more markedly "benevolent."

CHAPTER VIII

SPAIN'S BENEVOLENT NEUTRALITY

I

Spain's denial of invaluable wolfram to the Germans from February, 1944, onwards, and its conclusion with us of the favorable agreement of April 29, 1944, did not coincide with any spectacular triumph of Allied arms in Europe. General Franco doubtless appreciated that the offensive in the war as a whole was passing from the Axis to the Allies, and that he had been wise in adopting a policy of neutrality. Yet the concessions he made to us in the early spring of 1944 were in excess of demands of "strict neutrality." They partook of the nature of "benevolent neutrality." The peremptory closing of the consulate at Tangier was an open affront to Germany, and the almost complete shutting off of wolfram exports could only be a major contribution to Germany's eventual military collapse.

These events occurred, let me emphasize, before we had gained any remarkable military success in Europe. The Russians, it is true, were gradually reconquering some of the territory they had previously lost to Germany; they had retaken Kiev in November, 1943, and they retook Odessa in April, 1944. But not until mid-May did they clear the enemy out of the Crimea, and it was July when they recovered Minsk, and could advance toward the Vistula beyond their old frontiers. As for the British and Americans, they had landed in southern Italy in September, 1943, and captured Naples on October 1. But for months afterwards the Germans held them on the "Gustav Line," which was not decisively breached until the Allied success at Monte Cassino in May, 1944, full three weeks after the conclusion of our agreement with Spain. Even then, we had a considerable way to go before reaching Rome; and as yet a landing and offensive by us in France, though much discussed, was a project rather than a reality.

Since the Tehran Conference of Messrs. Roosevelt and Churchill with Marshal Stalin, at the beginning of December, 1943, and the announcement, at the end of that month, of the designation of General Eisenhower as supreme commander of American and British forces in Europe, it was universally expected that some time in the spring of 1944 the Allies would attempt a big landing in France and the establishment in the west of a "Second Front" against Germany. But how successful would such an attempt be? Optimism in the United States and in our Embassy in Madrid was not wholly shared by more disinterested persons, especially military people, on the European Continent. These knew that the Germans still had large and powerful armies in France, that they were steadily strengthening their defenses along the coast, and that they were beginning to direct new "secret weapons"—the rocket bombs—against England with serious results. Of course, the Germans, as well as everybody else, expected us to attempt a landing in France in the spring of 1944, and this fact explains why they accepted Spain's agreement with us with merely verbal protests. They had to keep all their available forces in France to try to ward off the expected invasion.

"D-Day"—the day of our first actual landing on the coast of Normandy—was June 6, 1944.[1] On instructions from Washington, I informed the Spanish Government a few days previously, not about the precise date or place, but about what in general impended, by requesting of Count Jordana two special facilities. One was the evacuation of Allied casualties out of southern France across Catalonia, and from the port of Barcelona. The other was the establishment of Barcelona as a "free port" for the entry and transport of foodstuffs and other supplies for the civilian population in France. To both requests, the Foreign Minister, after consultation with General Franco, readily acceded.

Neither of these facilities was immediately utilized. They would certainly have been highly useful to us if the landing in Normandy had been followed fairly soon, as our military authorities had originally planned, by a landing on the French Mediterranean coast,

[1] Our forces in Italy finally entered Rome two days before, on June 4.

and if this had met with stiff German resistance. Actually, however, matters worked out differently. The invasion of Normandy on June 6, though successful in first instance, and strong enough to withstand desperate German efforts to repel it, made slow progress during the next two months. Not until August did it achieve spectacular and decisive success by flooding out of Normandy in all directions and reaching Paris. Meanwhile, the contemplated landing on the Mediterranean coast between Marseille and Nice was delayed until August 15, and by this time the Germans, who were retiring northward, were in no position to offer serious resistance to it.

In June, 1944, we reached a significant agreement with Spain about another matter. This had to do with the firing of Spanish anti-aircraft guns at Allied planes which, on patrol duty, frequently violated Spanish neutrality by flying over coastal towns in Spanish Morocco and the Canary Islands. Our Chargé at Tangier, Mr. Rives Childs, first made a happy arrangement with General Orgaz, the High Commissioner for Spanish Morocco, whereby our planes might fly over Spanish territorial waters in pursuit of German submarines and our patrol blimps might be blown by adverse winds over Spanish soil without drawing fire from Spanish batteries under the Commissioner's jurisdiction. This arrangement our Embassy succeeded in having ratified by the Foreign and Air Ministers at Madrid and extended to the Canary Islands.

Another matter to which we devoted special attention in June, with considerable success, was the choking off not only of wolfram but of all other supplies to Germany. We obtained a woolen goods embargo until September 1, a temporary embargo on skins, and a practical embargo on olive oil. We could finally have obtained in June the "complete and permanent" embargo on wolfram exports if Washington had agreed to make available to Spain, after the war, certain hydro-electric equipment it greatly needed. At any rate, the Germans were effectually deprived, during their last months in France of all helpful trade with Spain, a situation which their eventual expulsion from France rendered permanent.

Affairs by the end of June were so favorable that, with the

approval of the President and Secretary Hull, I laid plans for finally making my long-deferred visit home "for consultation" as soon as we had duly celebrated "the Fourth" and I had had an opportunity to make a farewell call on General Franco. The 1944 "Fourth of July"—my third in Spain—brought to the Embassy the biggest crowd yet: practically the whole Spanish Foreign Office, the Spanish chiefs of staff, other high Spanish officials, all the Allied and neutral diplomats, numerous representatives of Spanish church, university, society, press, art, etc. It was a beautiful day.

On July 6, by appointment, I had an hour and a quarter's conversation with General Franco at the Pardo, in the presence of Count Jordana and the Baron de las Torres (the official interpreter). I noticed that since my last interview with the Caudillo, in July, 1943, the large autographed photographs of Hitler and Mussolini, which had previously adorned his reception room, had been removed and only the one of Pope Pius XII remained. "Sic transit . . . ," I thought to myself.

We discussed at some length the measures being taken to implement the agreement of April 29th, and I particularly urged that Spain not only intensify its precautions against possible smuggling of wolfram but also, in its own interest and on its own initiative, decline to avail itself of any further token shipments of wolfram such as the agreement of April 29th had authorized. The Caudillo said he was taking the utmost precautions against any illicit or clandestine escape of wolfram to Germany. The considerable German stocks at Irun and other points near the border were being moved a hundred kilometers inland and kept under the strictest guard. Two small vessels attempting to smuggle some of the ore from the Galician coast to Portugal had been apprehended and placed under naval guard, and their captains imprisoned. He was resolved that everything possible should be done to penalize anybody engaged in smuggling or benefiting from it. He imagined the wolfram problem would not plague us or Spain any longer, as he had reliable information, he said, that the French transportation system was now so badly disorganized and broken as to prevent the Germans from bringing any appreciable amount of goods out of the Iberian Peninsula.

The Caudillo talked freely about the war, and expressed interesting opinions. He thought German defeat was assured and would occur within a year. Germans kept telling him that they still had large reserves of munitions and also new and secret weapons which would turn the tide, and that the national morale was very high. He doubted whether the new rocket bombs were doing as much damage in England as the Germans claimed, and he wondered, if the Germans had an abundance of munitions and new weapons, why they didn't use them with some effectiveness in Italy, Normandy, and Russia. He had been told a year before, when our heavy air bombing of Germany started, that the German High Command greatly feared its effect on civilian morale. His latest information on this point was that civilian morale inside Germany, though lowered by the first shock of our blitz, had since risen again. This suggested that the Germans were getting used to it, as the British had done back in 1940–1941, and that air bombardment of itself could not bring a nation to terms. Of course, it might very seriously interfere with production and transport of munitions, and in this way be an extremely important adjunct to military success. He opined that the German General Staff would recognize defeat and wish to stop the war sooner than civilians or fanatical Nazis.

Problems confronting us immediately after the war, he believed, would be more acute than those now facing us. They would include not only feeding people throughout most of Europe, rebuilding towns and rehabilitating the countryside. The gravest problem would be how to prevent civil wars within the various countries. The solution of this, he thought, lay in Allied military occupation of the countries. But if the occupation were too short or too slight, on account of war weariness among Allied peoples, it would be ineffectual. Or if it were too prolonged or too harsh, it would be likely to arouse troublesome opposition in the occupied countries. A happy mean might be military occupation, coupled with a curb on political activities, for a term of five years, pending internal reconstruction and getting a people into the habit of working together.

General Franco did not stress the "menace of communism" as much as in earlier conversations with me. He distinguished between a "disciplined" popular communism within Russia and a "revolutionary" communism of minorities in other countries of Europe. The former, he said, was constructive; the latter, destructive.

He expressed the hope that in our victory we would safeguard Germany against Russia and against German communists. There was, he said, a sizable section of the Nazi party which was fundamentally sympathetic with communism, and he had reliable secret information from Germany that leaders of this section would prefer to have Germany surrender to and be occupied by Russia rather than England and the United States. He also had information that the Japanese were working hard to arrange an understanding and settlement between Germany and Russia, and that this was favored by a part of the Nazi leaders, though opposed by Hitler. He imagined that, in this respect, the majority of Germans were with Hitler. He thought it possible that Russia, after undoing the results of the war of 1914–18 and recovering the territories of the old Russian empire in Europe, might presently turn against Japan and seek to undo the results of the Russo-Japanese War of 1904–05 in the Far East.

He supposed, he said, that the war in the Pacific would last at least a year after the termination of the war in Europe. We could then concentrate our naval and air strength against Japan and sever its communications with the Philippines, the Dutch East Indies and China.

He expressed regret about the impending fate of Finland, Rumania and Poland. He had recently talked, he said, with the Ministers of Finland and Rumania. Each had explained the impossible position of his nation, with Germans, who were heartily disliked, in practical military occupation; with Russians, who were similarly disliked, ready for invasion and occupation; and with terrible civil strife impending between domestic partisans and adversaries of communism.

In conclusion, General Franco charged me to assure President Roosevelt that the United States could count on sincere and continuing cooperation of himself and of Spain.

In taking leave of the Caudillo, I expressed, in Count Jordana's presence, my high appreciation of the latter's constantly helpful efforts in behalf of good relations between our two countries. It was to be the last time I should ever see Count Jordana.

II

On July 8, 1944, I left our Counselor, Mr. Butterworth, in charge of the Embassy, and departed for America. I motored to Gibraltar. After a pleasant call on the British Governor and an interesting conversation with Lord Gort (who had just arrived from Malta), I flew in a navy plane from Gibraltar to Casablanca in the incredibly brief space of an hour. At Casablanca I was delightfully cared for by our naval commander and his aides, and visited by our Consul and the local French officials. Thence, I took off in a big plane of the Army Transport Command at one o'clock in the morning of Monday, July 10, and, after stops at the Azores and in Newfoundland, reached LaGuardia Field in New York at nine o'clock that evening.

My young son, Carroll, who had returned to the United States a year before in order to continue his schooling in his own country, and who would soon be entering the American army, met me at the airport, in company with personal friends of ours, Mr. and Mrs. Robert L. Hoguet. My wife and daughter remained in Spain, and during my absence made a lengthy excursion by motorcar throughout the northwestern provinces.

On July 12 I went on by train from New York to Washington, and during the ensuing three or four weeks I alternated conferences in the Capital with conferences in New York City. I saw Secretary Hull, Under Secretary Stettinius and most of their major associates in the State Department, and likewise various officials of the Departments of War, Agriculture, Commerce, and the Treasury, and representatives of FEA, OWI, OSS, the Board of Civil Aeronautics, and the War Refugee Board. To my personal delight, I found that Willard Beaulac and his wife had not yet left for Paraguay but were still in Washington, and I had the pleasure of seeing them anew, as well as other friends. In New York, too, I saw a number of my

Columbia colleagues, and spent a week-end with Dr. and Mrs. Nicholas Murray Butler at Southampton.

I also saw a number of journalists, including the Overseas' Writers' Club in Washington, and talked with them informally and "off the record." From them, as from all our Government officials, I received only the most courteous and considerate attention. As I wrote Mr. Hull, after my return to Madrid, "the many conversations and conferences in which I participated were extremely helpful to me and to the mission in Spain, and I hope they may have been helpfully informing to you and to the Department."

Until this trip of mine in July, 1944, I had not been in the United States since May, 1942, when the country had first gone on a full war-footing. I expected greater changes in the intervening two and a quarter years than I found. Everything seemed to be about the same as before, except speeded up and "more so." More uniforms everywhere. More congestion, on railways, in hotels, in restaurants. More munition factories. More restrictions on food, clothing, gasoline, etc. More employees in more governmental offices and agencies. But the same firm determination to carry on and win the war, coupled now, it struck me, with a determination not to shirk responsibility for establishing and maintaining future peace. The same idealism, but with it more genuine realism.

The newspapers—and the American people in general—appeared to me a bit over-optimistic about the duration of the war. The Allied breakthrough in Normandy and the following quick advance of our motored forces into Brittany and toward Paris were interpreted as signifying the speedy complete collapse of all enemy resistance not only in France but in Germany also. It was widely assumed, despite warnings of high government officials, that the end would come in Europe by autumn and in the Pacific by midsummer of the next year. Anyone who questioned such predictions was apt to be regarded as lacking in intelligence, if not in patriotism.

I was impressed also by the dearth of solid information about the situation in Spain and the facilities the Spanish Government was affording us. The propaganda of Spanish exiles and of the extremist element in our press had obviously implanted in the American mind a hostile stereotype, in the nature of a caricature, which the silence of our Government had served to confirm. It was not my business or my intention to engage in controversy or to "defend" Spain. In my informal talks with newspaper men, I was interested only in presenting unadorned facts and letting them speak for themselves. I must say I found these men, without exception, anxious to get at the truth and respectful of the candor with which I invariably spoke.

Persons in the State Department encouraged me—and also Mr. Beaulac—to participate in these "off-the-record" conversations. The same persons cooperated with Messrs. Ernest Lindley and Edward Weintal, of the staff of *Newsweek*, who wished to write an article on our Spanish policy, by furnishing them with certain documents from the Department's files. I knew before I returned to Spain that some such article was contemplated, but did not know what was going into it and I read no part of it until after its publication in *Harper's Magazine* in December, 1944.

While I was still in the United States, and at the moment stopping in New York, I was grievously shocked to read in the evening newspapers of August 3 of the sudden death of Count Jordana at San Sebastian, where he had recently arrived for the usual summer sojourn of the Spanish Foreign Office. I at once cabled condolences to Countess Jordana and to General Franco. Later I learned that the Foreign Minister had suffered a fall while on a hunting party, but that he had insisted upon treating it lightly and on making the scheduled trip to his beloved San Sebastian. The immediate cause of death was a thrombosis.

During the almost two years of official and personal contacts with Jordana, from September, 1942, to July, 1944, I had come to know him well and to feel for him no little respect and real personal affection. He was an honest and a kindly man. What he lacked in brilliance and daring, he made up for in pertinacity. And, though a Spanish patriot above everything else, he was unmistakably pro-Ally, especially pro-American, in personal attitude and public policy. It was indeed a godsend that he was Spain's Foreign Minister in the critical period of 1942–1943. On the day of his funeral,

August 5, I read, again in the New York newspapers, with special satisfaction, an official communication from the State Department expressing the "great regret of officials of this Government" and re-counting major occasions on which his actions had been particularly helpful to us. It was due and just.

A week afterwards, when I was once more in Washington, news came that General Franco was appointing as Count Jordana's suc-cessor Señor José Felix de Lequerica, who had been Spanish Ambas-sador to France since 1939, and as such had latterly been closely asso-ciated with the regime of Pétain and Laval at Vichy. This fact, to-gether with stories about Lequerica's alleged pro-Axis sympathies in 1940, caused considerable uneasiness in the State Department and some foreboding in me as to our future relations with him. Al-though I couldn't quite bring myself to believe that any Spanish Foreign Minister would try, at this late date, to reverse Count Jor-dana's policy, I was very curious to discover first-hand, and as soon as possible, what manner of man we would now have to deal with. Arrangements were speeded up for my return to Spain.

I took off from LaGuardia Field in New York, in an A.T.C. plane, on the afternoon of August 16, 1944, and after the usual stops at Newfoundland and the Azores arrived at Casablanca on the afternoon of the next day. On August 18 Lieutenant Sheppard of our Naval Commander's Staff in Casablanca motored me to the border of Spanish Morocco, where I was met by officials of the Spanish Government and our Chargé at Tangier, Mr. Rives Childs, and taken in the latter's car to a sumptuous luncheon in Larache and thence to our Legation in Tangier. The luncheon was given by the Spanish Military Governor of that district, a Moor himself, and on my left, among the guests, was the son of that famous old Moorish chieftain and brigand, Raisuli, concerning whom President Theodore Roosevelt years ago had addressed to the Sultan of Morocco the laconic ultimatum, "Perdicaris alive or Raisuli dead."

At Tangier, I was most hospitably received by Mr. and Mrs. Childs. At dinner in their attractive Legation, I met several mem-bers of the American staff and also the veteran British Consul-General, Mr. Gascoigne, and afterwards, in company with Mr.

Childs, I paid courtesy calls on the local Spanish officials, including the High Commissioner of Spanish Morocco, General Orgaz. My secretary, Michael George, had been vacationing in Tangier, and with him I took passage on the Spanish Iberia plane on August 19. In two hours we flew over the Strait of Gibraltar and halted at Sevilla. In another two hours we were in Madrid.

Then, after a few days at the Embassy, "catching up" on current business, holding conferences and taking needful action, I went on, with my wife and daughter, to San Sebastian. We arrived in the "summer capital" on August 25.

III

The American and indeed the whole diplomatic "lay-out" at San Sebastian was quite different in August, 1944, from what it had been in the summer of 1943. In the meantime, the State Department had accepted recommendations which the Embassy had long been urging for the establishment [1] at San Sebastian of a regular American consulate, where we would have adequate offices and security. Consequently, this year, unlike the year before, we were enabled to transact our business outside of hotel rooms and to utilize the services of a local consular staff (headed by an experienced Foreign Service Officer, Mr. Willard Galbraith) and also of officers and clerks temporarily transferred from Madrid. From August 1, when the Foreign Office removed to San Sebastian, until September 15, when it returned to Madrid, it was constantly attended and reported upon by a most sagacious and inquiring First Secretary of the Embassy, Mr. Fayette Flexer. While I was at San Sebastian, he was my right-hand man; and by means of the secret codes we were able, this year, to communicate immediately and safely from San Sebastian to Madrid and to Washington.

This year, too, the British had a large building on the outskirts of San Sebastian, where Sir Samuel Hoare and Lady Maud were

---

[1] It was really a "reestablishment," inasmuch as in days of the Spanish Monarchy, the United States had had a consulate at San Sebastian. There certainly should be one there all the time.

residing, besides offices in town; and the French Mission was occupying a commodious villa. On the other hand, Axis diplomats were
few and inconspicuous. The Japanese Minister made no appearance,
at least in public. The Italian Ambassador, who came for only a
week, was now, of course, on the Allied side. And the satellite Ministers of Rumania, Bulgaria, and Croatia were keeping away from
the Germans and seeking contacts with us. The first of these I received in San Sebastian; the second, after my return to Madrid.

The Germans were practically isolated, and notoriously divided.
The Nazi "stalwarts" in their Embassy, headed by the Counselor,
von Bibra, were arrayed against the Ambassador, Dieckhoff. Apparently, they got the upper hand, for, shortly after my arrival in San
Sebastian, Dieckhoff received peremptory orders to report at once
in Berlin. With his wife and two or three aides, he left Spain in such
a hurry that he didn't even say goodbye to the Foreign Minister or
to the Caudillo. Off he winged for Germany at the end of August,
the third and last of Hitler's Ambassadors I was to see. Henceforth
there was no German Ambassador in Spain, only a Chargé d'Affaires.

I had arrived in San Sebastian on August 25, 1944. The next
morning I had my first interview with the new Foreign Minister.
I found him extremely affable and interesting. In most respects, he
presented quite a contrast to his predecessor. Lequerica was a
Basque, a native of Bilbao. He was a large man physically, and
mentally very alert and quick. He did not belong to either the
nobility or the army class, but rather to the industrial and financial
bourgeoisie of which he was a conspicuous and wealthy member.
He was essentially a "politico," and under the Constitutional Monarchy had been an elected member of the Cortes and a lieutenant
of the Conservative leader Maura. He was not a Falangist and took
no pains to conceal his dislike for the "Party." He was a Monarchist, of "liberal" rather than "Traditionalist" affiliation, although
during the Spanish Civil War he had adhered to the "Nationalist"
cause and become a supporter of General Franco.

For five years since, from 1939 to 1944, Lequerica had resided
outside of Spain as Ambassador to France, and at an earlier period

in his life he had lived in England and studied at the London School of Economics. He knew a good deal of history and of the world at large. He was a bachelor who enjoyed good food and had numerous hobbies. He spoke English, in addition to French and his native Spanish, and my conversations with him were in English, without aid or presence of an interpreter. He was quite informal, and reminded me much more of an American business-man than of a typical Spaniard. I felt, at my first meeting with him, that he would adjust himself to changing circumstances readily and vigorously. The very fact that he had been associated for four years with Vichy and was reputed to have been pro-Axis, at least in 1940–1941, was likely, I reasoned, to render him all the more anxious to cooperate with us now that our arms were triumphing in France.

At the first meeting on August 26, after preliminary interchange of greetings, I expressed anew to the Minister my deep regret at the death of his distinguished predecessor whom I had seen for the last time in company with the Caudillo when I called on the latter at the Pardo on July 6, on the eve of my departure for the United States. I said I had always felt about Count Jordana that, while he was most careful not to sacrifice any Spanish interest, he was a real and respected friend of myself and my country. I naturally assumed that Señor Lequerica would continue and develop Count Jordana's policy and would do so with greater promptitude and success by reason of the greater opportunity and greater need now manifest. The Minister replied that I could count absolutely on his pursuing just such a policy, and particularly he wished to draw Spain much closer to the United States and Great Britain.

At his request, I spoke briefly of my trip to the United States. From it, I said, I had derived certain definite impressions. On the one hand, there was evident an underlying popular regard for Spain as a country and for the Spanish people. On the other hand, there was a practically universal conviction that the Spanish Government had not moved fast enough in adjusting its foreign and domestic policies to the rapidly changing military situation throughout the world. I frankly stated that the American people did not like the Falange and did not understand why this essentially Fascist organization was maintained and upheld in Spain at the very time when Fascism was rapidly disappearing everywhere else in the world.

I said I was sure the United States Government had no wish to interfere in the internal affairs of Spain and no intention of interfering, but the Minister, and the Caudillo likewise, should not harbor any illusion that the American people were sympathetic with the Falange. Furthermore, the American people at large did not understand why, in the face of the rapidly approaching complete defeat of Germany, the Spanish Government did not align itself with the United States and Great Britain in every respect short of active participation in the war. Some of us could understand why, back in 1940 and 1941, Spain might have felt obliged to pursue an opportunist policy of benevolent neutrality towards Germany, but no American could understand why, during the past six months at least, Spain should adhere to a legalistic neutrality when it should so obviously, in the light of military developments, be benevolently neutral toward the Allies. Spain, in many respects, was a more important country than Switzerland, Sweden, Portugal or Turkey, yet its policy, I feared, was lagging behind these countries. The Minister said he was glad to have my frank statements, that he himself felt there was need of quicker and more effective reorientation of Spanish foreign policy. He expected, he said, to collaborate closely with the British Ambassador and with myself.

I said I had a number of specific matters to take up with him, involving what I hoped would be the first steps towards effective implementation of the policy he was championing for Spain. I appreciated that this first interview with him was not the occasion for detailing all of them. There were two or three, however, of peculiarly pressing character, which, with his permission, I would present now, leaving the others for later discussion.

I brought up the subject of the press censorship in Spain, and recounted to him the specific complaints about its arbitrariness and partiality with which the chief correspondents of the A.P. and the U.P. in Spain had just furnished me. If this sort of thing continued, I said, the American press could justifiably conclude that the Spanish Government was trying to keep the Americans in ignorance of developments within Spain. The Minister said he was quite aware of this difficulty. He had already received the leading correspondents of the A.P. and U.P. and was convinced they had been discriminated against. He had accordingly given orders for a drastic liberalizing of the censorship. He did not want unfair or malicious reports going out about internal affairs, but he could see no reason why our correspondents should not report freely and fully on the progress of the war, and on developments within Spain.

I also took up with Lequerica, in this first interview, the matter of French-Spanish relations. I asked him if Spain was withdrawing recognition of the Pétain Vichy regime. Two days before, he said, he had informed the Spanish Chargé at Vichy and also the Spanish Legation at Bern, for communication to Marshal Pétain, that, in view of changed circumstances and the force employed by the Germans against the Marshal, Spain could no longer have diplomatic relations with the Vichy Government, now allegedly at Belfort, and that all Spanish diplomats accredited to it were to return immediately to Spain. He had also informed M. Piétri of the decision taken, with the result that the latter, with the approval of the Spanish Foreign Office, had issued a press release stating that his mission in Spain was at an end.

I said this raised an interesting point, inasmuch as I had noted in M. Piétri's statement a clause to the effect that while his mission was terminated he would continue temporarily to protect French interests in Spain. I said it seemed to me that this responsibility should pass automatically to M. Jacques Truelle, the official representative of the French Committee of National Liberation, with whom Spain already had de facto diplomatic dealings about all matters affecting French North Africa, which should now be extended to cover metropolitan France.

The Minister said he expected henceforth to deal exclusively with M. Truelle about all French interests. The day before, Truelle had brought him a statement to this effect, which the Minister had approved and which consequently appeared in this morning's newspapers. Piétri, he added, had been a close personal friend of his for many years, and had routed him out of bed at two o'clock this morning to protest against the publication of any statement by Truelle. The Minister had plainly informed Piétri at that "ungodly hour" that he would not halt the publication of the statement and that henceforth the Spanish Government would deal officially with Truelle and not with Piétri.

In conclusion, I requested the Minister to arrange an interview for me with General Franco, so that I might report to him on my trip to America and discuss with him the current international situation. Señor Lequerica said he would get in touch with the Caudillo at once by telephone, and seek an interview for me at the earliest possible date.

General Franco was vacationing at the time in Galicia. It was promptly arranged, however, that as soon as he returned to Madrid he would receive me at the Pardo. The date was fixed for September 11.

The brief time I actually spent at San Sebastian in 1944, at the end of August and the beginning of September, was packed full with interesting and important developments.

It was the time when the Germans were finally withdrawing their forces from along Spain's Pyrenean frontier, and when our armies were making advances in France from Normandy and the Mediterranean coast. Paris was liberated on August 25. A major offensive was started in the Marne valley on August 28. Toulon was occupied on August 28. Brussels and Antwerp were entered on September 4. A first incursion onto western German soil occurred on September 11. Simultaneously, the tide of battle in the East rolled at quickening tempo toward Germany. The Russians outflanked Warsaw on August 22. Rumania deserted the Axis and joined the Allies on August 23. Finland quit the war on September 4.

The Spanish Foreign Minister moved with despatch, during these days, to adjust Spain's international relations to the changing military situation. He not only practically abolished the censorship on our press correspondents and expedited the transfer of French representation from Vichy to General de Gaulle. He sent for, and officially received, the Chiefs of Mission of the various "occupied" countries—Holland, Belgium, Norway, Poland, Czechoslovakia,

Greece, and Yugoslavia. He issued, in collaboration with the Ministry of Marine, instructions for the internment of German ships which sought refuge in the Spanish ports of Pasajes and Bilbao on the Bay of Biscay. He also gave earnest attention to a variety of important requests which in a series of interviews I presented. What these were, I shall here merely mention. What happened to them will be detailed later.

First, we wanted Spain to cut the one remaining link the Germans still had with the Iberian peninsula, the Lufthansa air service from Stuttgart to Barcelona, Madrid and Lisbon.

Second, we wanted Spain to give assurances that it would not receive or harbor Axis "war criminals," or provide a haven for looted property.

Third, we wanted Spain to expel or intern German agents.

Fourth, we wanted Spain to conclude a definite air agreement with us.

Fifth, we wanted direct radio-telegraphic communication between Spain and the United States.

Sixth, we wanted a just settlement of long-standing difficulties between the Spanish Government and the American-owned Spanish Telephone Company.

Seventh, we wanted the release of the Italian warships which, following the agreement of April 29, and in accordance with it, had remained interned in the Balearic Islands.

IV

San Sebastian is only a half-hour's drive from the "International Bridge" at Irun, which separates Spain from France. A year before, in August, 1943, Mr. Beaulac and I had motored up to the Bridge and seen on its far side detachments of German soldiers and frowning German artillery. To the query of a Spanish guard on the near side of the Bridge whether we wished to cross, Beaulac had said: "Not now, thanks; but next year we will."

And now, a year later almost to the day, I crossed the "International Bridge," though without Beaulac. This memorable excursion on Sunday afternoon, August 27, 1944, marked the first official visit of Allied representatives from Spain to liberated France. It was arranged by the French Mission, and consisted of a little cavalcade of three motor cars, with an escort of French "Maquis" on motor cycles. One car carried the French Minister, M. Truelle, with members of his staff and two Spanish officials. In the second rode the British Ambassador, Sir Samuel Hoare, with his Military Attaché and a Secretary. I was in the third, with Fayette Flexer, Mgr. Boyer-Mas, and Michael George.

Over the Bridge we passed, receiving Spanish salutes at one end, and *French* at the other. The swastikas and the Germans were gone. On we went, through Hendaye and St. Jeane de Luz, to Biarritz. The road was lined with cheering crowds of French people—men, women, and children, peasants and townsfolk, priests and nuns, wounded veterans and "resistance" youths. Where all the American and British flags came from, I don't know, but they were everywhere, and occasionally, too, a Russian flag. Heaps of flowers were tossed into our path and through the car windows, and when we were halted by the press of people, babies were handed in to be kissed.

On arriving at the townhall in Biarritz, we passed in review a company of Maquis, ranging in age from 16 to 60, in an odd assortment of improvised uniforms and with every sort of weapon from a machine gun to a pitchfork, but all looking very soldierly. The Mayor greeted and led us into the building, where brief speeches were made by Sir Samuel and myself, and toasts were drunk in real French champagne. From chats with the Mayor and several Maquis, I learned something of the general situation in southwest France and of the urgent need for emergency food supplies and also for arms with which to overcome comparatively large German forces still in the vicinity of Bordeaux.

As soon as we were back in San Sebastian, I began arranging with the French Mission for release to it of American food supplies then at Cadiz, and with the Spanish authorities for their free transport *via* Barcelona to southern France. It took time to complete the arrangements, but eventually the food got over the Pyrenees and helped to relieve the almost famine conditions there prevailing.

At the time, the Allied High Command paid little attention to southern France and the Pyrenean border. It was concentrating its efforts further north or further east along direct routes toward Germany itself. This left "pockets" of German armed forces, especially on the western coast, which the poorly armed local French forces could not reduce. It also left much of southern France in a state of virtual anarchy. From August to November, this region had only slight and slow communication with Paris, and was in the hands, not of regular officials of the de Gaulle Government, but of self-constituted and frequently violent groups of Maquis. These were, of course, the militants of the French underground, who had done a splendid job against the Germans but who tended to regard as "collaborationists" those fellow Frenchmen that were less militant than themselves and to treat them pretty roughly. Some of the Maquis—though not all—were Communists, and these, being better organized and the most militant, practically exercised dictatorships in such cities as Toulouse, Carcassonne, and Perpignan, and arbitrarily put a considerable number of persons to death.

Relatively few disorders occurred in the western sector of southern France adjoining the Pyrenees—the sector including the *Départements* of Landes, Gers, Basses and Hautes Pyrenées. But in the central and eastern sectors, Communist influence was stronger, and disorders more common. Here, too, were congregated several thousand Spanish (chiefly Catalan) Republican exiles, many of whom were Communist or Anarchist. These had joined the Maquis and given valorous aid in clearing the French Pyrenean area of Germans. But once this was accomplished they were less intent upon continuing the fight northward against our Axis enemy than upon enlisting French Maquis support for incursions of their own southward against Franco Spain.

The Communist-controlled radio at Toulouse, echoing the radio at Moscow, broadcast a series of tirades against General Franco and his Government and such sensational stories as the following: There were uprisings in Spain. "Loyalist" armed forces were operating in Estramadura and Asturias, and were in possession of Málaga. There were riots at Barcelona, where 1,500 were slain in street fighting, and at Bilbao and Sevilla. Armies of Spanish exiles were

crossing the Pyrenees and making rapid progress in Catalonia and
Aragon. General Franco recognized that the "jig was up," and was
hurrying to the Pyrenees to arrange terms of surrender with representatives of the "Spanish Government in Exile" (which the Republican Maura, at Paris, claimed he was to head). Meanwhile, still
according to the Communist broadcasts, Spain was shipping quantities of petroleum, arms, and foodstuffs to the beleaguered German
garrisons at La Rochelle and other places on the coast of France.

From such Toulouse broadcasts, the "news" reached London,
and thence was transmitted by cable or radio to New York. Presently, staid conservative newspapers in Britain and America were
carrying columns of what amounted to Communist propaganda
about Spain. And the extremist press outdid itself, still regaling
readers at the end of October with "facts" of Spain's continuing
huge war exports to Germany.

During the two weeks I was in San Sebastian and the following
two months in Madrid, everybody in Spain knew about troubles in
southern France. But the reported troubles in Spain were quite
unknown to anyone in the country during the period. There were
absolutely no uprisings or riots or disorders in any city. With the
exception of a few parcels carried by the Lufthansa commercial
airline, no supplies of any sort left Spain for Germany. Even if the
Spaniards had wished to send supplies, there was now no means of
doing so. The Allies held the intervening roads and railways across
France. There may possibly have been some smuggling of supplies
by boat from Galicia or across the Bay of Biscay to beleaguered
German garrisons on the French coast, but if so it must have been
extremely slight, for by this time the whole coast was being blockaded and patrolled by the British.

The single grain of truth in the Communist-inspired news-
stories was the incursion of Spanish Maquis over the Pyrenees. A
few hundred of these did attempt to get over and to incite popular
uprisings in Catalonia and Aragon. They didn't get far, however,
and they failed utterly to enlist recruits on Spanish soil. They only
managed to be killed or taken prisoner or to escape back to France
with some cattle and sheep pilfered from peaceable peasants. The

reaction within Spain was, at first, one of alarm and fear; then, of annoyance and disgust, and finally, of relief. This was not confined to the Government and its supporters. It was shared by the majority of "Leftists," who were equally opposed to any resumption of civil war. At least temporarily, the border-raids strengthened, rather than weakened, the Franco regime. Eventually the raids ceased altogether, as the Spanish frontier guards were reenforced by regular troops, and as conditions on the French side became more orderly. By November, General de Gaulle had obtained a measure of control in the South and incidentally deprived the Communists of their radio station at Toulouse.

V

Meanwhile, on September 9, 1944, I returned from San Sebastian to Madrid, in order to keep the appointment with General Franco at the Pardo on the 11th. On this occasion, in company with the Foreign Minister and the official interpreter (Baron de las Torres), I was with the Caudillo an hour and a half, and he appeared in especially good health and spirits. I repeated to him substantially what I had said to Señor Lequerica on August 26 [1] concerning my trip to the United States and the impressions I gathered from it. I then specified several matters on which we hoped Spain would take action in the near future as a "benevolent neutral."

First, there was the matter of German commercial airline service to and from Spain. In view of the fact that France and northern Italy and the intervening Mediterranean were now a theatre of Allied military operations, we felt, I said, that Spain should not permit itself to be used as a base for any German planes flying over this theatre and carrying questionable German passengers and information. A year ago we had requested Spain to establish an airline of its own over France to Switzerland, and I knew that Count Jordana would have complied with that request had not the German Government positively refused to allow Spanish planes to fly over France, which was then a German military theatre. Why, now, for

[1] See above, pp. 251–252.

a similar reason, should not the German planes be stopped by Spain? General Franco replied that he and his Foreign Minister had been discussing this very matter the hour previously and that they were to continue discussion of it during the afternoon. He expected ways and means would be found of complying with our request.

Second, I said, my Government hoped and expected he would see fit to give speedy public notice that Spain would refuse to receive any Axis leaders, military or civilian, who might seek refuge here, and would take effective steps to implement the notice. It would be a most practicable guarantee against future embarrassing demands upon Spain from the Allies, and it would be something which, if now volunteered by Spain, would redound to its benefit in the post-war period. General Franco said that, according to his best knowledge, no Axis leaders contemplated seeking refuge in Spain. Certainly none had arrived to date and he imagined they would be killed off by suicide or assassination or taken captive by us before they could ever get away from Germany or North Italy. He didn't think the matter very pressing for Spain. I expressed dissent from this view, and said I feared Spain might presently be faced with a most embarrassing *fait accompli*. The action already taken by Sweden, according to information I had just received, might be more foresighted. He asked me about the Swedish action and I told him that Sweden had declared it would not receive Axis leaders, and to implement this declaration it was preparing detailed instructions to the Swedish army, navy, police, coast guards and customs officials. The Caudillo said this was very interesting and he would study the matter jointly with the Foreign Minister.

There was still another matter, I continued, to which I would call attention. Already Señor Lequerica had taken steps, no doubt with the Caudillo's approval, to accord recognition to the French Provisional Government of General de Gaulle and to resume full diplomatic relations with the representatives of nations now being liberated—Belgium, the Netherlands, Norway, Poland, Czechoslovakia, Yugoslavia, and Greece. General Franco said I was quite right; that was exactly what Spain was doing. I said I believed it excellent, but I would suggest, as a further important step, the rupture, in the near future, of Spain's diplomatic relations with Japan and its puppets of Manchukuo and Nanking China. The war in Europe would be over in the near future. The war against Japan would probably last another year. Spain had important interests in the Philippines which had not been respected by the Japanese. Moreover, when the war was over the independence of the Philippines would be assured, and thus there would be another member of the family of Spanish-speaking nations in the world. Spain, I felt sure, would wish by some impressive gesture to evince its solidarity with the Philippine Commonwealth and the United States in their joint struggle against Japan. Besides, I would recall the remarks which the Caudillo had made to me a year ago about Japan and about Spain's sympathy with the United States in the war of the Pacific.

The Caudillo said he would repeat, with all the emphasis at his command, what he had said to me a year ago about Japan. I could be assured, and my Government likewise, that his sympathies and those of all Spain were solidly with the United States in the war against Japan. He did not like or trust the Japanese and he would be quite prepared at the right moment to rupture diplomatic relations with Japan. Over a year ago he had flatly turned down the third petition of the Japanese Government to raise its Legation at Madrid to an Embassy, and since then he had on two occasions threatened the Japanese Minister with the rupture of diplomatic relations and the refusal of Spain to continue to represent Japanese interests anywhere abroad: once, when he heard of the treatment of certain Catholic bishops in the Philippines and Guam, and the second time when he heard of attacks on Spanish citizens and property in the Philippines. On each of the two occasions the Japanese had promised redress. He was by no means sure it had been forthcoming, and he wanted me to know that the possibility of a rupture of Spanish relations with Japan was constantly in his mind. He wished further to state that he had the highest possible opinion of the fair way in which the United States had always treated Spanish citizens and Spanish interests in the Philippines throughout the whole period of American occupation.

I thanked General Franco for what he had just said, and we then discussed the long-standing questions between the Spanish Government and the American-owned Telephone Company. He assented to my suggestion that the Government name an official representative or commission with full power to negotiate a settlement with the Company. He was quite emphatic that Spain needed more, rather than fewer, American investments, and that they must be treated fairly and honorably.

At the end of the conversation, General Franco remarked upon our military campaign in France and Belgium. It was magnificent, he said. He believed that Generals Patton and Bradley would go down in history as two of the greatest generals the Second World War had produced. He felt very happy, he said, about our success. It was a great relief to Spain, which was thereby finally freed from the grave fear of foreign invasion that had haunted it for almost five years. Moreover, Spain could rejoice that France was now being happily liberated and restored, in concert with the United States and Great Britain, to its traditional position as a bulwark of western civilization. Spain, which had been through harrowing experiences for eight years past, could henceforth breathe more easily. I took leave of the Caudillo at two o'clock in the afternoon, and returned to the Embassy for what, even for Spain, was a late luncheon.

Two days after this interview with General Franco, I addressed a note to the Foreign Minister, in accordance with instructions from Washington, inviting Spain to participate in the International Conference on Civil Aviation, scheduled to open in Chicago on November 1, 1944. Señor Lequerica informed me on September 22 that Spain gladly accepted the invitation and would send to the Conference a strong delegation representing the Foreign Office, the Air Ministry, and the Ministry of Industry and Commerce.

On this same date, September 22, likewise on instructions from Washington, I conveyed to the Foreign Minister the United States Government's gratitude for the friendly and hospitable reception accorded by the Spanish Government to the American technical commission which had visited Spain in July in order to obtain needful data preliminary to any implementing of the landing rights for American commercial airlines that Spain had granted us "in principle" in November, 1943.[1] I explained that my Government was

[1] See above, pp. 167, 202–203.

now prepared to negotiate a definite air agreement with Spain, on a reciprocal basis, and that we would like provision in it for three American air routes: (1) from New York to Lisbon, Madrid, Barcelona, Marseille, and points beyond, and return; (2) from New York to Lisbon, Madrid, Algiers, and points beyond, and return; and (3) from New York to South America, West Africa, Rio de Oro, Sevilla, Madrid, Paris, and return. The Minister said he was most sympathetic with our proposal and would do everything in his power to expedite the conclusion of a bilateral air agreement. Accordingly, on September 28, we submitted a tentative draft. This was acknowledged by the Foreign Minister on October 3, and served as the basis for ensuing detailed negotiations which were most skillfully handled, on our side, by Mr. George Haering, First Secretary of the Embassy, and which proceeded apace with full Spanish cooperation and without serious hitch.

Simultaneously, distinct progress was made in meeting other important desires of ours. On the subject of "war criminals," the Foreign Minister gave me assurances on September 28. As a result of discussion between himself and General Franco, he said, I could inform my Government that if the Allied Powers formally adjudged a given person to be a war criminal and if he sought refuge in Spain, the Spanish Government would interpose no obstacle to delivering him to justice outside of Spain.

Already the thousand or more German guards, soldiers, and nurses who entered Spain in August at the time of the general German withdrawal from southern France, had been expeditiously interned in the camp at Miranda de Ebro. Moreover, a considerable number of German agents, against whose presence in Spain the British and ourselves had complained to Lequerica, were arrested, and either sent home on the Lufthansa plane from Barcelona or interned at Miranda. Though stories were current that this or that top Nazi or Fascist—Himmler or Ribbentrop, even Mussolini or Hitler—was on the way to Spain, or had already arrived, none of these appeared. It would in fact have been impossible for any such persons to enter the country without being detected by one or another of the Allied intelligence services or by some Spaniard who would have informed us. And, even if they got into Spain, we had the Spanish Government's pledge to deliver them to us.

The Spanish Government also took steps to discourage the importation of looted property and assets. It seized a quantity at Irun in September. It stiffened its customs inspection at the border. It furnished helpful information to Embassy officers who, under Mr. Ackerman, our Commercial Attaché, were engaged in tracking down German investments in Spain.

In pressing the Foreign Office for stoppage of the German commercial airline between Barcelona and Stuttgart, we were handicapped in two ways. On the one hand, the British Ambassador was at first very reluctant to support our efforts. Still concentrating on the subject of "German agents," Sir Samuel thought they should be sent home rather than interned in Spain, and they could be sent home only by the German air service. On the other hand, Washington was slow to appreciate or to accept what the Spanish Government regarded as a necessary prerequisite to its stopping the air service to Germany.

I am sure that, despite British half-heartedness about the matter, we could have obtained in September, 1944, the severance of this single remaining German link with Spain, if we had assured to Spain an alternative means of communication with Switzerland. Every time I pressed Lequerica for stopping the Lufthansa, he pointed out that Spain had to have some means of keeping in touch with its diplomatic missions and its nationals in central Europe. On September 28 he referred to the proposal we had made over a year before that the Spaniards or the Swiss, or both, should operate an airline between Spain and Switzerland,[1] and said that if this were now put into effect, Spain would immediately ground the German commercial planes. He further suggested that the planes on the proposed Spanish-Swiss line could land at some point in France, to be designated by us, for inspection and control of passengers and freight carried by them. In this way, he said, we could make certain that the new line was serving strictly neutral, and not German, interests.

[1] See above, pp. 155–156.

The French Mission in Madrid was favorably impressed by Lequerica's proposal and recommended to General de Gaulle its acceptance. The British Embassy, too, came to view it with favor, and so reported to London. But our military authorities had many other things to think about and apparently the State Department did not press them for a favorable decision on this matter. So nothing came of the proposal.

There was still another proposal of the Spanish Government. If we wouldn't permit air communication between Spain and Switzerland, wouldn't we at least permit courier service by rail or motor between the two countries? This would enable Spain to do without the German airline. For several months, however, we could get no approval of such an arrangement. Indeed, it was not until just after my final departure from Spain in January, 1945, that approval was forthcoming and the German commercial airline finally grounded.

Meanwhile, lacking means of stopping the line, we did our best to minimize its usefulness to Germany. Through our intelligence services, we obtained day-to-day information of the passengers and parcels that went out on it to or from Barcelona, Madrid, and Lisbon. We could not be sure that in the "diplomatic pouches" passing between Germany and the German Missions in Portugal and Spain there was not transfer of important securities southward and of military reports, industrial diamonds, etc., northward. But as a result of vigorous representations at the Foreign Office, we eventually succeeded in getting Spain to limit the number of pouches thus carried and also to withhold outbound cargoes of food concentrates, vitamins, and other commodities of conceivable military assistance to Germany.

VI

In the preceding chapter I mentioned the "International Institute for Girls in Spain," and the negotiations which led, on July 1, 1944, to the evacuation of its large building in Madrid by the Falange.[1] The building was then leased by the State Department

[1] See above, pp. 205, 232.

from the American board of trustees for an obligatory term of five years, with an option for another five years, and extensive renovation and repairs were executed under the supervision of Messrs. Larkin and Amateis of the Department and First Secretary Sydney Redecker of the Embassy. Finally, on September 23, we were able to move and to collect in this one convenient and spacious building the hitherto dispersed and cramped offices of the Embassy.

With wolfram and "preemptive buying" now matters of purely historical and archaeological interest, the USCC began folding up and, like the Arabs, silently stealing away. Several months later, nevertheless, they were returning in order to supervise the purchase of materials we wanted for our armed forces and the civilian population in liberated areas of Europe.

By September, 1944, it was perfectly obvious that certain things which we had been doing in Spain we needed to do no longer, and that other things which hitherto had been of little importance now required more attention. Thus, while we could dispense with the section of the Embassy having to do with preemptive buying, we had to build up new sections for detection of "looted property" and for "supply purchases." Altogether, the economic and commercial responsibilities of the Embassy increased, rather than lessened.

Our intelligence service no longer had work to do in maintaining "chains" over the Pyrenees into France and reporting enemy movements there, nor were there any more Allied airmen or refugees coming into Spain to be cared for by us.[1] A shrinkage could prop-

---

[1] Altogether, from November, 1942, to June, 1944, Spain saved us over 1,100 American airmen. Concerning the fate of one of the very last, the wife of our Consul at Bilbao, Mrs. Harry Hawley, wrote Mrs. Hayes on June 12: "Yesterday we buried the body of a young American aviator which was washed up by the sea not far from here. It was a really beautiful funeral. The British colony turned out nearly one hundred per cent and the Spanish sent a large contingent of air force and naval officers. The flowers couldn't have been lovelier if the boy had been one of our own sons. I think we all felt that this was a symbol, representing so much. My husband read the Episcopal burial service as the boy's identity disk said he was a Protestant, and there is no chaplain here. The British cemetery is a very pretty spot, a few miles outside Bilbao, and there Albert Smith of Pennsylvania's poor battered body lies under the pine trees next to a British and a Canadian aviator who also were washed against the Spanish coast. We were greatly touched that Spanish officials turned out in such numbers for the funeral."

erly be effected in the offices of the Military and Naval Attachés and the OSS.

It was similar with the OWI. We no longer had to wage psychological and propagandist warfare against the Axis in Spain. We had already won it, and all Spain knew that the unconditional surrender of Germany was approaching. There was no need, I thought, of our continuing to spend large sums of money on the printing and distribution of war propaganda. Our large staff at the Casa Americana should be drastically reduced. At the same time I perceived long-term advantages in maintaining and developing offices of a Press Attaché and of a Cultural Relations Attaché, which would continue within the Embassy and under the State Department after such an emergency wartime organization as the OWI should have disappeared. To this end, I despatched to the State Department in September a fairly elaborate report, containing specific recommendations. With these, Mr. T. L. Barnard, the Overseas Director of OWI who visited us at Madrid in early October, · expressed himself as being in agreement. It was accordingly arranged that, while Mr. Emmet Hughes and a few other members of the local OWI Outpost would remain for a time, their functions would be gradually curtailed, and the Outpost would be subordinated to a Press Attaché chosen from among Foreign Service Officers in the Embassy. To this post, I appointed First Secretary Philip Bonsal in October. He proved, I believe, a happy choice.

Thanks to the State Department, we had an especially competent and devoted corps of consular officers throughout Spain. Since my arrival, I had made it a practice to call the chiefs of the several consulates to Madrid for an annual three-day conference, in order that the Embassy might have the benefit of their personal experience and counsel, and that they, in turn, might know at close range the manifold functioning and activities of the Embassy. Such conferences had been held at Thanksgiving time in 1942 and in 1943. Now, in 1944, it seemed advisable to move up the date of the conference to the week of October 12. The progress of our arms in France and the changing circumstances in Spain called for a reorientation of our strategy and tactics, affecting the Consulates as

well as the Embassy. Besides, I had already decided that the wartime
job for which I had come to Spain was accomplished and that, as
soon as the Presidential election was over, I would present my resignation as Ambassador and return to my university work at Columbia. For the moment I kept this decision to myself, but I did want
to see the Consuls again before I resigned. I liked them all, and
they had been very kind to me and invariably cooperative.

The Consular Conference of 1944 was attended by Key from
Barcelona, Hawley from Bilbao, Quarton from Málaga, Hamlin
from Sevilla, Galbraith from San Sebastian, Cowles from Vigo,
Anderson from Valencia, and Furnald from Las Palmas in the
Canaries, together with wives of most of them. Messrs. Butterworth
and Ackerman and numerous other members of the Embassy assisted, as did also our Military and Naval Attachés. Sessions were
held in the new Chancery and in the Casa Americana, and a reception and dance and a dinner were given in the Embassy residence.
Altogether, it seemed to me a particularly pleasant conference, and
profitable to all concerned.

October 12, a top day in the Conference, was broken into, so
far as I personally was concerned, by a Pan-American celebration
at the Spanish Foreign Office. The whole American diplomatic
corps (and the Portuguese Ambassador) were invited to a reception
and book-exhibit at noon and to a state dinner in the evening.
Señor Lequerica surpassed himself in hospitality, and at the reception made a brief address in which he paid graceful tribute to the
three "makers" of America—Spain, Portugal, and the United
States.

In the same month, the long mission of my British colleague
came practically to an end. Sir Samuel Hoare, in making his farewell call on me at our Chancery, explained that he felt he was no
longer needed in Spain and that he was anxious to get back into
active political life in England where he might be wanted for a
cabinet post and where a general election would occur before many
months. He would probably return to Spain very briefly, perhaps
in early December, in order to take formal leave of the Chief of the

Spanish State, but to all intents and purposes his mission was now terminating.

There was something of sadness in this departure of Sir Samuel. He was especially saddened, I perceived, by the failure of his hopes and efforts for the restoration of the monarchy in Spain. "I have never known so many professed monarchists," he said, "who didn't really want a king." And in spite of differences between Sir Samuel and myself about tactics in a number of matters during the past two and a half years, I regretted the going of a familiar figure.

The British Embassy in Madrid was henceforth presided over by its Counselor, Mr. James Bowker, as Chargé d'Affaires, and we in the American Embassy could not have had a more friendly or cooperative colleague than he.

When I first came to Spain, in May, 1942, I had been, of course, the last of the Ambassadors in order of precedence. Ahead of me had then been, besides the Papal Nuncio, the Ambassadors of Portugal, Germany, Italy, France, Great Britain, Brazil, Argentina, Chile, and Peru. Since then, however, there had been many changes in the ambassadorial corps. Only the Portuguese and Chilean Ambassadors now remained the same. Three German Ambassadors had gone, and there had been none at all since August, 1944. Two Italian Ambassadors had been recalled, the last, our good friend Paulucci, having recently been replaced by a Chargé. Since M. Piétri's enforced withdrawal in August there was no French Ambassador, only the de Gaulle Minister, M. Truelle. The former Brazilian and Peruvian Ambassadors had also been replaced, and since the departure of Palacios Costa a year ago there had been no Argentine Ambassador. And now the British Ambassador was gone.

A month after Sir Samuel Hoare's departure, and immediately after the November elections in the United States, I urgently requested President Roosevelt to relieve me of the mission in Spain and let me return to regular university work at home. It was not until the following January, however, that I was able finally to leave Spain. In the meantime, certain pending negotiations with the Spanish Government were brought to a satisfactory conclusion.

VII

In November, 1944, Spain participated in two international conferences in the United States. One was the unofficial Business Conference at Rye, New York. The other was the official Conference on Civil Aviation at Chicago. Our Embassy helped to arrange and expedite the trip of the Spanish delegates to these conferences. For the aviation delegates, we gave a party on October 19, attended by the Foreign Minister and other high officials of the Government. There is no doubt that both delegations benefited greatly from their sojourns in America and returned to Spain with sincere and high appreciation of our country and of the courtesies shown them in it.

There had been hope that a bilateral air agreement might be concluded between the United States and Spain before the assembling of the International Aviation Conference in Chicago on November 1, 1944. A year before, in November, 1943, Spain had agreed "in principle" to grant landing rights to American commercial airlines,[1] and in July, 1944, an American committee of technical experts had visited Spain and gathered data, with remarkably friendly collaboration of officials of the Spanish Air Ministry, on which could be based detailed proposals for implementing those "landing rights." [2] The proposals, in the form of a draft agreement, were then prepared in Washington, and despatched to us in Madrid in September. On September 28 I submitted the draft to the Foreign Minister, who acknowledged it on October 3. On October 9, I addressed to him the following personal letter:

My dear Mr. Minister and friend:

I greatly appreciate Your Excellency's most courteous letter of October 3rd advising me that the proposed draft of an air agreement between our Governments has been referred to competent Spanish authorities for information and study.

In this connection, I should like to state that I have informed my Government that Your Excellency's remarks in the course of our conversation on September 22 indicated that we hold in common the

[1] See above, p. 202.   [2] See above, p. 262.

view that it would be mutually desirable and beneficial for the United States and Spain to reach a definite accord about the matter before the assembling of the international air conference at the beginning of next month.

The United States Government has been gratified by the Spanish Government's cooperative attitude in aviation matters and would welcome the strengthening of aviation ties between the two countries. Indeed, my Government is prepared to arrange for technical collaboration, with an attendant release of equipment, whereby the development of large-scale facilities in Spain for international traffic could be promptly expedited, and it is also giving close attention to the requirements of Spanish airlines. I can state that an immediate start will be made to assure early results from such cooperation, despite difficulties currently arising from war conditions.

Consequently, and in view of our joint desires, the only obstacle to the conclusion of an air agreement before the international aviation conference convenes would seem to be the time element. It has occurred to me that this obstacle might be overcome by having an authorized representative of the Spanish Government and a similar representative of the American Embassy meet without delay to concentrate upon the detailed negotiation of the air agreement through continued frequent sessions which would permit the reaching of an accord within the limited period which is still at our disposal before the international conference begins.

If this suggestion meets with Your Excellency's approval, I shall be glad to have Mr. Haering, our First Secretary, act as the Embassy's representative.

With the highest personal regards, I am, etc.

Señor Navasques was promptly designated as the chief Spanish representative, and during the ensuing two months both he and Mr. Haering devoted practically all their time to detailed discussion with each other and with experts in the Ministries of Air, Industry and Commerce, and Foreign Affairs. And from time to time, of course, the Embassy had to consult Washington on specific questions. It was obvious, from the start of these negotiations, that the Spanish Government was as anxious as ours to reach an early agreement. But the details were too numerous and complex to be fully agreed to before November 1. The Spaniards submitted a draft of counter proposals to us at the end of October, and a compromise between this and our original draft was formulated at Washington and discussed with the Spanish delegation at the Chicago Conference in mid-November. On November 21, I submitted the new draft to the Foreign Minister.

The only obstacle to Spain's acceptance of the revised draft was a question about the interpretation of certain clauses referring to "most-favored-nation treatment." This was surmounted by authorization we obtained from Washington to supply the Spanish Foreign Office with the clarification it desired through an exchange of notes simultaneously with the signing of the agreement itself.

Finally, on December 2, 1944, while the International Aviation Conference was still in session in Chicago, the bilateral air agreement between Spain and the United States, with its supplementary clarification, was formally concluded at Madrid through an exchange of Notes between Señor Lequerica and myself. The Notes were ceremoniously signed at the Ministry of Foreign Affairs in the presence of high governmental dignitaries and of representatives of the American, British, French, and Spanish press. Mr. Butterworth and Mr. Haering accompanied me to provide an official American representation in keeping with the occasion.

Our air agreement with Spain was a major achievement. It set a precedent and a norm for other air agreements of the future. Its immediate advantage to us is indicated in the next chapter.

The State Department most kindly wired me on December 11 that it "wishes to commend you and the members of your staff, particularly Mr. Haering, for the successful negotiation and conclusion of the Air Agreement with Spain." At the same time arrangements were made for sending to Spain another group of American experts to advise with the Spanish authorities concerning necessary alteration and improvement of airfields at Madrid, Barcelona, and Sevilla, and concerning requisite supplies and equipment for carrying the Agreement into effect. Likewise we undertook to forward the desire of the Spanish Iberia airline to resume its services to the Balearic and Canary Islands and to obtain equipment it needed from the United States.[1]

[1] Shortly after I left Spain, the Iberia service to the Balearic Islands was resumed.

There had long been considerable American investments in Spain which it was the duty of our Embassy to safeguard against possibly arbitrary or unjust actions on the part of the Spanish Government. In the main, it must be said, the regime of General Franco was better disposed toward foreign capital than had been the Republican regime from 1931 to 1936; and there was no indication, during my stay in Spain, of discrimination by the Government against Allied investments or in favor of those of the Axis. I have no reason to doubt the complete sincerity of General Franco's statement to me on September 11, 1944, that "Spain needed more, rather than fewer, American investments, and that they must be treated fairly and honorably." [1]

There was, of course, a continuing distinct trend in Spain, as elsewhere, toward the nationalization of public utilities, in which foreign capital was apt to be largely invested, and an insistence that subsidiaries of foreign business corporations should be organized as Spanish companies and fully subject to Spanish law. In general, the Franco Government's policy in these respects was to seek such a nationalization as would ensure Spanish control and majority-ownership, under state regulation, while not disturbing minority foreign investment and a certain amount of foreign management and technical service.

Occasionally, however, some radical element or agency of the Government, in order to speed up the process of nationalization, would impose especially onerous conditions on foreign-owned or foreign-managed companies. Thus, we had occasion to protest about the imposition of a virtually confiscatory fine, for an alleged infraction of Spanish law, on the Singer Sewing Machine Company, and also about the refusal of a rate-increase necessary to save from bankruptcy the American-owned Gas and Electricity Company of Palma de Mallorca. In entering our protests, the Embassy sedulously refrained from judging the cases or demanding any particular settlement. We were not a collecting agency for private American business. We merely sought, with all the energy at our command, to ensure that American investments had fair treatment and were

[1] See above, p. 262.

not confiscated or discriminated against. In the instances I have just cited, our protests were sympathetically received, and favorably acted upon, by the Spanish authorities.

Complaints reached us from the moving-picture industry in the United States concerning heavy taxes and other burdens which Spain placed on the importation and showing of American films. With the approval of the State Department, I submitted notes on the subject to the Foreign Office on August 28 and October 6, 1944, and our Commercial Attaché, Mr. Ackerman, discussed it repeatedly and at length with the Minister of Industry and Commerce, Señor Carceller. We got little satisfaction on this score, and in existing circumstances we couldn't expect much. There was, in fact, no "discrimination" against American films; and despite what could be regarded as excessive taxes, many more films were actually being imported and shown from the United States than from any other country. Besides, Carceller was quite convinced that the number of foreign films brought into Spain should be still further restricted, rather than increased, not only to protect and build up home industry but also to husband Spanish trade balances abroad. Any spare funds of Spain in the dollar area, he insisted, should be spent on essential goods such as petroleum, hydro-electric equipment, tractors, etc., instead of on a luxury item like moving pictures.

By far the largest American investment in Spain was that of the International Telephone and Telegraph Company. This controlled and efficiently managed the monopolistic Spanish Telephone Company which had been created back in 1924 during the dictatorship of Primo de Rivera and which had since functioned under a highly favorable twenty-year contract with the Spanish Government. The contract had been seized upon (I suspect unjustly) by Spanish "Leftists" as one of their indictments against Primo de Rivera, and under the Republic a serious, though eventually unsuccessful, attempt was made to annul it and to nationalize the Spanish Company. A similar attempt was made by the Franco regime in its early days, and for a time the American officers of the Company were deposed. Though this attempt was presently abandoned, and the officers reinstated, many difficulties continued between the Company and the Government. Some of these were aggravated by abnormal conditions resulting from the Civil War and the ensuing World War; others, by the impending expiration of the contract in 1944 and the doubt concerning what would then happen to the Company and the large American interest in it.

One incidental aspect of the Telephone matter had engaged our attention for some time. The original arrangements between the I. T. and T. and the Spanish Government had provided for possible radio-telegraphic circuits, in conjunction with the Mackay system, between Madrid and Buenos Aires and between Madrid and New York, and the former of these had been duly established. But for a long time the establishment of the direct circuit between Madrid and New York was blocked by the Telecommunications Section of the Ministry of the Interior (Gobernación), ostensibly for technical reasons, but chiefly (there is reason to believe) because of pressure from rival British interests. The Telephone Company carried the case to the Spanish Supreme Court, which in April, 1942, handed down a decision affirming the Company's right to operate the circuit to New York. In August of the same year the Ministry of Gobernación instructed the Telecommunications Section to execute the Supreme Court judgment as soon as four technical points should be satisfied by the Company.

To satisfy these points took time, but eventually, in October, 1943, the Company notified the Ministry that they were satisfied and it was ready to open the circuit. But Gobernación or Telecommunications still withheld requisite authorization, and at this point I appealed to the Foreign Minister (then Count Jordana) who secured in January, 1944, a Cabinet order for the Ministry of Gobernación to act and issue the authorization. Still no action.

As soon as the wolfram crisis was passed, in May, 1944, I renewed and repeated representations about the circuit at the Foreign Office and to General Franco himself. In October, 1944, Señor Lequerica informed me that the Ministry of Gobernación, through the Caudillo's personal intervention, was finally granting the authorization, and not long afterwards direct radio-telegraphic service between Spain and the United States became a reality. We thus obtained towards the end of 1944 what we had unsuccessfully sought from the Monarchy in the 1920's and from the Republic in the 1930's.

The matter of the direct circuit was one in which the United States Government was especially interested. But, as I have said above, it was incidental to the much more complex and vexatious matter of the Telephone Company itself. In this matter the Embassy did not presume to pass upon the pros or cons or to engage in detailed negotiations looking to a settlement. We simply made clear to the Spanish Government that we wanted and expected such honest direct negotiations between it and the Company as would lead to speedy settlement equitable for all concerned, including American investors, and that we strongly objected to the use of compulsion against the Company. To this end, I addressed a series of Notes to the Foreign Office in 1944: April 4, May 6, July 7, August 12 and 24, September 12 and 30, October 16. To the same end, I discussed the matter repeatedly with Señor Lequerica, and on September 11 with General Franco.

I shall not here detail the many complex difficulties or the negotiations. Early in December, 1944, the Foreign Minister notified me that the Caudillo had designated Señor Carceller as the Government's plenipotentiary to deal with the Telephone Company, and on December 6 Señor Carceller formally opened negotiations with Mr. Frederick Caldwell of the Company in the presence of our Commercial Attaché, Mr. Ackerman. As soon as the negotiations were fairly under way, Mr. Ackerman withdrew. It was soon obvious that both sides really wanted a settlement, and a mutually satisfactory one was finally reached in March, 1945. Spain would purchase, on reasonable terms, the majority stock controlled by the I. T. and T., and would continue, under a new contract, to obtain from it certain technical and managerial services.

Another and quite different economic matter engaged our attention in the winter of 1944–1945. This was the matter of utilizing Spain as a supplier of commodities such as textiles and certain foodstuffs for our armed forces and for the civilian population in liberated areas of Europe. Although the Germans still had the military strength in the last weeks of 1944 to launch a counter-offensive toward Liége, it was generally recognized as a despairing effort which could only delay and not ward off the ultimate Allied triumph throughout Europe. And as our triumph neared, it became all the more needful to mobilize the resources of the neutrals as well as of the victors for the ensuing tasks of relief and rehabilitation.

On instructions from Washington, I personally presented to the Foreign Minister, Señor Lequerica, on January 4, 1945, a Note requesting the Spanish Government to authorize and facilitate the purchase of relief supplies by an agency of our Government and to exempt such purchases from customary taxation. The response was favorable; and in due course the USCC and also our military authorities availed themselves of the assurances I had received and did a large amount of helpful buying in Spain.

VIII

Meanwhile, we were profiting from Spain's "benevolent neutrality" in other respects. On November 13, 1944, in accordance with instructions from the State Department, I expressed to the Foreign Minister the hope that, as the war in the Pacific proceeded and areas were liberated from Japanese domination, Spain would decline to take under its diplomatic protection any consulates or missions of Japan or of puppet governments which Japan might have set up in those areas. Señor Lequerica assured me that the United States could count on full and hearty compliance by Spain with the request. He reminded me of what the Caudillo had said about Japan in July, 1943, and again in July, 1944,[1] and added that the breaking-point had just about been reached in Spain's relations with Japan.

I was not at all surprised to read, just after my final return to America in the early spring of 1945, that the Spanish Government had ruptured all diplomatic relations with the Japanese Govern-

---

[1] See above, pp. 161, 261.

ment and its puppets. It had been clearly foreshadowed by General Franco in July, 1944.

In the course of the conversation with Señor Lequerica on November 13, I said again, what I had said in numerous earlier conversations with him and with Count Jordana, that while my Government had no intention of interfering in Spanish internal affairs, the continuing Falangista dictatorship was repugnant to my people and hence an impediment to thoroughly cordial Spanish-American relations. The Minister remarked, on this occasion, that he and the Caudillo were mindful of the problem and were definitely aiming at an evolutionary solution in the near future.

It may be, curiously enough, that the execution of whatever plan General Franco and Señor Lequerica were then considering for a modification of the regime, was delayed as a result of Lord Templewood's brief "farewell" visit to Spain in the first week of December.[1] The British Ambassador took no pains to conceal his disappointment that the monarchy was not being restored. He expressed it, with considerable bitterness, not only in personal conversation with me and other members of the diplomatic corps and in final interviews with the Caudillo and the Foreign Minister, but also in a quasi-public speech he made at a large dinner given in his honor by the Portuguese Ambassador and attended by well-known Spanish Monarchists. The Caudillo was reported to have been immensely annoyed, and some very sarcastic articles about Lord Templewood appeared in the Spanish press.

On the other hand, in a conversation I had with the Foreign Minister on December 14, Señor Lequerica declared that the Caudillo was giving most serious attention to the problem of effecting an evolution in the existing regime without weakening the state. The United States and Great Britain should bear in mind, he said, that a majority of the Spanish people had supported General Franco in the Civil War and had won the victory and that the victorious majority simply could not and would not abdicate to the minority and let it start a new civil war or a new chaos. He said

[1] Sir Samuel Hoare had just been raised to the peerage as Viscount Templewood of Chelsea.

he couldn't tell me just how the problem was going to be solved, but he could assure me that steps would shortly be taken toward an evolution. He recognized that the Falange in its current form and trappings was very unpopular both in the United States and in Great Britain. Something should be done about it. Nevertheless, one must face the fact that no mere evolution of the existing Spanish regime, including even an abolition of the Falange, would satisfy certain extremist public opinion in the English-speaking countries which could be satisfied only by the renewal of civil war in Spain and the triumph of the forces of violence and chaos. At the same time, one might hope that an evolution could be brought about which would satisfy a larger and more reasonable public opinion in our countries and thereby enable our Governments to accept close collaboration with Spain. The central desire in Spain, the Minister concluded, was to work closely with the United States.

One last thing I greatly wanted to achieve before I finally left Spain—the release of the Italian warships interned in the Balearic Islands. They had been there since September, 1943, and I felt that we could have secured their release in the winter of 1943–1944 if at that time the British Ambassador had earnestly supported our representations or if Washington had reenforced them in London. As it was, both our Government and the British consented, in the general agreement with Spain of April 29, 1944, to leave the question of the Italian warships to future arbitration.

In September, the Italian Ambassador at Madrid, with the concurrence of his Government in Rome, proposed to me and to the British Ambassador that we inaugurate negotiations with the Spanish Foreign Office looking toward the promised arbitration. I was more than willing, but Sir Samuel Hoare deemed the time not yet propitious for reopening the question.

Reopen it I did, nevertheless, on October 9, just as Sir Samuel was relinquishing his post and departing for home. On that day, I told the Foreign Minister I wished to speak informally with him about the Italian warships and to express the thought that the changed military situation might now make it possible and desirable for the Spanish Government to take a less legalistic attitude toward the ships and to release them. My Government, I knew, had no thought of repudiating the agreement of April 29th, and, if Spain insisted, it would adhere to the principle of arbitration. Yet I must point out that if the arbitration should go against Spain, as I believed it would, Spain would be liable for payment of heavy expenses and damages resulting from unjustified internment of the ships. The Italian Ambassador, I understood, had already pointed this out to the Minister.

I further argued that the early release of the Italian warships would enable Spain to express, in a practical way, its sympathy with the United States in the war against Japan. If we could use the Italian ships in European waters, we could concentrate that many more of our own naval forces in the Pacific.

Señor Lequerica was evidently interested and impressed. He said he would look into the case, and if he could find grounds, consonant with international law, for releasing the Italian ships, he would release them. He would give the matter careful study in the near future.

The day after this conversation with the Foreign Minister, the State Department wired me that it would support the Italians in the matter and that it was asking the British to do likewise. With this backing, I continued the discussion with Señor Lequerica on November 2. He said he had been looking into the matter, as he promised on October 9, and reading all the pertinent documents. As a result he had formed the opinion that much could be said, from the standpoint of international law, on both sides, and he was minded to release the ships as a special gesture of goodwill to the Italian Government and to the Allies.

On November 13, the Foreign Minister assured me the Italian warships would positively be released, though he couldn't specify any date. On November 30, he suggested arbitration by competent persons, possibly under the chairmanship of the Portuguese Ambassador.

On December 5, when I informed the Minister of my contemplated departure from Spain in another month and requested the agrément for my successor, he said he would do his utmost to see that "I left Spain with the Italian warships on a silver platter." He then made a definite proposal about procedure. He would appoint as arbitrator a distinguished Spanish professor of international law, if acceptable to the chiefs of the American, British, and Italian missions in Madrid.

It was an unusual sort of arbitration, and required some thought and discussion. Eventually, on December 29, an agreement was reached through an exchange of letters between Señor Lequerica and myself, with confirmatory letters of Mr. Bowker, the British Chargé, and Mr. Mascia, the Italian Chargé. Already the Foreign Minister had designated as arbitrator Señor Don José de Yanguas Messia, professor of international law in the University of Madrid, member of the Institute of International Law, and late Spanish Ambassador to the Vatican.

During the Christmas and New Year holidays, Professor Yanguas Messia prepared an exhaustive, scholarly study of the international law involved, concluding with the decision that, while Spain as a neutral had not been under obligation to release the Italian warships, it was under no obligation to intern them, and that they might now be given twenty-four hours in which to refuel and depart.

The decision was officially withheld from us until we could get the necessary fuel to the ships in the Balearics and the Italian naval authorities could get the ships and their crews ready to sail. Then, on my last evening in Madrid—the evening of January 14, 1945—there met with me, in the Goya room in the Embassy, Professor Yanguas Messia, the Under Secretary of the Spanish Foreign Office, the British and Italian Chargés, and the American Counselor, Mr. Butterworth. Here the decision was officially pronounced and the formal documents presented. Before dawn the next morning all the Italian warships were off on a free and safe voyage to home ports.

On January 15 Captain Giuseppe Marini, the commander of the squadron, radioed me from aboard his flagship: "At the moment at which I leave Spain with the Royal Italian ships under my command, I take the liberty of sending to Your Excellency the most profound and sincere assurance of my gratitude for the admirable and tenacious work devoted to the restitution of ships and men to Italy, ships and men now ready for combat in the common cause."

The release of the Italian warships was the climax of my wartime mission in Spain. Spain's neutrality was unquestionably "benevolent."

CHAPTER IX

HOW I LEFT SPAIN

I

During the first two years of my mission in Spain—that is, from May, 1942, to May, 1944—there was always a considerable possibility that German armed forces might invade the Peninsula and create a disconcerting if not disastrous military situation for the Allies, and, of course, for Spain. Nevertheless, despite this chronic possibility, the Spanish Government as well as the Spanish people gave increasing evidence of a determination not only to resist any attempted invasion but also to accord helpful facilities to the Allies. Spain passed, during those two years, from "non-belligerency" to "neutrality," and thence to a "benevolent neutrality" in our favor.

By the spring of 1944 the critical and essentially *wartime* phase of my mission in Spain was over. With the conclusion of the wolfram agreement of April 29 and the successful Allied landing in Normandy on June 6, there disappeared any real danger that the Germans might strike across the Pyrenees or even extract strategic materials from the Peninsula.

I had come to Spain with a certain predilection for the country and its people, born of a familiarity with Spanish history and Spanish literature. The longer I remained, the more this predilection was confirmed and strengthened by personal contact and practical experience. I found Spain fascinating, and the Spanish people "simpatico." After two years in their midst, I knew I would part from them with sincere regret.

Yet I wanted to return to America and to my university. My life and work were there, not in Spain or in a diplomatic career. The mission to Spain was a strictly wartime mission.

On April 17, 1944, I wrote to the Secretary of State, Mr. Cordell Hull, suggesting that I be replaced in Spain. The Secretary replied on May 8: "I have conveyed to the President the suggestion which you made in your letter. . . . The President . . . desires me to assure you that there is not the remotest thought that you should step aside from your post at Madrid where you have done such a splendid job."

The result was that I remained a third year in Spain, amid developments which have been narrated in the preceding chapter. It was a year of harvesting a crop of benevolent neutrality, and on the whole, therefore, a pleasant and agreeable year. But long before its expiration, I was quite convinced that the work for which I had been sent to Spain was fully accomplished and that immediately after the presidential election on November 7, 1944, I would press for acceptance of my resignation as Ambassador to Spain.

Consequently, on November 9, I addressed the following letter to Mr. Hull:

Dear Mr. Secretary:

I have the honor to enclose a letter for transmission to the President and a copy of it for yourself, containing my resignation as Ambassador to Spain.

It is customary, I believe, after a presidential election and before the beginning of the new administration, for chiefs of mission to tender resignations. In my case, I would not wish the resignation to be deemed in any sense *pro forma,* for reasons set forth in the letter. I feel simply that the work I was sent to Spain to do has been done and that henceforth I can be of greater service at home.

You, and indeed the Department of State as a whole, have been most considerate, and I shall always remember with the greatest pleasure and satisfaction the opportunity I have had to be associated with you and the Department at a critical time in our national history. I am delighted, of course, that our people in Tuesday's election gave such vigorous and unmistakable endorsement to the foreign policies championed by President Roosevelt and yourself. What a relief to have this assurance that the same leadership and the same direction will be continued not only on through the remainder of the war but on into the even more difficult period of peacemaking.

I trust that arrangements may conveniently be made so that I can properly relinquish the post here and return home in January.

With the highest regards and the best personal wishes, I am,

Faithfully yours,

Carlton J. H. Hayes.

The accompanying letter to President Roosevelt, also dated November 9, 1944, was as follows:

Dear Mr. President,

In the spring of 1942, you honored and entrusted me with a war-time mission as your Ambassador to Spain. This mission, I believe, has now been discharged. Spain not only did not enter the war on the side of the Axis or jeopardize Allied military operations in North Africa in 1942, in Italy in 1943, or in France in 1944, but has actually accorded us, during the past two years and a half, an increasing number of facilities helpful to our war-effort.

Now that our favorable position in Spain has been decisively confirmed and buttressed by our great military successes on all fronts, the mission in Spain properly loses its wartime emergency character, and I would accordingly ask to be relieved of it. It has been performed gladly by me, in the knowledge that I was serving you and our country and that I had your confidence and support. Frankly, however, it has been costly and wearing for me, and I eagerly look forward to resuming my semi-private life and work at Columbia University.

Will you therefore please accept my resignation as Ambassador to Spain, effective at your convenience and so as to enable me to return home at the beginning of the new year?

To this request, I would add expression of my very grateful appreciation of the trust you have reposed in me and of the unfailing assistance I have had from you and from the Secretary and Department of State.

With the highest personal regards and continuing loyalty, I am,

Faithfully yours,

Carlton J. H. Hayes.

At the same time, I confidentially informed Dr. Nicholas Murray Butler about the matter and suggested to him that if it were agreeable to him and to the Columbia Trustees I would like to resume my regular university connections in the spring of 1945. He responded immediately, and it was arranged that I should have the spring as a "sabbatical," during which I would do some writing, and should return to full-time teaching in the autumn of 1945.

On November 22, President Roosevelt replied:

I have read with genuine regret your letter of November 9th in which you tender your resignation as Ambassador to Spain. You have carried out a mission of great difficulty with outstanding success and in doing so you have made a contribution to the war effort of the highest importance. I am mindful of the personal sacrifices and the personal cost which this contribution has involved for you. In reluctantly accepting your resignation for the personal reasons which you describe and effective at such time in January, 1945, as may be convenient to you, I wish to thank you most warmly and to assure you of the lasting gratitude of the Government which you have served at a critical period of our history with such distinguished loyalty and efficiency. With best wishes for the future, I am,

Faithfully yours,

Franklin D. Roosevelt.

On November 30, Mr. Hull, writing from the hospital, added this kindly message:

I want you to know that I deeply appreciate your never-failing cooperation and support. I also want to say that you personally have made a magnificent contribution to the welfare of our country, and I share the pride I know 'you must feel at your outstanding record of public service. With every good wish for your health and happiness in the future,

Sincerely yours,

Cordell Hull.

On December 3, 1944, I received a telegram from the Department, stating that the President wished to appoint the Honorable Norman Armour as my successor and asking me to seek the requisite *agrément* of the Spanish Government. I did so in an interview with the Foreign Minister, Señor Lequerica, on December 5.

I explained to the Minister that I had been American Ambassador to Spain for almost three years, that the position had been a difficult one, especially in 1942 and 1943, that affairs were now obviously improving, that I was not a career diplomat but a scholar and university professor who had undertaken the ambassadorship at the urgent request of President Roosevelt and in order to meet an emergency, that this emergency was now passed and I wished to return to my customary life and usual pursuits, and that I had so informed President Roosevelt a month ago just after the presidential election in the United States. Now I had word that the President was kindly complying with my request and asking me to seek the *agrément* of the Spanish Government for my successor. I was greatly pleased by the designation of Mr. Norman Armour, a career diplomat and one of the most distinguished in our service. I then went over with the Minister Mr. Armour's diplomatic career and left with him a memorandum about it.

The Minister was good enough to express what seemed to be very real regret at my forthcoming departure. He assured me he would consult General Franco at the earliest possible moment concerning the *agrément* and he hoped to be able to advise me shortly. At the moment, the Caudillo was away on a hunting trip and would probably not return until the end of the week or the beginning of the next.

Señor Lequerica utilized the occasion to expatiate upon his favorite theme, the desirability of the United States and Spain drawing much closer together. Spain, he said, was a natural bridgehead between the American continents and Europe. Spain desired to have the closest possible ties with all of America and to play its part in discouraging any possible friction between North America and South America. On the other hand, he felt that if the United States, now obviously the greatest military nation in the world, was to play its proper role in the postwar period, it should realistically utilize Spain as a special bulwark in Europe. He even hoped there might be special understandings between the United States and Spain—economic, political, military. Such understandings could be arrived at within the framework of any world organization that might be established after the war and without any derogation to British interests in Spain.

He said he appreciated that the chief obstacle in the way was hostility of public opinion in the United States toward the existing Spanish Government. He could assure me there would be, in due course, a very considerable evolution of the existing Spanish Government, and this would be expedited if the United States Government would show signs of seeking Spanish friendship. In the last analysis the form of government in Spain—whether a military dictatorship, a restored monarchy, or a socialistic republic—was of secondary significance in the whole general world set-up. There would always be a Spain, regardless of its form of government, and a Spain which could be of great service to the United States.

On December 11 the Foreign Minister notified me that General Franco had just returned from his hunting trip and had at once assented to our request for the *agrément* for Mr. Armour. I so cabled the State Department on the same day, and immediately afterwards the President formally designated him as my successor and the Senate duly confirmed the nomination.

By some of the public press in America, it was assumed that I had been "recalled," and that this, coupled with Sir Samuel Hoare's final return to England, foreshadowed a radical change of policy of the American and British Governments toward Spain. As the record shows, however, there was no actual connection between the resignations of Sir Samuel Hoare and myself. He had practically surrendered his post, on his own initiative, in early October. My own resignation had been contemplated several months previously and was quite independently pressed by me a month afterwards. And the very fact that a new Ambassador to Spain, as distinguished as Mr. Norman Armour, was appointed so speedily, scarcely indicated a change of policy on the part of our Government.

I was very happy both that I was going home and that Mr. Armour was coming to Spain. He was a veteran of our Foreign Service and an experienced and sympathetic negotiator with Spanish-speaking people. In addition to long service in our missions in Paris, Rome, and Tokio, he had been our Ambassador in turn to Chile and to Argentina, and latterly had been acting chief of the division of American Republics in the State Department. I could think of none better qualified to carry out, with dignity and success, the friendly policy of our Government toward Spain and the Spanish people.

To a congratulatory message I sent him, Mr. Armour replied on December 18: "I cannot tell you how much I appreciated your kind letter, which has just reached me, and your good wishes on the new assignment. You are more than generous in your reference. . . . I plan, unless you and the Department advise to the contrary, to spend some time [in Washington] reading up on Spain, probably getting off by plane towards the end of February. This would, I hope, give me the opportunity for several meetings with you, which would be most helpful to me. . . ."

II

I arranged to leave Spain by boat, with my wife and daughter, about the middle of January, 1945. The only available boat scheduled for that time was the Spanish liner, the *Marqués de Comillas,* sailing from Bilbao and arriving at New Orleans in mid-February. Through the good offices of the president of the line, Count Ruiseñada, we were able to secure desirable reservations on the ship.

Meanwhile, much had to be done. There was a good deal of current Embassy business to be attended to, including the important pending negotiations for air agreement, release of Italian warships, etc., which have been described in the preceding chapter. Besides, the final month of our sojourn in Spain was extraordinarily full of "farewell" parties and social engagements.

Protocol required exchange of "goodbye calls" with chiefs of all the Allied and neutral missions in Madrid. And special luncheons or dinners were tendered us by many of them, notably the Portuguese, Peruvian, and Brazilian Ambassadors, the Ministers of Poland, Holland, and Venezuela, the Chargés of Cuba and Belgium.

Spanish hospitality was displayed in traditionally prodigal fashion not only by government officials but also by a large number of friendly private citizens. As much as possible we tried to reciprocate at the Embassy.

At the same time, we had enjoyable visits from our colleagues at Lisbon, Ambassador and Mrs. Harry Norweb; a dinner in honor of Colonel Sharp, our retiring Military Attaché, and of his successor, Colonel Johnson; and a luncheon for the Pan-American diplomatic corps.

With no little regret and poignancy, I made a farewell call on our old friend, Señor Pan de Soraluce, who had been the respected

Under Secretary of Foreign Affairs during almost all of my stay in Spain, but who was now retired and confined to his home by serious illness. Also, Mrs. Hayes and I paid a similar last call on Countess Jordana.

On December 30 the Foreign Minister gave a luncheon for me, at which were assembled the leading figures in Spain's cultural life. On January 10, we gave a farewell reception at the Embassy, attended by some eight hundred Spaniards, in addition to our American staff and colony and members of Allied and neutral missions. The next day I had my last official conversations at the Foreign Office. On January 12, after farewell calls by me on the Caudillo and by Mrs. Hayes on Señora Franco, at the Pardo, we attended a luncheon of the Foreign Minister for the entire American diplomatic corps (together with the Portuguese Ambassador), and in the evening a party given by our Embassy staff in the Chancery.

On Saturday, January 13—our last full day in Madrid—we concluded our goodbyes. The final call I made was on the French Minister, M. Jacques Truelle, whose mission I had had a hand in launching two years before and for which I retained a kind of fatherly affection. In the evening I had five guests for an intimate dinner at our Embassy: the Foreign Minister, Señor Lequerica; the distinguished painter, Señor Zuloaga; the British Chargé, Mr. James Bowker; the Portuguese Ambassador, Dr. Pereira; and our Counselor, Mr. Walton Butterworth, who would be American Chargé from my departure to Mr. Armour's arrival.

Spanish weather, usually good, turned bad during our last days in Madrid. One snowstorm followed another, reaching blizzard proportions and evoking from historically-minded Spanish journalists the comment that it was the worst winter Spain had had "since 1567." Snow impeded traffic in the streets of Madrid, and completely blocked the highways across the mountains to the north. In the circumstances we had to abandon all thought of motoring to Bilbao and to content ourselves with going by train. Even so, the train on which we left Madrid on Sunday evening, January 14, had to be assisted by snow plows, and we arrived at Bilbao only after twenty hours of heatless and foodless riding.

At Bilbao, we were pleasantly received by our Consul, Mr. Harry Hawley, and his wife, and by local state and steamship officials and other Spaniards. After attending several social functions and inspecting a large up-to-date factory of the Firestone Rubber Company, we boarded the *Marqués de Comillas* at noon on Thursday, January 18, and began our month's voyage homeward. The ship was not large, but it was clean and comfortable. Its officers and crew were competent and most courteous, and its table was excellent. Among our fellow passengers were the Costa Rican Chargé; a Salvadorean Consul-General; a Basque pelota team bound for a series of matches in Cuba and South America; and two members from the staff of the American Consulate-General at Barcelona, one—Mr. McKinney—being transferred to the post of Consul General at Winnipeg, and the other—Mr. Joseph Caragol—on his way to join the army.

After a rough trip out from Bilbao and around Cape Finisterre, we put in on Friday evening, January 19, at Vigo, our last Spanish port of call, where we were greeted by the Military and Civil Governors, the Mayor, and our Consul, Mr. Marelius, with his staff. Here the ship remained until Monday evening, the 22nd, and the interval was filled with enjoyable experiences for us. On Saturday we lunched with our Consular staff at Vigo, and dined with excellent Spanish friends, the Señores Davila. On Sunday we had an excursion with Mr. and Mrs. Marelius to the famous cathedral- and shrine city of Santiago de Compostelo. On Monday we were shown about the city of Vigo and its delightful suburbs and entertained at luncheon by the Mayor and Civil Governor.

As we were leaving Vigo, and with it Spain, on that Monday evening, I sent farewell telegrams to the Spanish Chief of State and the Spanish Foreign Minister. To General Franco I wired: "Permit me, as I leave Spanish territory, to convey to Your Excellency the assurance of my high appreciation of the courtesies which you and the Spanish people have shown me during my mission in this country and to express the sincere hope that the bonds of friendship between Spain and the United States may be continually strengthened to the advantage of both." To Señor Lequerica, the message read: "At the moment of my leaving the last Spanish port *en route* to my own country, I would express my sincere thanks for the many courtesies and kindnesses which you have constantly shown me, and my continuing best wishes for yourself and for Spain."

Tuesday afternoon, January 23, we arrived at Lisbon and remained there until Wednesday evening. In the Portuguese capital we were pleasantly surprised to receive flowers from Dr. Salazar as well as from Nicolas Franco,[1] and a call from the charming family of our good friend the Portuguese Ambassador to Spain, Dr. Pereira. Our Ambassador to Portugal, Mr. Harry Norweb, had just left by plane for the United States, but Mrs. Norweb and members of the Embassy staff were most hospitable and showed us every attention.

At Lisbon I saw Mr. Perry George, who had just arrived by plane from America and who told me he was charged by the State Department with the special mission of persuading the Portuguese and Spanish Governments to permit our army planes (those of the Army Transport Command) to cross and land in the Peninsula. I said that, so far as Spain was concerned, I didn't think he would have a bit of trouble, provided the request was related to our air agreement of December 2 and presented as a temporary means of implementing it.

Subsequently I learned that this prophecy proved quite true. The Spanish Government readily granted the desired privilege for our military planes—a privilege it had never accorded to Axis military planes, even in those days when the fortunes of war had appeared most favorable to the Axis. It was on an A.T.C. plane that my successor, Mr. Norman Armour, would make his initial entry into Spain in March, 1945. The Spanish-American Agreement of December, 1944, was bearing early and good fruit.

[1] Brother of General Franco and his Ambassador to Portugal.

III

In leaving Spain, I took with me a portrait by Don Ignacio Zuloaga which the Spanish Government had insisted upon his painting and presenting to me when I had made clear that I could not accept any of the decorations customarily conferred on departing Ambassadors. It was a magnificent work of art, in Zuloaga's best and most mature manner, and I shall always treasure it as a fine memento of the great and living culture of a country which had been my home for almost three years and for which I felt sincere admiration and respect.

Innumerable were the Spanish courtesies and kindnesses accompanying us on our final departure—flowers, messages, letters, souvenirs. Practically every Spanish newspaper published some kind of tribute and good wishes. I hope I may be pardoned for reproducing one or two of these in English translation. For I regard them as evidencing not merely a liking for a particular American Ambassador like myself but a real desire for sympathetic understanding of Spain in the United States; and the hyperbole in them, being simply natural to the Spanish language and character, can be discounted without questioning the sincerity underlying it.

Said the Madrid newspaper *Ya*, in a special article on January 13:

The Spanish Government has desired to testify, with an admirable portrait by Zuloaga, to its esteem and sympathy for the Ambassador of the United States, who has shown such cordial understanding of our country, its customs, and its historical development. Mr. Hayes has made every effort to come close to our traditional personality and has displayed an exceptional appreciation of our character, of our special conception of life, and of the permanent traits of our culture. This explains the echo of profound sympathy that the work of the Ambassador has created in our country, which is aware of the diplomatic mission of drawing the United States and Spain closer together, a mission that has been brilliantly forwarded by Mr. Hayes.

We venture to hope that the gift of the Spanish Government will be welcome to one who has proved himself profoundly sensitive to the unfading charm of Spain. The beautiful picture for Mr. Hayes, on his departure, is, by reason of Zuloaga's happy interpretation, something more than a portrait. It is a coincidence of psychology and history, in which the personality of the Ambassador is revealed to us with the halo of the cordial esteem of an entire nation.

On January 14 the *Gaceta del Norte* of Bilbao published an extensive interview which I had given its Director, Don Antonio Gonzalez, in the previous November and which had since been corrected and proof-read by our Press Attaché, Mr. Philip Bonsal. The interview was reprinted, in full or in part, in a large number of newspapers throughout Spain, including *Madrid* of January 16 and *ABC* of January 18. The most quoted passage was one expressing views of mine regarding the relative interests of the United States and Spain in the Western Hemisphere:

We [Americans] have learned a great deal about Spain from our increasingly close relations with the other American Republics. Our knowledge of the language, culture and institutions of free Republics of the Western World has, of course, developed our knowledge and increased the affectionate respect with which we regard Spain. Spanish influence and Spanish character are facts in those Republics. There is nothing inconsistent or inimical between that influence and character and the economic and political basis upon which the defense of the Western Hemisphere in this great world struggle has been achieved. Nor is there anything inconsistent or inimical between the continued devotion of the people of those countries to the artistic and cultural heritage which they derive from the Peninsula, and their increasing awareness of the cultural achievements of the English-speaking nations. Surely there is room in this world for both Lope de Vega and Shakespeare.

I am willing to venture the prophecy that in the future the relations between Spain and her children in the Western World and those between the United States and the sovereign Republics of America will develop and become increasingly fruitful, side by side. In this development there is implicit, of course, increased understanding between the people of Spain and the people of the United States. Many great Spaniards and many great Americans have shown us the path which we must follow.

I would also mention two letters which especially touched me as I left Spain. One was from Ramón Pañella and Francisco Font, president and secretary, respectively, of the American Chamber of

Commerce in Spain. To this I replied: "One of the most heartening and helpful associations I have had during my three years' sojourn in Spain has been with the officers and members of the Chamber. While I am happy at the prospect of returning to my normal university life and work in the United States, I cannot conceal the very real and deep regret I feel at leaving Spain and these most pleasant personal associations. . . . I am very happy that President Roosevelt has designated as my successor such a very able and distinguished diplomat as Mr. Norman Armour. Mr. Armour tells me, in a letter I have just received from him, that he expects to arrive in Spain in March. You will find him, I know, most cooperative and agreeable. With profound gratitude and continuing best wishes to both of you and to all your colleagues in the Chamber, I am," etc.

The other letter was addressed by the Brazilian Ambassador in Washington to our Secretary of State, dated January 29, and read as follows: "In execution of instructions, I have the satisfaction of expressing to Your Excellency my Government's gratitude to His Excellency Ambassador Carlton Hayes for the great services he rendered, during his mission in Spain, to our Embassy in that country. The spirit of cooperation and friendship which always guided the relations of His Excellency with our Ambassador in Madrid and the confidence with which he honored him at a difficult time such as the one through which we are passing at present are properly appreciated by the Brazilian Government which, through me, requests Your Excellency to express its thanks to Ambassador Hayes."

Little need be said about the last stage of our long voyage home on the *Marqués de Comillas*. From Lisbon, which we left on Wednesday evening, January 24, it partook of the nature of a summer holiday cruise. On Friday, February 2, we sighted the French island of Martinique in the West Indies, and, after sailing down the west side of the Lesser Antilles, we dropped anchor on the evening of February 3 at Port-of-Spain in the British island of Trinidad off the Venezuelan coast. This was a "control port," where, during the war, British officers made inspection and search of neutral ships, their crews and passengers. Apparently nothing improper was found on our Spanish ship, but while its search was going on, I had leisure for calling on the Governor of Trinidad, Sir Bede Clifford, and having Sunday luncheon with him, for making a tour of the magnificent American naval base in company with its commander, Commodore C. C. Boughman, and his aide, Lieutenant Tanner, and for visiting the American Consulate in Port-of-Spain.

Leaving Trinidad on Tuesday evening, February 6, we sailed on through the Caribbean, rounding the western end of Cuba on Sunday evening, February 11, and reaching Havana the next morning. Here we were met by the Counselor of our Embassy in Cuba, Mr. John Muccio, who was an admirable guide for us during our two-day stop in port. We had the pleasure of dining with Ambassador and Mrs. Spruille Braden and also of greeting Spanish friends we had known in Madrid: Señor Garcia Olay, the present Chargé of the Spanish Embassy; and Marqués de Rialp, official representative of General Franco at the recent inauguration of the new Cuban president, together with the Marquesa, a Cuban herself.

On Wednesday afternoon, February 14, precisely a month after our departure from Madrid amid a wintry blizzard, we sailed from Havana in tropical calm. On the morning of the 16th we arrived at the mouth of the Mississippi and that evening at New Orleans. We docked and landed the next morning. We were once more, and safely, in our own country.

Newspaper people at New Orleans besought me for comments on Spain, but I resisted their importunities. I was still "official," and the subject was much too complex to clarify in a few words. We simply rested a day in New Orleans, having pleasant conversation with the Condés Fontenar, friends of ours who were on their way back to Spain, and with Mrs. Butterworth, the mother of our Counselor in Madrid, while the local agent of the State Department efficiently arranged for the transportation of ourselves and our luggage to New York.

We reached New York, by train, on Tuesday, February 20. The next day Mrs. Hayes had a conference with Mrs. Norman Armour about arrangements in the Embassy at Madrid; and on the next day, Mr. and Mrs. Armour were fellow passengers with me on a train from New York to Washington. I spent several days in Washington, winding up my official affairs and having a number of agreeable conversations with Ambassador Armour, with Under Secretary Joseph Grew and other officials of the State Department, and with representatives of a variety of governmental agencies. With the President I left a personal memorandum, summarizing our relations with Spain during the three years of my mission at Madrid, and indicating what in my opinion should be our future long-term policy toward Spain.

The President wrote me on March 24:

I have been much interested in your February memorandum on the "Spanish Situation with Special Reference to Relations between Spain and the United States." I value most highly your views and recommendations and I am sure that they will be most useful and helpful to the State Department. Your work in Spain was outstanding and I want you to know how much I appreciate your help.

Very sincerely yours,

Franklin D. Roosevelt.

It was to be the last letter I should ever receive from Franklin Roosevelt. It was written after I and my family had reestablished ourselves at our country home, Jericho Farm, in Afton, New York, and its signature was so patently weaker and more shaky than the signature on earlier personal letters of his as to give me the tragic conviction that Franklin Roosevelt was a very ill man. He died only two weeks afterwards.

IV

Let me now set forth certain conclusions from my wartime experience and reflection in Spain.

Throughout my entire residence there, from May, 1942, to January, 1945, I had constant evidence that the large majority of the Spanish people greatly desired (1) to stay out of the international struggle, (2) to avoid recurrence of civil war, and (3) to be friendly with the English-speaking democracies, especially with the United States. These desires have been common, not only to the mass of "Leftists" (Republicans and Socialists), but also to most of the "Rightist" groups which supported General Franco in the Spanish Civil War (Liberal Monarchists, Traditionalists, and the Conservative following of Gil Robles) and consequently to members of these groups who held office in the existing Government (which was essentially a coalition rather than a single-party Government).

General Franco is in a curious position. He is a cautious politician with strong military backing, and, though doubtless the large majority of Spaniards, "Rightist" as well as "Leftist," would ideally prefer another Chief of State (if it could be arranged in an orderly fashion), many of them recognize, with varying degrees of gratitude, that by virtue of his cautious policy he succeeded in keeping Spain free from foreign and domestic war during an extraordinarily trying period.

So long as Axis victory seemed to him inevitable, so long as almost the whole continent of Europe was at the mercy of Germany, with German armies massed near the Pyrenees and German submarines infesting the seas adjacent to Spain, General Franco let Hitler and indeed the world believe that he was pro-Axis. Nevertheless, whatever may have been his inmost thoughts and personal fears in the matter, the fact remains that at least from the date of his dismissal of Serrano Suñer from the Foreign Office and the leadership of the Falange, in September, 1942, General Franco guided or backed the responsible officials of his Government in approximating Spain's official position to the pro-Allied position of the large majority of the Spanish people.

From September, 1942, to June, 1943, while the Spanish Government was still ostensibly "non-belligerent" and hence technically "unneutral," it not only placed no obstacle in the way of our landings and military operations in North Africa and southern Italy but gave us significant facilities, such as *de facto* recognition of the French Committee of National Liberation at Algiers and of its official representatives in Spain; free transit through Spain of over 25,000 volunteers (chiefly French) for active service with our armed forces in North Africa; non-internment of several hundreds of our forced-landed military airmen and their evacuation through Gibraltar; immediate delivery to us, quite uncompromised, of secret equipment on forced-landed planes; and freedom and full opportunity to carry on economic warfare with the Axis on Spanish territory by means of preemptive buying of wolfram, mercury, fluorspar, skins, woolen goods, etc., and blacklisting of Spanish firms doing business with the Axis.

From July, 1943, to May, 1944, the Spanish Government shifted its declared position from "non-belligerency" to "neutrality," and gradually increased the facilities it was according us to the detriment of the Axis. It not only curbed the discrimination against us in the Falangist-controlled press of the country, withdrew the Blue Division and Blue Air Squadron from the Eastern front, and replaced pro-Axis with pro-Allied diplomatic representatives in countries of Europe and Latin America, but it permitted the commercial sale of American propaganda magazines, granted us control of all passenger traffic, by Spanish airplanes as well by ships, between Spain and Spanish Morocco, and withheld recognition of Mussolini's "Social Republican" Government in North Italy.

Moreover, it speeded up the evacuation of Allied refugees and forced-landed airmen, arranged for the escape to Spain of a considerable number of Jews from Hungary, Germany, and the Low Countries, and tolerated, even to the point of abetting, the very important clandestine activities of our secret espionage services directed toward obtaining from across the Pyrenees invaluable military information about German troop movements and dispositions in France. Finally, as the result of a series of negotiations, pressed by us and vehemently opposed by Germany, Spain embargoed all exports of wolfram to the Axis from February to May and agreed to allow thereafter only token shipments (which stopped altogether after our landing in France in June, 1944). Simultaneously, the Spanish Government agreed to submit to arbitration the question of the internment of Italian warships which had been held for several months in the Balearic Islands, to close the German Consulate at Tangier, and to expel its staff and other Axis agents suspected of espionage or sabotage against us.

From July, 1944, the Spanish Government repeatedly indicated, by word and likewise by deed, that its policy toward us was one of "benevolent neutrality." It authorized our use of Barcelona as a free port of entry for supplies for France and other "liberated" areas. It expelled or interned several hundred German agents. It assured us it would not harbor persons adjudged by competent Allied tribunals to be "war criminals." It rescinded practically all censorship restrictions on American journalists in Spain and arranged with the United Press to utilize this American news service for the Spanish press.

It was the first foreign government to make a general air agreement with ours, and under this, we obtained transit and landing rights in Spain for three different American air lines and also for our army planes. It finally put into effect between Madrid and New York the direct radio-telegraphic circuit which had been the object of protracted and fruitless negotiations by us with the Spanish Monarchy prior to 1931 and with the Spanish Republic prior to the Civil War. On the eve of my departure from Spain, in January, the Foreign Minister notified me that his Government had released the interned Italian warships. Already the outstanding, and long-standing, difficulties between the Spanish Government and the American-owned Telephone Company were the subject of amicable negotiations which issued, just after I left, in a mutually satisfactory agreement. Moreover, the Foreign Minister had already agreed to stop the carrying of any merchandise by the German airline between Barcelona and Stuttgart (the only means left to Germany of getting goods from or to Spain), and had expressed a desire to discontinue this German line altogether if only we would consent to the maintenance of some sort of communication between Spain and Switzerland. This also was accomplished shortly after I left Spain. Furthermore, both the Foreign Minister and General Franco himself repeatedly made clear, not only in conversation with me, but by inspired articles in the Spanish press, their hostility to Japan and their intention, in due course, of breaking diplomatic relations with it. This, too, they did soon after I left.

In trying to assess the reasons for Spain's swing toward us and the increasing facilities it granted us from 1942 to 1945—in other words, the reasons for whatever success my wartime mission had— I arrive at four basic considerations. First and foremost Spain acted, as any nation would act, in what it conceived to be *its own interest*. In its own interest, Spain needed and desired to stay out of the war. To have joined the Axis in 1940 would sooner or later have brought it into the war. To have shown any partiality for the Allies prior to the end of 1942 would have brought the Germans into Spain, and consequently Spain into the war. To have flouted reasonable requests of the Allies from 1943 onwards might well have led to hostile action on their part and thus brought Spain into the war. In any of these cases, Spain would have lacked foresight and failed to serve its own greatest interest. The tactic of our diplomacy was to establish and enlarge a common area of Spanish interest and of our own. For we were not in Spain to oppose Spaniards or their Government, but to get them to help us oppose the Axis.

Second, I must emphasize the *economic weapon* which we and the British possessed. Spain simply had to have certain commodities from us, most notably petroleum, which it could not obtain in satisfactory quantities elsewhere. These we were able and ready to furnish or to withhold. With what telling effect we wielded this weapon, even before we had any military victories to our credit, must already be sufficiently clear. It should be borne in mind, however, that the mere withholding of a commodity like petroleum was in itself no weapon at all. Only when it was associated with a willingness to furnish the commodity, under conditions reasonably satisfactory to us, did it constitute an effective weapon.

Third, we owed no little of our success in Spain to Axis, and particularly *German, misjudgment of Spanish character*. The Nazis were at first too sure they had Spain in their pocket, and afterwards they overworked their propaganda and threatened too much. They neither invaded Spain, when they could, nor ceased trying to dictate to it, when they should. Moreover, their regimentation, their superior airs and patronizing attitude, and their deadly seriousness were repulsive, when not merely ridiculous, to the large majority of a nation notoriously individualistic, proud and stubborn. The tactic which certain of our journalistic critics in America urged us to adopt toward Spain was essentially the German tactic. It is fortunate we didn't follow it, and I sincerely hope, in our own national interest, it never will be followed.

Fourth, and by no means least, we were immeasurably aided by our *moral* ascendancy over the Axis. Spain came to recognize that when we made pledges, as, for example, to respect its territorial integrity or to furnish it with some commodity, we meant to keep our pledges, whereas the Axis relied on brute force and made promises only to break them. To maintain our moral position intact is vitally necessary to our prestige in any foreign country and hence to the successful conduct of all our international relations. When we have requests to make of another country, we must support them with reasons that are fair and honorable. If we had acted otherwise in Spain, we should have gravely weakened our moral position and thereby greatly handicapped ourselves.

V

My mission in Spain was rendered peculiarly difficult by reason of prevailing popular sentiment in the United States against the Spanish Government of the time, that of General Franco. And contemporary and future Spanish-American relations are likely to be troubled for similar if not the same reasons.

Our American Government, being democratic, is naturally and necessarily responsive to public opinion. And public opinion in the United States, as crystallized or reflected by our journalists and publicists, has been, and still is, predominantly hostile to the existing regime in Spain, expectant of its speedy collapse, and opposed to any measure or indication of a collaboration with it which might conceivably serve to strengthen or prolong it. This opinion is reenforced, moreover, by a somewhat similar attitude prevalent in England, by the partisan propaganda of exiled refugees from the Spanish Civil War residing abroad, and by the interested and denunciatory propaganda emanating from Soviet Russia and its inspired press and radio.

The central and most widespread popular notions in the United States about the Franco regime have been that it was forced upon Spain by Hitler and Mussolini, that it has been thoroughly Fascist, and pro-Axis, and that, as one of our newspapers has recently said, "if diplomatic and economic support were withdrawn from Franco by all the United Nations, his government would fall through spontaneous action by the masses of the Spanish people whom he has exploited and tortured for nearly a decade." [1] I, of course, hold no brief for General Franco's Government. I am an American and a democrat, and I most certainly would not wish to see his type of government installed or copied in the United States, or indefinitely continue in Spain or anywhere else. Yet I have had to face the fact, just as our own Government still has to face it, that if one wishes to deal with Spain one must deal with the existing Spanish Government, whatever it is, and that in order to deal with it wisely and advantageously one must be realistic about it and not the victim of wishful thinking or of fables.

Actually the Franco regime owes its origin only in part to military aid it received from Italy and Germany during the Civil War. This aid has been much exaggerated, as that of Russia and France to the "Loyalists" has been minimized. The Civil War was primarily a *Spanish* affair, in which a half of the Spanish nation and more than half of the Spanish army supported General Franco.

Actually, too, as the historical record in this book reveals and as Mr. Churchill plainly stated in the House of Commons in May, 1944, the Spanish Government of General Franco has not been "thoroughly pro-Axis," but, rather, has long accorded a large number of important facilities to the Allied war-effort. Spain's contributions to us in this respect compare favorably with those of any other neutral—Sweden, Switzerland, Turkey, or Portugal. Nor, as I have previously explained, has General Franco's dictatorship been inspired by Nazi ideology or directed solely by Fascists; it has been more in the nature of a military dictatorship traditional to Spanish-speaking peoples. [2]

Actually, also, it is difficult to understand why "the exploited

[1] Dayton (Ohio) *Daily News*, May 28, 1945.   [2] See above, pp. 54–56.

and tortured masses of the Spanish people" must await the withdrawal of foreign diplomatic support from their government before they "spontaneously" rise up and overthrow that government. Surely they don't fear that France and Russia and England and China and the United States would interfere to *prevent* them from overthrowing Franco. No, there must be a sizable number of Spaniards who don't regard themselves as "exploited" or "tortured," or who prefer a quiet *evolution* of the Franco regime to stormy *revolution* and the uncertainty of succeeding alternatives.

There has been a curiously recurrent expectation in America of an automatic collapse of the Franco regime. It was loudly voiced by journalists and publicists in the spring of 1943, just after our military successes in North Africa; more loudly in September, 1943, when Mussolini was ousted and Italy signed the armistice with us; and still more loudly in the spring of 1944, when we entered Rome and landed in Normandy. Thenceforth, in continuous chorus it has been affirmed that the triumph of Allied arms must mean the speedy abdication and disappearance of General Franco and his supporters.

The curious feature of all this is that what actually happened in Spain did not correspond at all to the expectations abroad. Instead of weakening his position within the country, the external events in the spring of 1943, in September, 1943, and in the spring of 1944 served rather, at least for the time being, to strengthen it. By now, it should be evident that one is seriously misinformed and unrealistic if one takes for granted that the Spanish Government's collapse is inevitable and imminent—unless, of course, we are ready to employ Allied pressure to collapse it. It is not likely to collapse through voluntary abdication, or, so far as I can see, through any general mass revolt of the Spanish people. The domestic opposition to it is too divided, too broken into quarrelsome groups of Monarchists, Republicans, Socialists, Syndicalists, Anarchists, Communists, and Basque and Catalan Nationalists, and too lacking in experienced and respected leadership. The memory of the horrors of the late Spanish Civil War is still much too vivid, and the fear of doing anything to precipitate its recurrence is, with the exception of the Communist minority, almost a national obsession.

After all, the existing regime represents that part of the Spanish nation which finally won a three-year civil war; and it would indeed be quite a novelty in human history if the victors in such a war should say to the vanquished only five or six years afterwards: "We are sorry; we shouldn't have won; we have made a mess of things; we will now restore you to power and welcome back your former leaders and let them do to us what they will." Imagine General Grant saying anything like that to the leaders of the Southern Confederacy in the midst of our own post-Civil War Reconstruction!

Of course, the United Nations could almost certainly exert sufficient joint pressure, through rupture of diplomatic relations and more especially through economic boycotts, to bring about the disintegration of General Franco's Government. It might be, moreover, that in such an event the half of the Spanish nation which was on the "Loyalist" side during the civil war would temporarily overlook its factional differences and unitedly acclaim the return to Spanish soil of the Government-in-Exile constructed at Mexico City. But it would be extremely dubious whether the initial acclaim and unity could be long maintained, whether the acquiescence of the other half of the Spanish nation, including the army, could be secured, and whether the United Nations could show the same harmony in continuously supporting a new regime as in getting rid of the present one.

Every major nation, I suppose, would like to see every other nation fashioned in its own image and likeness. Most Americans would doubtless like to see Spain a democratic republic functioning under a constitution and bill of rights akin to ours; and some Americans may hope that sooner or later our Government will employ its economic power and, if necessary, its military force to replace the existing political regime in Spain with just such a democratic republic. But on the other hand, Soviet Russia and Communists elsewhere in the world hope that Spain will be transformed into a Soviet state, into a "dictatorship of the proletariat," with Dr. Negrin, or someone like him, forcibly substituted for General Franco; while the statesman who served as British Ambassador at Madrid from

1940 to 1944 has repeatedly expressed the hope that constitutional monarchy of the English type might be "restored" in Spain.

From my experience and observation in Spain, I am extremely dubious about an early, happy realization of such hopes. The masses of the Spanish people are largely indifferent, if not hostile, to the Bourbon monarchy, and if it were restored by some military *coup* it would lack needful popular support and could be maintained in the long run only with foreign (presumably British) assistance. On the other hand, large numbers of Republican and Socialist "Leftists" blame the Communist minority, no less than the "Rightists," for the tragedy of the Spanish Civil War, and at least some of them would make common cause with the entrenched and not inconsiderable strength of the "Right" against any Communist regime, with the result that this would have to be forced upon Spain with foreign (presumably Russian) aid.

It might be that a democratic republic could be established with a large measure of popular support. But we should be under no illusions about the difficulties which would beset it and which would militate against its orderly functioning according to American traditions and ideals. Spaniards have no such political tradition as ours. Their two experiences with republican governments—the one in the 1870's and the other in the 1930's—were not fortunate and have not made all of them enthusiastic about seeking a third experience. Moreover, any majority of Spaniards who might support a Republic would not consist of two big and moderate parties, like the Republican and the Democratic in our own country, but would comprise a variety of factions so disparate as to render extremely difficult the maintenance of a united and really democratic front against Communist advocates of a "proletarian dictatorship" on one side, and "Rightist" champions of monarchy or a military dictatorship on the other. Dictatorship, in one form or another, is no novelty, but an old habit, in Spanish political life, and historically it has been exercised from the "Left" as well as from the "Right."

Some Americans seem to think that the United States should follow up the Allied defeat of Fascist Italy and Nazi Germany by engaging in a kind of worldwide crusade against any and every government which we don't like or which someone dubs "fascist" or "totalitarian." Now *if* it is an aim of ours to overthrow all dictatorships throughout the world, we should intervene in Spanish affairs and use all possible means to overthrow General Franco's dictatorship. For this purpose, I imagine, we could count on the cooperation of the Soviet Union, possibly on that of France, and barely possibly on that of Great Britain. But would there be continuing agreement among the Allies as to who or what should take General Franco's place?

And *if* we are going to intervene in Spanish affairs and use all possible means to overthrow General Franco's dictatorship, why should we stop there? A goodly number of other countries in the contemporary world, including some of the United Nations, are subject to dictatorships, military or even totalitarian. What about Portugal? What about Turkey? What about Brazil? What about a half-dozen or more Spanish-American countries? What about China? What about the Soviet Union itself? Marshal Stalin was not notably helpful to the democracies from 1939 to 1941.

In the circumstances it would seem statesmanlike, at least from the standpoint of the United States, to ensure a peaceful resolution of current political difficulties and conflicts among peoples recently liberated from Fascist Italy and Nazi Germany before interfering in Spain or in any other neutral or allied country. My own conviction is that we should not concern ourselves with the internal affairs or form of government of any foreign country, unless that country becomes, or clearly threatens to become, a menace to the peace and independence of its neighbors and hence of the world and of ourselves. I never liked the Nazi regime in Germany or the Fascist regime in Italy, or, for that matter, the Communist dictatorship in Russia. These have all seemed to me fundamentally of the same ilk and quite antithetical to the democracy I know and like in America. Yet so long as they kept the peace and did not go on the warpath, or threaten our security, I believe our Government acted wisely in having diplomatic relations with them and in leaving to their own peoples any question of their internal affairs and form of government. When Nazi Germany and Fascist Italy did become menacing and aggressive against their neighbors, we had reason to break with them and to oppose them; we finally did so when they joined Japan in an attack upon us.

Non-interference in the internal affairs of foreign countries is not merely personal counsel of mine. It is a long-standing, and at least used to be a generally accepted, American public policy. One of its classic expressions was President James Monroe's in 1823, which I quoted at the beginning of this book and which, for emphasis, I here quote again: "Our policy in regard to Europe . . . remains the same, which is, not to interfere in the internal concerns of any of its powers; to consider the Government *de facto* as the legitimate Government for us; to cultivate friendly relations with it, and to preserve those relations by a frank, firm, and manly policy, meeting, in all instances, the just claims of every power; submitting to injuries from none." This was the policy which President Franklin Roosevelt reaffirmed in specific pledges to Spain, and the policy in accordance with which our wartime mission in Spain was discharged. I don't believe it should lightly be changed.

Frankly, I would leave Spain to the Spaniards. Left to themselves, they are no menace to their neighbors or to the peace of the world, and they are a people whose tradition and temperament are inflexibly opposed alike to domestic regimentation and to interference from abroad. The existing regime is regarded by the mass of Spaniards, "Rightist" as well as "Leftist," and is admitted by General Franco himself, to be but "temporary." Eventually there is sure to be a change in it. But change is more likely to be impeded than expedited by foreign intervention or interference, which would probably involve additional suffering for the Spanish people and lead to serious divisions among the major Allied Powers.

Meanwhile, with the existing Spanish Government, as with any Spanish Government which, through evolution or internal revolution, may succeed it, the United States would do well, in my opinion, to pursue a policy of friendly relations. Spain and the Spanish people can be, regardless of their form of government, very serviceable to American interests at the present and in the future.

There remains, of course, a public opinion in the United States, besides other public opinions in Great Britain and Russia, hostile to the pursuit of such a policy. But the most hostile of this public opinion is, I am sure, a peculiarly ill-informed, or a most selfishly interested and propagandist-directed, public opinion. There can be no doubt of the need and importance of public opinion in a democracy. But if a democracy is to act wisely, especially in the domain of foreign policy, and at the same time to reflect, as it should, the major public opinion of its people, it is of supreme importance that democratic public opinion be well-informed and truthful and honest. Public opinion which is fashioned and propagated otherwise must of necessity lead a democracy like the United States into the most foolish and dangerous paths.

As the United States projects its worldwide leadership into post-war reconstruction and the organization and maintenance of international peace and security, it becomes all the more desirable that our Government, particularly our Department of State, should greatly strengthen and make much more effective its liaison with the American press and other fashioners of American public opinion and thereby contribute actively toward making and keeping that opinion well and wisely informed. This, I hope, would apply to our relations with Spain as with other countries.

VI

Spain desires to cultivate especially friendly relations with the United States. I firmly believe that for the future, regardless of what its Government may be, whether one evolved from General Franco's or a restored monarchy or a republic, we should reciprocate and should cultivate especially friendly relations with Spain.

In support of such a policy on our part, I would advance some five basic considerations:

(1) Spain (with Portugal) occupies a most important geographical position in respect of commercial aviation of the present and future, particularly between the American Continents and Europe. There is no need of laboring the generally recognized significance of the airplane for post-war communication and transport

between nations and continents, or the rivalry which most probably will develop among great industrial nations for primacy in the construction of planes and the proliferation of air routes throughout the world. For the United States, it would appear that one of its first objectives in the development of any world-program of aviation should be the Iberian peninsula. Spain perceives advantages to herself in this, and is quite prepared to cooperate closely with the United States in aviation matters if she can count upon fair and considerate treatment in return.

(2) Spain (with Portugal) also occupies, as the present war has amply demonstrated, a peculiarly strategic position in relation to any major threat to the peace of Europe and hence of the world. If Spain had joined Germany in 1940 or could have been relied upon to offer no resistance to German invasion and occupation, it is reasonable to suppose that the German war machine would have reduced Gibraltar, closed the Strait, and thereby dealt a mortal blow at Britain in the Mediterranean and North Africa before we could have sent any effective aid or been in any position to undertake a counter-offensive against the "soft under-belly" of Europe. In that case, the war might have been gravely prolonged and the final outcome far more dubious.

It should by now be clear to Americans that any Power, whether Napoleonic France or Hitlerian Germany or some other madly ambitious power of the future, which goes on the warpath in Europe and attempts to dominate that Continent, automatically endangers the peace and security of the rest of the world and is sure, sooner or later, to involve the United States in a horribly costly overseas conflict. It behooves us, therefore, to cultivate and maintain especially friendly relations with nations which of themselves are not likely to provoke such a conflict but which can provide, in case of emergency, a convenient European bridgehead for our armed forces. Spain is just such a nation; and especially friendly future relations with her should not undermine, but rather buttress, any policy or program of collective world security. But to make a friend of Spain requires being a friend to Spain.

(3) Many ills in Spain derive from economic backwardness.

This is fully recognized by the Spanish Government and by thoughtful Spanish businessmen and farmers, who look particularly to the United States to supply machinery, materials, and technicians for the industrial and agricultural betterment of their country. Most Spaniards are industrious and hard-working; and economic assistance from the United States would prove profitable to both countries. In the immediate future, Spain could be utilized as an important supplier of textiles, tires, and foodstuffs to our armed forces and the liberated areas in Europe, if only she could get from us the requisite raw cotton, rubber, and fertilizers. She has the factories and the workmen. Instead of trying to force on Spain exports from the United States which are deemed luxuries by her Government and which eat up her dollar-balances, we might, much more helpfully to ourselves and to the well-being of the Spanish people, remove some of our restrictions on the export of materials vitally needful to the domestic and foreign economy of Spain, and at the same time lower our tariff on the imports with which Spain must pay us.

Spain particularly wants a large number of motor trucks, a large amount of hydroelectric equipment, a large miscellany of agricultural implements and machine tools and spare parts. She wishes to import them from the United States, and if we meet her halfway, we shall have in her a good customer as well as a good neighbor.

(4) Some ills in Spain derive from lack of sufficient popular and technical education. Here, too, thoughtful Spaniards, regardless of political affiliation, look to the United States for aid and example. They want to know what is being done by Americans, both scientifically and practically, in agriculture, in medicine, in chemistry, in vocational guidance, in the industrial arts. In turn, Spain has arts and literary and historical scholarship from which Americans should increasingly profit. A sympathetically developed program of cultural relations between Spain and the United States, on the scale of that between the United States and Hispanic America, would be mutually beneficial.

(5) I do not believe that we can successfully pursue one policy

in Hispanic America and another in Spain. If we continue to convey the impression that we are a "bad neighbor" to Spain, we shall increase the difficulties and hazards of remaining a "good neighbor" to the other American Republics. Contemporary Spain, I am sure, has absolutely no political objectives on the American Continents, but she does have a huge *cultural* empire there. Her history and enterprise, for four and a half centuries now, have been more fruitfully associated with America than with Europe. She faces westward, rather than northward or eastward. She has given to eighteen of the twenty-one American Republics her language, her religion, her art, her men and mentality, her virtues and vices. I have yet to encounter a family in Spain, whether of nobility or peasantry, of professional or artisan class, which does not have relatives and interests in Spanish America. There are hundreds of thousands of first-generation Spaniards actually living in such cities as Buenos Aires, Montevideo, Lima, and Havana, and, for good or ill, exerting influence upon the social, economic, cultural, and political life of American Republics to the south of us.

Nor is the traffic one-way. Indeed, I have been astounded by the Spanish-American numbers and influences in Spain. Along with France, Spain has been, and is most likely to remain, the main magnet for tourists and students, artists and athletes and journalists, from Latin America. Almost every well-to-do Spaniard has a wife or mother or at least an aunt who hails from Cuba or Peru or Mexico or Argentina; and in every important Spanish city the "colony" of nationals of each major Spanish-American country outnumbers any other "foreign" colony, German, French, or British.

There are many differences, of course, between Spain and her daughter-nations in the New World—differences between an old, long-settled country, of monarchical tradition and relatively homogeneous population, and a group of pioneering "frontier" countries with republican and separatist traditions and with very heterogeneous populations. But such differences are, I think, less than those obtaining between England and the United States, and they should not be exaggerated. Throughout both Spain and Hispanic

America there are strikingly similar political and social, as well as cultural, characteristics. The social structure is similar, and so, too, are the political currents: the complexity and individualism of party politics; the endless conflicts between "Rightists" and "Leftists," between "clericalism" and "anti-clericalism," between federalism and centralization; the recurrent revolutionary movements and the equally recurrent resorts to military dictatorship. Such currents in one Spanish-speaking country are reflected, sooner or later, to greater or lesser degree, in the others. Here, again, by reason of close cultural and personal contacts, Spain cannot be unaffected by developments in Spanish America, or *vice versa*.

I assume that the "good-neighbor" policy of the United States toward the countries of Spanish America involves our securing the utmost cooperation with and from them for mutual defense and commercial advantage, without impairing their independence or interfering in their internal affairs. If they tend towards "Right" or towards "Left," that is their concern and not ours, so long as they are friendly and cooperative and do not endanger the basic purposes of the good neighbor policy. If this policy is to produce the most salutary and enduring effects, then I would conclude from the foregoing that it should be extended to embrace not only the Spanish-American countries and Brazil but also Portugal and Spain.